# *Writing*
# ACADEMIC ENGLISH

## Third Edition

Alice Oshima
Ann Hogue

**Writing Academic English, Third Edition**

Addison Wesley Longman, 10 Bank Street, White Plains, NY 10606

Editorial director: Allen Ascher
Acquisitions editor: Louisa Hellegers
Director of design and production: Rhea Banker
Development editors: Artelia Court, Françoise Leffler
Production manager: Alana Zdinak
Production supervisor: Liza Pleva
Senior manufacturing manager: Patrice Fraccio
Manufacturing supervisor: Edie Pullman
Managing editor: Linda Moser
Production editor: Lynn Contrucci
Photo research: Diana Nott
Cover design: Curt Belshe
Text design adaptation: Curt Belshe
Electronic production supervisor: Kim Teixeira
Text composition: Kim Teixeira

Photo credits: See page 269
Text credits: See page 269

**Library of Congress Cataloging-in-Publication Data**

Oshima, Alice
    Writing academic English/Alice Oshima, Ann Hogue.—3rd ed.
        p.      cm.

    Includes index.

    ISBN 0-201-34054-2 (alk. paper)

    1. English language—Rhetoric—Handbooks, manuals, etc.  2.
English language—Grammar—Handbooks, manuals, etc.  3. English
language—Textbooks for foreign speakers.  4. Academic writing—
Handbooks, manuals, etc.  5. Report writing—Handbooks, manuals,
etc.  I. Hogue, Ann.  II. Title.

PE1408.073    1998

808'.042—dc21                                          98-23607
                                                          CIP

3 4 5 6 7 8 9 10—BAH—03 02 01 00 99

# Contents

# Preface

*Writing Academic English,* Third Edition, is a comprehensive rhetoric and sentence structure textbook/workbook. It has been written for intermediate to advanced college or college-bound international and English as a Second Language students. It can also be used by native speakers of English who need to develop their basic composition skills or to brush up on sentence structure and mechanics.

The book teaches writing in a straightforward manner, using a process-oriented approach. At the same time, the structure of paragraphs and essays and their important components are taught in small, learnable steps. Clear, relevant models illustrate each step, and varied practices reinforce each lesson. Sentence structure, with special emphasis on subordinated structures, is taught in a separate section.

Because most academic writing is expository in nature, we have purposely limited the rhetorical components to exposition. The models and practices feature current and general academic topics relevant to students' interests in a rapidly changing world. Many also provide practice using English in technical, scientific, and business contexts.

Other features of the book include four appendixes offering punctuation rules with exercises, a comprehensive chart of transition signals, a chart of correction symbols, and a list of topic suggestions for in-class "writing under pressure" practice. Uncommon vocabulary items are glossed, and each chapter ends with a convenient review of the main teaching points and a writing or editing assignment. A Peer Editing Checklist ends Chapters 2 through 8.

## What's New in the Third Edition

Instructors familiar with the second edition will find these changes:

- The book now has three main sections instead of four. The chapter on library research has been deleted. A revised chapter on quotations, summary, and paraphrase has been renamed Concrete Support II.

- The Writing under Pressure assignments, formerly found at the end of each chapter in Part I, have been consolidated in Appendix C.

- A list of correction symbols has been added to the appendixes (Appendix D).

- Interactive Peer Editing Checklists now accompany each writing assignment.

- Important teaching points, rules, and examples appear in charts within the text for quick, easy reference.

- Small boxes cross-referencing relevant sections of the book appear in the margins.

- Other boxes offering computer tips are sprinkled throughout the book.

- Compositions to edit for specific sentence errors have been added to the end of each sentence structure chapter.

Finally, models have been updated, practice material freshened, and explanations streamlined, always with the intention of making the material more accessible to our students.

### Order of Lesson Presentation

*Writing Academic English* is intended to be covered in one 15-week semester, with classes meeting five days a week. The chapters in Part I, Writing a Paragraph, and Part II, Writing an Essay, should be taught in sequence. The sentence structure chapters in Part III should be taught alongside the chapters in Parts I and II on the paragraph and essay in order to encourage students to write a variety of complex structures. Chapter 10, Types of Sentences, should be taught at the beginning of the course; subsequent chapters may be taught in any order. Wherever possible, instructors should integrate sentence structure with rhetoric. For example, adverbial time clauses in Part III may be taught simultaneously with chronological order in Part II.

### Topic Suggestions

The topics listed for each writing assignment are only suggestions. Keep an eye open for interesting topics from current events or for interesting graphs, photographs, and charts in newspapers on which to base other assignments.

### In-Class Writing

Group brainstorming and in-class writing of first drafts are especially helpful in the early stages because you are available for immediate consultation. Also, you can check to make sure everyone is on the right track. Pair and group collaboration is appropriate for brainstorming and editing work; however, writing is essentially an individual task even when done in class.

### Writing under Pressure

Appendix C suggests topics for writing under pressure. These assignments are to be done in class under time pressure to simulate the experience of writing essay examinations. We feel that this is valuable practice for college-bound students.

### Practice Exercises

The final practice exercises of the sentence structure chapters usually ask students to write original sentences. Because these practices prove whether the students understand the structures and can produce them correctly on their own, we hope that you are not tempted to skip them.

### Peer Editing

Interactive Peer Editing Checklists appear with each writing assignment. One method of using these lists is to ask pairs of students to exchange books as well as first drafts of compositions. Each student in a pair edits the other student's work and writes comments and suggestions about the other's composition in that student's book. A second method is to provide photocopies of the checklists for peer editors to record their comments. A third method is to have each student read his or her draft out loud to a small group of classmates and then to solicit oral comments and suggestions by asking the checklist questions. The student who has read then writes down the group's suggestions in his or her own book. Of course, the instructor can also respond to student writing by commenting on photocopies of the checklists.

### Photographs

The photographs introducing each chapter of the book depict some of the forms of written communication used by diverse cultures throughout the evolution of civilization.

# To the Student

Many people have the mistaken idea that being able to write well is a talent that one either has or doesn't have. This idea is not necessarily true. You can learn to write effectively if you are willing to learn some strategies and practice them.

Good writing in English requires the ability to write good sentences and to organize them logically into paragraphs and essays. In this book, you will learn how to do both. Nine chapters will help you write good paragraphs and essays, and five chapters will help you write good sentences.

We hope you will enjoy the teaching approach and writing challenges offered in our book. If you study each lesson carefully and do all of the practices thoughtfully, not only will your writing skills improve, but you will also develop greater confidence in your ability as a writer.

# Acknowledgments

Many people contribute to the making of a book. We especially thank Artelia Court, whose expert editing resulted in countless instances of improved clarity and consistency; Diana Nott, whose diligent research provided the photographs that greatly enhance the book; our editors at Addison Wesley Longman, Louisa Hellegers, Françoise Leffler, and Lynn Contrucci, whose experience guided everyone through the various stages of book production; and our families and friends, who suffered uncomplainingly through the process with us once again. To everyone, we are truly grateful.

# Writing

## ACADEMIC ENGLISH

# PART I

# Writing a Paragraph

# CHAPTER 1

# The Process of Academic Writing

Native American symbols from Alaska

## *Introduction*

Academic writing, as the name implies, is the kind of writing that you are required to do in college or university. It differs from other kinds of writing such as personal, literary, journalistic, or business writing. Its differences can be explained in part by its special audience, tone, and purpose.

Whenever you write, consider your specific audience, that is, the people who will read what you have written. Knowing your audience will help you to communicate clearly and effectively. In academic writing, your audience is primarily your professors or instructors.

In addition, you should also consider the tone of your writing, which depends on your subject matter and on your audience. Tone is your style or manner of expression. It is revealed by your choice of words and grammatical structures and even the length of your sentences. The tone of a piece of writing can be, for example, serious, amusing, personal, or impersonal. Academic writing is formal and serious in tone.

Finally, the purpose of a piece of writing determines the rhetorical form[1] chosen for it. A persuasive essay will be organized in one way and an expository[2] essay in another way. In this book, you will learn the basic rhetorical forms of academic writing, from single paragraphs to multiparagraph essays.

As you write each assignment in this course and in other college courses, keep in mind your audience, tone, and purpose so that the message your reader will receive is the message you intend to convey.[3]

## *The Writing Process, Stage I: Prewriting*

**COMPUTER TIP**

Writing is so important in academic life that some universities have on-line writing centers. These sites offer extra writing advice and information. Ask your instructor how to find them.

Writing, particularly academic writing, is not easy. It takes study and practice to develop this skill. For both native speakers and new learners of English, it is important to note that writing is a *process*, not a "product." This means that a piece of writing, whether it is a composition for your English class or a lab report for your chemistry class, is never complete; that is, it is always possible to review and revise, and review and revise again.

There are four main stages in the writing process: prewriting, planning, writing and revising drafts, and writing the final copy to hand in. Each stage will be explained and practiced in Part I of this book. In this chapter, you will concentrate on prewriting techniques, which are activities to help you generate[4] ideas for your writing assignments.

### *Step 1: Choosing and Narrowing a Topic*

If you are given a specific writing assignment (such as an essay question on an examination), then, of course, what you can write about is limited. On the other hand, when you are given a free choice of topics and can write about something you are interested in, then you must narrow the topic to a particular aspect of that general subject. Suppose you are interested in the environment. It would be impossible to cover such a big topic in a paragraph. You would have to narrow the topic to perhaps environmental pollution, if that is your interest. Environmental pollution, however, is still too broad a topic for a paragraph, so you might even further narrow the topic to a type of environmental pollution, such as pollution of the oceans. However, writing about ocean pollution is still too broad because it would include pollution by oil, chemicals, sewage, and garbage. Therefore, you might decide to write about oil as a source of ocean pollution. Finally, you might make this topic even narrower by writing only about the effects of oil spills on sea life. The point is, you must narrow the subject of your paragraph to a specific focus so that you can write about it clearly and completely.

The diagram on page 4 illustrates the process of narrowing a general topic to a specific one.

---

[1]**rhetorical form:** organizational form and style
[2]**expository:** explanatory; one that explains
[3]**convey:** express
[4]**generate:** produce

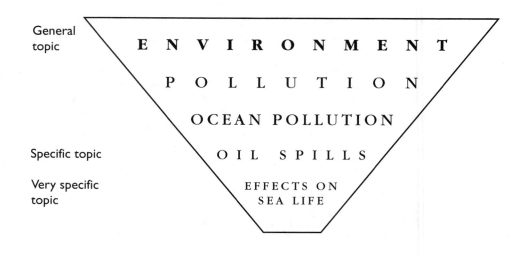

General topic

Specific topic

Very specific topic

**PRACTICE I**

*Choosing and Narrowing a Topic*

Individually, in a small group, or with your whole class, narrow each of the following general topics to one specific aspect that could be written about in one paragraph.

School          Entertainment
Television     Food
Sports

## Step 2: Brainstorming

After you have chosen a topic and narrowed it to a specific focus, the next prewriting step is to generate ideas. This is done by a process called brainstorming. Although these brainstorming activities may seem unnecessary at first, after doing them a few times, you will realize their usefulness. Brainstorming for ideas can get you started writing more quickly and save you time in the later stages of the writing process.

Three useful brainstorming techniques are *listing*, *freewriting*, and *clustering*. Learn how to do each of them and then decide which is the most productive for you.

### Listing

Listing is a brainstorming technique in which you think about your topic and quickly make a list of whatever words or phrases come into your mind. Your purpose is to produce as many ideas as possible in a short time, and your goal is to find a specific focus for your topic.

Follow this procedure:

**1.** Write down the general topic at the top of your paper.
**2.** Then make a list of every idea that comes into your mind about that topic. Keep the ideas flowing. Try to stay on the general topic; however, if you write down information that is completely off the topic, don't worry about it because you can cross it out later.
**3.** Use words, phrases, or sentences, and don't worry about spelling or grammar.

Here is an example of the listing technique on the topic of the culture shock experienced by international students in the United States.

**MODEL**

*Listing*

---

### Culture Shock

communication problems

poor verbal skills

children disrespectful

new language

American family life

families seldom eat together

lack vocabulary

show affection in public

Americans talk too fast

they are friendly

people are always in a hurry

use slang and idioms

families don't spend time together on
    weekends and holidays

children are "kings"

lack confidence

American food is unhealthy

everyone eats fast food

homeless people shocking sight

American students

classroom environment

unclear expressions

public transportation is not good

need a car

use first names with teachers

college professors wear jeans

students ask questions

no formal dress code

no one takes time to cook good meals

professor's role

children spend more time with friends
    than with parents

use incomplete sentences

poor pronunciation

Americans difficult to understand

students can challenge professors

---

**4.** Now rewrite your list and group similar ideas together. Cross out items that don't belong or that are duplications.

---

| Group A | Group B | Group C |
|---|---|---|
| (communication problems) | ~~homeless people shocking sight~~ | (American family life) |
| poor verbal skills | American students | families seldom eat together |
| new language | (classroom environment) | families don't spend time together on weekends and holidays |
| lack vocabulary | ~~public transportation is not good~~ | children are "kings" |
| ~~show affection in public~~ | ~~need a car~~ | children disrespectful |
| Americans talk too fast | use first names with teachers | children spend more time with friends than with parents |
| ~~they are friendly~~ | college professors wear jeans | ~~American food is unhealthy~~ |
| ~~people are always in a hurry~~ | students ask questions | ~~everyone eats fast food~~ |
| use slang and idioms | no formal dress code | |
| lack confidence | ~~no one takes time to cook good meals~~ | |
| use incomplete sentences | professor's role | |
| poor pronunciation | students can challenge professors | |
| Americans difficult to understand | | |
| unclear expressions | | |

Now there are three lists, each of which has a central focus. The central focus in each new list is circled: *communication problems, classroom environment,* and *American family life.* The writer can choose one list to be the basis for a paragraph.

**PRACTICE 2**

*Brainstorming by Listing*

Brainstorm by listing ideas on one of the following topics. Follow the four steps outlined on pages 4–5.

How to be a good student
How television is a learning tool
The characteristics of a good teacher
My favorite leisure-time activity
Tourist attractions in your country or city
One of the topics from Practice 1: Choosing and Narrowing a Topic on page 4

## *Freewriting*

Freewriting is a brainstorming activity in which you write freely about a topic because you are looking for a specific focus. While you are writing, one idea will spark[1] another idea. As with listing, the purpose of freewriting is to generate as many ideas as possible and to write them down without worrying about appropriateness, grammar, spelling, logic, or organization. Remember, the more you freewrite, the more ideas you will have. Don't despair[2] if your mind seems to "run dry." Just keep your pencil moving.
    Follow this procedure:

1. Write the topic at the top of your paper.
2. Write as much as you can about the topic until you run out of ideas. Include such supporting items as facts, details, and examples that come into your mind about the subject.
3. After you have run out of ideas, reread your paper and circle the main idea(s) that you would like to develop.
4. Take that main idea and freewrite again.

    In the following model, the student is supposed to write a paragraph about one major problem at his college. The student doesn't have any idea of what to write about, so he starts freewriting about some of the problems that come to mind.

**MODEL**

*Freewriting 1*

> ### Problems at Evergreen College
>
> What is the biggest problem at Evergreen College? Well, I really don't know. In fact, I can't think of one particular problem although I know there are many problems. For one thing, the classrooms are usually overcrowded. At the beginning of this semester, Science Hall 211 had 45 students although there were only 31
> 5  desks. A few of the seats attached to the desks were broken, so about 20 students had to sit on the floor. Besides, the classrooms are poorly maintained. In several of my classes, there are broken chairs and litter on the floor. Students even leave their dirty cups and other garbage on the desks. So the rooms are messy. The library is too small and always crowded with students. Not all students really study in the
> 10 library. Sometimes they talk a lot and this is really quite distracting to me and other

---

[1]**spark:** cause to start coming to mind     [2]**despair:** be discouraged

serious students who want and need a quiet place to study. So the present library should be expanded or a new library should be built. Oh yes, I think that (another) (problem is parking near the campus.) The college has a big parking lot across from the west side of campus, but it is always full. So, many times students have to park

15 their cars in the residential areas, which could be so far away from the campus that they have to run to class to make it. Yes, parking is a big problem that many students face every day. I have a car, and many of my friends have one. We really have a problem. So, I think the biggest problem at Evergreen College is not enough parking spaces near the college campus. . .

After he finished freewriting, the student reread his paper and circled the main ideas, one of which he will consider as the major problem at Evergreen College.

Let's say that the student has decided to choose parking as a major problem at Evergreen College. Now that the student knows the topic that he wants to write about, he will again brainstorm by freewriting; only this time, the specific topic will be on the parking problem only. His freewriting paper might look like this.

**MODEL**

*Freewriting 2*

### The Parking Problem at Evergreen College

I think finding a parking space close to the campus at Evergreen College is a major problem. There are not enough parking lots for students to park their cars. Therefore, students have to come early to get a parking space, and even then, sometimes they are unlucky and can't get a good parking space. Once I couldn't

5 find a space in the west-side parking lot, and I had to drive in the streets for a half hour before I found one. So, I was late for class. Some students are late to class almost every time the English class meets. Some even drop the class, not because they can't handle it, but because they can't find a place to park close to the campus. The teacher warns them time and time again not to be late, but they can't

10 help it. . . . What is the solution to the parking problem? Maybe the college should spend some funds to construct a multilevel parking lot that will accommodate three times as many cars as the present parking lot holds. . . .

The student can continue freewriting as long as he can generate ideas related to the topic. Then after completing that task, he can reread it and develop certain points, add some more ideas, or even delete others. The student can do this freewriting activity several times until he is satisfied with what he has written.

**PRACTICE 3**

*Brainstorming by Freewriting*

Brainstorm by freewriting on one of the following topics. Follow the four steps outlined on page 6.

Problems of working students
Problems of international students
Problems with learning English in my country
A topic of your own choice

### *Clustering*

Clustering is another brainstorming activity that you can use to generate ideas. Here's how to use this technique: In the center of your paper, write your topic and draw a "balloon" around it. This is your center, or core, balloon. Then write whatever ideas come to you in balloons around the core. Think about each of these ideas and make more balloons around them.

For example, suppose you had to describe a person who is close to you in some way. Using the clustering technique to get ideas, you might end up with a paper such as the following.

**MODEL**

*Clustering*

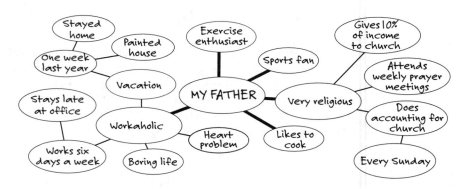

The largest cluster of balloons was generated from the "workaholic" balloon, so this would be a good focus for this student's paragraph about his father.

**PRACTICE 4**

*Brainstorming by Clustering*

Use the clustering technique for ten minutes to generate ideas about a member of your family.

## *The Writing Process, Stage II: Planning (Outlining)*

In Stage I, you chose topics and narrowed them, and you generated ideas by brainstorming. Now you are ready for Stage II in the process of writing, the planning stage. In the planning stage, you organize the ideas you generated by brainstorming into an outline.

Turn back to the model about culture shock on page 5. The student had developed three different lists of ideas: communication problems, classroom environment, and American family life. She decided to write a paragraph about communication problems.

**Step 1: Making Sublists**

The first step toward making an outline is to divide the ideas in the "communication problems" list further into sublists and to cross out any items that don't belong or that aren't useable.

**MODEL**

*Sublists*

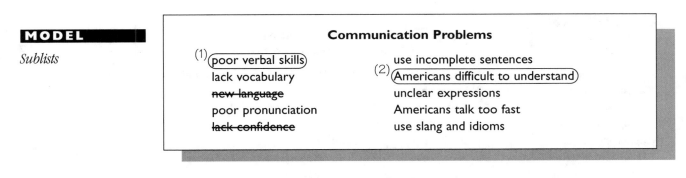

**Communication Problems**

(1) ~~poor verbal skills~~ *(circled)* poor verbal skills
lack vocabulary
~~new language~~
poor pronunciation
~~lack confidence~~

use incomplete sentences
(2) Americans difficult to understand *(circled)*
unclear expressions
Americans talk too fast
use slang and idioms

The ideas listed under "communication problems" could be divided further into two sublists—those that describe international students and those that describe Americans. Two items, (1) *poor verbal skills* and (2) *Americans difficult to understand,* can serve as titles for the sublists. *New language* and *lack confidence* didn't fit in either sublist, so they were crossed out. The remaining items could be put under 1 or 2. When you have grouped all of the points into their appropriate sublist, you have created a preliminary outline for a paragraph.

**MODEL**

*Preliminary Outline*

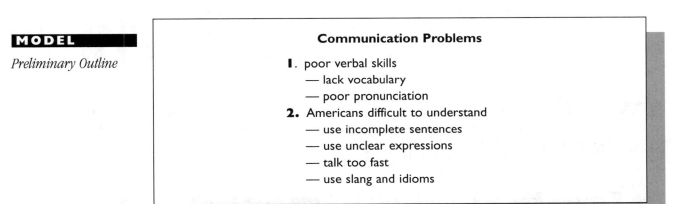

**Communication Problems**

1. poor verbal skills
   — lack vocabulary
   — poor pronunciation
2. Americans difficult to understand
   — use incomplete sentences
   — use unclear expressions
   — talk too fast
   — use slang and idioms

### Step 2: Writing the Topic Sentence

Finally, write a topic sentence. The topic sentence is the most general sentence in a paragraph, and it expresses the central focus of the paragraph. The topic of Group A is clearly communication problems. Therefore, a possible topic sentence might be as follows.

**MODEL**

*Topic Sentence*

One problem that many international students face in the United States is communication with Americans.

or

International students in the United States face communication problems with Americans.

### Step 3: Outlining

An outline is a formal plan for a paragraph. In an outline, you write down the main points and subpoints in the order in which you plan to write about them. The following is an example of an outline of the topic "communication problems."

**MODEL**

*Outline*

    *Topic Sentence*
    *Supporting point*
        *Supporting detail*
        *Supporting detail*
    *Supporting point*
        *Supporting detail*
        *Supporting detail*
        *Supporting detail*
        *Supporting detail*

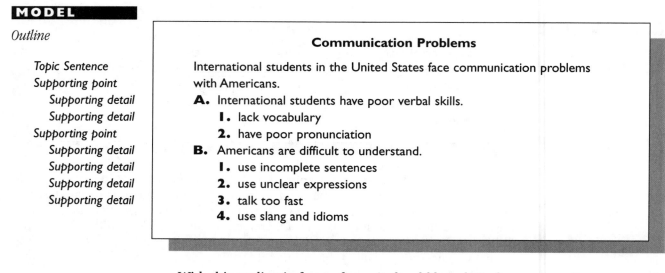

**Communication Problems**

International students in the United States face communication problems with Americans.
**A.** International students have poor verbal skills.
   **1.** lack vocabulary
   **2.** have poor pronunciation
**B.** Americans are difficult to understand.
   **1.** use incomplete sentences
   **2.** use unclear expressions
   **3.** talk too fast
   **4.** use slang and idioms

With this outline in front of you, it should be relatively easy to write a paragraph about international students' communication problems with Americans. There is a topic sentence, two main supporting points, two supporting details for the first main point, and four supporting details for the second main point. You could, of course, add some examples and a concluding sentence if you wanted to, but the main planning for the paragraph has been completed.

**PRACTICE 5**

*Outlining*

Develop outlines for the other two groups, *classroom environment* and *American family life*. Follow the three steps outlined above. Each outline should contain a topic sentence, one or two main supporting points, and one or two supporting details for each main supporting point. Add a title to your outline.

## The Writing Process, Stage III: Writing and Revising Drafts

Stage III in the writing process, after prewriting (Stage I) and planning (Stage II), is writing and revising several drafts until you have produced a final copy to hand in. Remember that no piece of writing is ever perfect the first time. Each time you write a new draft, you will refine and improve your writing.

### Step 1: Writing the First Rough Draft

The first step in the revision process is to write a rough draft from your outline. This is how to proceed:

- Write down the topic sentence and underline it. Doing this will remind you of the focus of your paragraph.

- Skip one or two lines per line of writing and leave margins of one inch on both sides of the paper. These blank spaces will allow you to add more details, information, examples, etc. in order for you to fully develop your points. Also, you can add comments such as "define —————," "check spelling," "add an example," and so on in the margins for your attention later on.

- Write your paragraph, following your outline as closely as possible. Try writing steadily. Don't hesitate to add ideas that aren't in your outline if you are certain they are relevant to the topic.

- Don't worry about grammar, punctuation, or spelling. This first rough draft does not have to be "perfect"; in fact, it won't be because your main goal is to write down as much information as you can, following the points in your outline.

While you are writing, you may not be able to think of a word or phrase, or you may be unable to complete a thought. Don't worry—just leave a space or a line. You can fill it in later. Also, while you are writing about one major point, you might come up with an idea for another major point. Don't risk forgetting it! Write it down in the margin of your paper near where it belongs.

Above all, remember that writing is a continuous process of discovery. Therefore, as you are writing, you will think of new ideas that may not be on your brainstorming list or in your outline. You can add new ideas or delete original ones at any time in the writing process. Just be sure that any new ideas are relevant!

## Step 2: Revising Content and Organization

After you write the rough draft, the next step is to revise it. When you revise, you change what you have written in order to improve it. You check it over for content and organization, including unity, coherence, and logic.[1] You can change, rearrange, add, or delete, all for the goal of communicating your thoughts more clearly, more effectively, and in a more interesting way.

During the first revision, do not try to correct grammar, sentence structure, spelling, or punctuation; this is proofreading, which you will do later. During the first revision, be concerned mainly with content and organization.

This is how to proceed:

- Read over your paragraph carefully for a general overview. Focus on the *general* aspects of the paper and make notes in the margins so that you can rewrite parts that need to be improved.
- Check to see that you have achieved your stated purpose.
- Check for general logic and coherence. Your audience should be able to follow your ideas easily and understand what you have written.
- Check to make sure that your paragraph has a topic sentence and that the topic sentence has a central (main) focus.
- Check for unity. Cross out any sentence that does not support the topic sentence.
- Check to make sure that the topic sentence is developed with sufficient supporting details. Be certain that each paragraph gives the reader enough information to understand the main idea. If the main point lacks sufficient information, make notes in the margin such as "add more details" or "add an example." Make sure that you haven't used general statements for support. (**Note:** Using concrete supporting details will be taken up in Chapters 6 and 7.)
- Check your use of transition signals.
- Finally, does your paragraph have or need a concluding sentence? If you wrote a final comment, is it on the topic?

Now rewrite your paragraph, incorporating all of the necessary revisions. This is your second draft.

---

[1] These terms are explained in later chapters.

**Step 3:
Proofreading
the Second
Draft**

The next step is to proofread your paper to check for grammar, sentence structure, spelling, and punctuation.

- Check over each sentence for correctness and completeness: no fragments and no choppy or run-on sentences.
- Check over each sentence for a subject and a verb, subject-verb agreement, correct verb tenses, etc.
- Check the mechanics: punctuation, spelling, capitalization, typing errors, etc.
- Change vocabulary words as necessary.

**Step 4: Writing
the Final Copy**

Now you are ready to write the final copy to hand in. Your instructor will expect it to be written neatly and legibly in ink or typed. Be sure that you make all the corrections that you noted on your second draft. After rereading the final copy, don't be surprised if you decide to make a few minor or even major changes. Remember that writing is a continuous process of writing and rewriting until you are satisfied with the final product.

The following models show you how one student worked through the process of writing and revising drafts before arriving at the final copy.

**MODEL**

*The First Rough Draft*

> **Communication Problems**
>
> *combine sentences* *add examples*
>
> [1]International students in the United States face communication problems with Americans. [2]It is a kind of culture shock to them. [3]They soon realize that their verbal skills are poor. ⓣ [4]They lack vocabulary, and they have poor pronunciation.
>
> [5]American people doesn't understand them. [6]They also speak too softly because are shy. [7]~~Students don't feel confidence when speaking English.~~ [8]Is difficult for foreign people to understand Americans. [9]Americans use incomplete sentences, ~~and~~ ⓣ ~~often they use unclear expressions.~~ [10]Americans talk too fast, so it is often imposible to catch their meaning. ⓣ [11]Americans also use a lot of slangs and idioms.
>
> [12]People do not know their meaning. *add concluding sentence*

After writing the first draft, the writer checked her paragraph for organization.

- First, she checked to make sure that her paragraph matched the assignment. The assigned topic was "culture shock." Although her second sentence mentions culture shock, her topic sentence does not, so she decided to combine the two sentences.

**CROSS-REFERENCE**

Use the correction symbols explained in Appendix D, pages 260–261, to mark grammar and sentence structure changes on your draft.

- The writer checked the paragraph for unity and decided that sentence 6, which she had added while writing the rough draft, was a good addition. However, she decided that sentence 7 was off the topic, so she crossed it out.
- Next, she checked to see if there were enough supporting details, and she decided that there weren't. She decided to add examples of poor pronunciation, an incomplete sentence, and an idiom. She couldn't think of an example of an unclear expression, so she crossed out her reference to unclear expressions in sentence 9.

- She also decided to add transition signals such as *first of all, for example,* and *also* to make her paragraph more coherent.
- Finally, she decided to add a concluding sentence.

Then she wrote her second draft.

**MODEL**

*The Second Draft*

---

**Communication Problems**

¹One kind of culture shock faced by international students in the United States ~~when they first arrive in the United States.~~ is ~~the~~ difficulty ~~they have~~ communicating with Americans. ²They soon realize that *sp* their verbal skills are poor. ³First of all, they lack vocabulary, and they have poor pronunciation. *so* ⁴American people ~~doesn't~~ *don't* understand them. ⁵For example, a few days ago, I asked an American student how to get to the library, but because I have trouble pronouncing *r*'s and *l*'s, the student didn't understand me. ⁶I finally ~~have~~ *had* to write it on a piece of paper. ⁷~~They~~ *International students* also speak too softly because *they* ~~are~~ shy. ⁸Is difficult *it* for foreign people to understand Americans, too. ⁹Americans use incomplete sentences, such as "Later" to mean "I'll see you later," and "Coming?" to mean "Are you coming?" ¹⁰Also, Americans talk too fast, so it is often imposible to ~~catch their~~ *sp* *understand* ~~them.~~ meaning ¹¹In addition, Americans also use a lot of slang and idioms. *whose meaning nonnative speakers* ¹²~~People~~ do not know ~~their meaning.~~ ¹³For example, the other day someone said to me, "That drives me up the wall," and I could not imagine what he meant. ¹⁴I had a picture in my mind of him ~~sitting in~~ his car *driving* ~~driving~~ up a wall. ¹⁵It didn't make sense to me. ¹⁶In short, communication is probably the first problem that international students face in the United States. ¹⁷After a while, however, their ears get used to the American way of speaking, and their own verbal ~~skills~~ *abilities* improve.

---

Next, the writer proofread her paragraph for sentence structure, grammar, mechanics (spelling, punctuation, capitalization, etc.), and vocabulary. These are the corrections she made:

*Sentence structure:*

1. This student knows that one of her writing problems is sentences that are sometimes too short, so she tried to find ways to lengthen her short sentences in this paragraph.
   - She added *When they first arrive in the United States* to sentence 2.
   - She combined sentences 3 and 4.
   - She combined sentences 11 and 12.

**2.** She crossed out three words in sentence 1 and changed *sitting in his car driving up a wall* to *driving his car up a wall* in sentence 14 to improve these sentences.

*Coherence:*

It was not clear who *They* referred to in sentence 7 (Americans or international students?), so she changed it to *International students.*

*Grammar:*

This student knows that she occasionally makes mistakes with verbs and omits subjects, so she checked carefully for these problems.
- She needed to correct *doesn't* in sentence 4 and *have* in sentence 6.
- She needed to add *they* in sentence 7 and *It* in sentence 8.

*Mechanics:*

The student writer found two spelling errors and added three missing commas.

*Vocabulary:*
- In sentence 10, because *catch their meaning* is not standard English and because she didn't want to use the word *meaning* in consecutive sentences, she changed the phrase to *understand them.*
- In sentence 11, *slang* is uncountable, so she crossed out the *-s.*
- In sentence 12, *people* is not very specific. *Nonnative speakers* is more appropriate.
- In the concluding sentence she didn't want to repeat the phrase *verbal skills,* so she wrote *verbal abilities* instead.

Then she wrote the final copy to hand in.

**MODEL**

*The Final Copy*

### Communication Problems

One kind of culture shock faced by international students in the United States is difficulty communicating with Americans. When they first arrive in the United States, they soon realize that their verbal skills are poor. First of all, they lack vocabulary, and they have poor pronunciation, so American people don't
5   understand them. For example, a few days ago, I asked an American student how to get to the library, but because I have trouble pronouncing r's and l's, the student didn't understand me. I finally had to write it on a piece of paper. International students also speak too softly because they are shy. It is difficult for foreign people to understand Americans, too. Americans use incomplete sentences, such as
10  "Later" to mean "I'll see you later," and "Coming?" to mean "Are you coming?" Also, Americans talk too fast, so it is often impossible to understand them. In addition, Americans also use a lot of slang and idioms whose meanings nonnative speakers do not know. For example, the other day someone said to me, "That drives me up the wall," and I could not imagine what he meant. I had a picture in
15  my mind of him driving his car up a wall. It didn't make sense to me. In short, communication is probably the first problem that international students face in the United States. After a while, however, their ears get used to the American way of speaking, and their own verbal abilities improve.

# *Review*

These are the important points you should have learned from this chapter:

1. Academic writing is a special kind of writing for college and university work. It is intended for a specific audience (primarily your instructors and professors).
2. Academic writing is formal in tone.
3. The purpose of academic writing is usually to explain or to persuade. The purpose of a piece of writing will determine its rhetorical form.
4. Prewriting activities are useful for narrowing a topic and generating ideas. Three useful brainstorming techniques are listing, freewriting, and clustering.
5. Plan your writing by preparing an outline.
6. Revision is an essential part of the writing process. Your first effort is called the rough draft. After revising it for content and organization (using the Peer Editing Checklists at the ends of most chapters), write your second draft. Proofread your second draft for sentence structure, grammar, mechanics, and vocabulary, and then write a final copy to hand in.

**WRITING PRACTICE**

Choose one of the topics for which you have completed the brainstorming step, and write a paragraph ten to fifteen sentences in length. Use your topic from one of these practices: Practice 2: Brainstorming by Listing (page 6), Practice 3: Brainstorming by Freewriting (page 7), or Practice 4: Brainstorming by Clustering (page 8).
Complete the remaining steps in the writing process:

**STEP 1**
*Prewriting*        Brainstorming: You have already completed this step.

**STEP 2**
*Planning*          Develop an outline, including a topic sentence.

**STEP 3**
*Writing*           Write a rough draft.

**STEP 4**
*Revising*          Edit your rough draft for content and organization.

**STEP 5**
*Rewriting*         Write a second draft, and proofread it for grammar and mechanics.

**STEP 6**          Write a final copy to hand in.

# CHAPTER 2

# What Is a Paragraph?
# An Overview

Egyptian hieroglyphics

## Introduction

A **paragraph** is a basic unit of organization in writing in which a group of related sentences develops one main idea. A paragraph can be as short as one sentence or as long as ten sentences. The number of sentences is unimportant; however, the paragraph should be long enough to develop the main idea clearly.

A paragraph may stand by itself. In academic writing, a paragraph is often used to answer a test question such as the following: "Define management by objectives, and give one example of it from the reading you have done for this class."

A paragraph may also be one part of a longer piece of writing such as a chapter of a book or an essay. You will first learn how to write good paragraphs, and then you will learn how to combine and expand paragraphs to build essays.

## Paragraph Structure

The following model contains all the elements of a good paragraph. Read it carefully two or three times, and try to analyze its structure.

**MODEL**

*Paragraph Structure*

### Gold

Gold, a precious metal, is prized for two important characteristics. First of all, gold has a lustrous[1] beauty that is resistant to corrosion.[2] Therefore, it is suitable for jewelry, coins, and ornamental purposes. Gold never needs to be polished and will remain beautiful forever. For example, a Macedonian[3] coin remains as
5   untarnished[4] today as the day it was minted[5] twenty-three centuries ago. Another important characteristic of gold is its usefulness to industry and science. For many years, it has been used in hundreds of industrial applications. The most recent use of gold is in astronauts' suits. Astronauts wear gold-plated heat shields for protection outside spaceships. In conclusion, gold is treasured not only for its
10   beauty but also for its utility.

### The Three Parts of a Paragraph

A paragraph has three major structural parts: a topic sentence, supporting sentences, and a concluding sentence.

The **topic sentence** states the main idea of the paragraph. It not only names the topic of the paragraph, but it also limits the topic to one or two areas that can be discussed completely in the space of a single paragraph. The specific area is called the controlling idea. Notice how the topic sentence of the model states both the topic and the controlling idea:

TOPIC                                                     CONTROLLING IDEA

<u>Gold</u>, a precious metal, is prized for <u>two important characteristics</u>.

**Supporting sentences** develop the topic sentence. That is, they explain the topic sentence by giving reasons, examples, facts, statistics, and quotations. Some of the supporting sentences that explain the topic sentence about gold are

First of all, gold has a lustrous beauty that is resistant to corrosion.

For example, a Macedonian coin remains as untarnished today as the day it was minted twenty-three centuries ago.

Another important characteristic of gold is its usefulness to industry and science.

The most recent use of gold is in astronauts' suits.

---

[1] **lustrous:** glowing
[2] **corrosion:** chemical damage
[3] **Macedonian:** from an ancient Mediterranean culture

[4] **untarnished:** unchanged in color
[5] **minted:** made, manufactured

The **concluding sentence** signals the end of the paragraph and leaves the reader with important points to remember:

> In conclusion, gold is treasured not only for its beauty but also for its utility.

## *Unity and Coherence*

In addition to the three structural parts of a paragraph, a good paragraph also has the elements of unity and coherence.

**Unity** means that you discuss only *one* main idea in a paragraph. The main idea is stated in the topic sentence, and then each and every supporting sentence develops that idea. If, for example, you announce in your topic sentence that you are going to discuss two important characteristics of gold, discuss only those. Do not discuss any other ideas, such as the price of gold or gold mining.

**Coherence** means that your paragraph is easy to read and understand because (1) your supporting sentences are in some kind of logical order and (2) your ideas are connected by the use of appropriate transition signals. For example, in the paragraph about gold, there are two supporting ideas: Gold is beautiful, and gold is useful. Each of these supporting ideas is discussed, one after the other, and an example is given for each one. This is one kind of logical order. Furthermore, the relationship between the ideas is clearly shown by using appropriate transition words and phrases such as *first of all, for example, another important characteristic,* and *in conclusion.*

In summary, a well-written paragraph contains five elements: a topic sentence, supporting sentences, a concluding sentence, unity, and coherence. In Part I of this book, you will study and practice each of these elements.

**CROSS-REFERENCE**

Consult Appendix B, Chart of Transition Signals, pages 255–257, for a comprehensive list of these signals.

## *The Finished Assignment Format*

Usually, instructors accept either handwritten or typed (on a typewriter or computer) assignments. Follow the instructions below to format the assignments you prepare for this class. Your instructor may assign other formats as well.

**Paper**

*Handwritten*: Standard 8½ by 11 inch white binder paper. Remember that the holes are on the left. Write on one side only.

*Typed*: Standard 8½ by 11 inch white typing paper. Type on one side only.

**Assignment Identification**

*Both handwritten and typed*:

- In the upper right-hand corner, write or type your name, the course title and/or number, and the due date.
- In the upper left-hand corner, write or type the practice number and/or name of the assignment and the page number.

**Title**

*Handwritten*: Center the title on the top line of the first page.

*Typed*: Center the title about 1½ inches from the top of the first page.

**Body**

*Handwritten*:

- Begin writing on the third line after skipping a line.
- Indent the first line of every paragraph about one inch from the margin.
- Write on every other line.

*Typed*:

- Begin typing after skipping four single-spaced lines.
- Indent the first line of every paragraph five spaces.
- Double space; that is, leave one blank line between each line of typing.

*Both handwritten and typed:*

- Leave one-inch margins on the left and right sides and at the bottom of each page.
- Number every page except the first page.

**MODEL**

*Assignment Format*

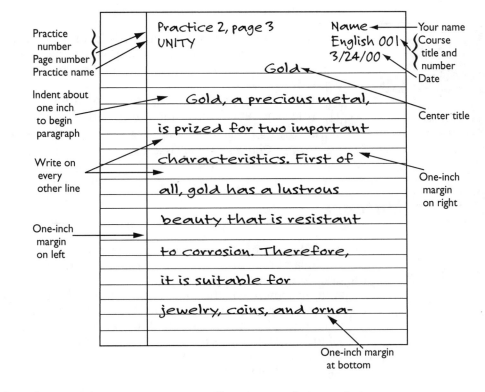

Practice number
Page number
Practice name

Practice 2, page 3
UNITY

Name
English 001
3/24/00

Your name
Course title and number
Date

Gold

Center title

Indent about one inch to begin paragraph

Gold, a precious metal, is prized for two important characteristics. First of all, gold has a lustrous beauty that is resistant to corrosion. Therefore, it is suitable for jewelry, coins, and orna-

Write on every other line

One-inch margin on right

One-inch margin on left

One-inch margin at bottom

## Writing on a Computer

If you have access to a computer and know a word processing program, you can use it for the complete writing process from brainstorming to writing the final draft. On the other hand, you may prefer to do the prewriting stages of your paper with pencil and paper and then use the computer for the writing, editing, and revising stages. Keep in mind that a paragraph written on a computer is formatted like a typewritten one.

Writing on a computer is the most efficient, timesaving method of reorganizing and improving the content of your paper. You can add, change, and delete words, phrases, sentences, or whole paragraphs with just a few keystrokes. You can also move items from one location to another in a flash, and if you don't like the change you just made, you can change it back instantly.

Another advantage of using a computer is that you can tell the computer to proofread your paper for spelling errors. Most word processing programs have spelling checkers built into them. Most also automatically correct errors in capitalization. However, you must still proofread your paper yourself because a computer may not find all of your errors.

As your word processing skills improve, you can start adding boldface and italic type or even photos, charts, and graphic designs to your papers. The possibilities are almost unlimited. It is well worth your time and effort to learn to use a computer for writing.

***How to Write a Title***

Single paragraphs do not usually have titles. Giving your practice paragraphs titles, however, may help you to organize and limit your thoughts. For longer essays or reports, though, the use of titles will become more necessary.

A title tells the reader what the topic of the paragraph is. It is usually a word or phrase, not a sentence. It should be brief, but not so brief that it doesn't tell the reader what to expect.

Remember these points when writing a title:

**COMPUTER TIP**

Use the centering icon to center the title of your writing at the top of the page.

**1.** The first, last, and all important words in a title are capitalized. Prepositions and articles are not considered important words in a title. Prepositions of more than five letters, however, may be capitalized. Articles that begin the title, of course, are capitalized.

**2.** The title of a paragraph or essay is not underlined.

**3.** The title is not enclosed in quotation marks, nor is it ended with a period.

| | |
|---|---|
| My Greatest Culture Shock | The Effects of Inflation |
| How to Choose a Good Used Car | Riding the Subway in New York |

# *The Topic Sentence*

Every good paragraph has a topic sentence, which clearly states the topic and the controlling idea of the paragraph. It is a complete sentence. It is usually (but not always) the first sentence in the paragraph.

A topic sentence is the most important sentence in a paragraph. It briefly indicates what the paragraph is going to discuss. For this reason, the topic sentence is a helpful guide to both the writer and the reader. The writer can see what information to include (and what information to exclude). The reader can see what the paragraph is going to be about and is, therefore, better prepared to understand it.

There are three important points to remember about a topic sentence.

**1.** A topic sentence is a *complete sentence;* that is, it contains a subject, a verb, and (usually) a complement. The following are *not* complete sentences:

> Driving on freeways.
> The importance of gold.
> How to register for college classes.

**2.** A topic sentence contains both a *topic* and a *controlling idea*. It names the topic and then limits the topic to a specific area to be discussed in the space of a single paragraph. The following examples show how a topic sentence states both the topic and the controlling idea in a complete sentence:

> Driving on freeways requires skill and alertness.
> Gold, a precious metal, is prized for two important characteristics.
> Registering for college classes can be a frustrating experience for new students.

**3.** A topic sentence is the most general statement in the paragraph because it gives only the main idea. It does not give any specific details.

The following is an example of a general statement that could serve as a topic sentence:

> The Arabic origin of many English words is not always obvious.

The following sentence, on the other hand, is too specific:

> The slang expression *so long* (meaning "goodbye") is probably a corruption of the Arabic *salaam*.

Sentences such as the following may be too general:

> English is a difficult language to learn.

**Position of Topic Sentences**

The topic sentence may be the first or last sentence in a paragraph. The topic sentence may also be the first *and* last sentence of the paragraph— "sandwich-style." A sandwich-style paragraph is especially helpful to your reader if the paragraph is very long. The second topic sentence in the sandwich-style paragraph also serves as a concluding sentence.

Study the following three paragraphs. Notice the different positions for the topic sentence in each. The topic sentences are underlined.

**MODEL**

*Position of Topic Sentences*

### Hurricanes

<u>Hurricanes, which are also called cyclones, exert tremendous power.</u> These violent storms are often a hundred miles in diameter, and their winds can reach velocities[1] of seventy-five miles per hour or more. Furthermore, the strong winds and heavy rainfall that accompany them can completely destroy a
5  small town in a couple of hours. The energy that is released by a hurricane in one day exceeds the total energy consumed by humankind throughout the world in one year.

### Medical Miracles to Come

By the year 2009, a vaccine[2] against the common cold will have been developed. By the same year, the first human will have been successfully cloned.[3] By the year 2014, parents will be able to create designer children. Genetic therapy will be able to manipulate genes for abilities, intelligence, and
5  hair, eye, and skin color. By 2020, most diseases will be able to be diagnosed and treated at home, and by 2030, cancer and heart disease will have been wiped out. <u>These are just a few examples of medical miracles that are expected in the next few decades.</u>

### Synonyms

<u>Synonyms, words that have the same basic meaning, do not always have the same emotional meaning.</u> For example, the words *stingy* and *frugal* both mean "careful with money." However, to call a person stingy is an insult, while the word *frugal* has a much more positive connotation.[4] Similarly, a person
5  wants to be slender but not skinny, and aggressive but not pushy. <u>Therefore, you should be careful in choosing words because many so-called synonyms are not really synonymous at all.</u>

---

[1] **velocities:** speeds
[2] **vaccine:** substance that prevents a specific disease such as smallpox or polio
[3] **cloned:** made an exact copy of
[4] **connotation:** positive or negative meaning

Remember, the topic sentence indicates the main idea of a paragraph and is the most general statement in the paragraph.

**STEP 1**   Decide which of the following sentences is the topic sentence of the paragraph.

**STEP 2**   Write TS on the line next to that sentence.

**STEP 3**   Decide the order of the supporting sentences and number them SS1, SS2, SS3, and so on.

**Paragraph 1**

_____ **a.** It enables customers to do several banking transactions twenty-four hours a day.

_____ **b.** In addition, a customer can transfer funds between accounts or get a cash advance on a credit card.

_____ **c.** An automated teller machine (ATM) is a convenient miniature bank.

_____ **d.** For example, a customer can use an ATM to deposit money and withdraw a limited amount of cash.

**Paragraph 2**

_____ **a.** After an attack by a great white, 462 stitches were required to sew up an Australian scuba diver.

_____ **b.** With their razor-sharp teeth and strong jaws, great white sharks are very dangerous.

_____ **c.** Nevertheless, one did just that near a public beach in Australia in 1985.

_____ **d.** Even when they attack humans, however, great whites do not usually eat them.

_____ **e.** In 1997, a great white shark bit a man surfing at a beach in California and left three shark teeth in his leg.

_____ **f.** It bit in half and totally devoured[1] a young female swimmer.

_____ **g.** Great whites do not usually attack humans, but when they do, they always cause serious injury and even death.

**Paragraph 3**

_____ **a.** Another important change was that people had the freedom to live and work wherever they wanted.

_____ **b.** The earliest significant change was for farming families, who were no longer isolated.

_____ **c.** The final major change brought by the automobile was the building of superhighways, suburbs, huge shopping centers, and many theme parks such as Disney World in Florida.

_____ **d.** The automobile revolutionized the American way of life.

_____ **e.** The automobile enabled them to drive to towns and cities comfortably and conveniently.

_____ **f.** In fact, people could work in a busy metropolitan city and drive home to the quiet suburbs.

---

[1] **devoured:** ate

**Paragraph 4**

_____ **a.** In time, this melted part rises as a magma.[2]

_____ **b.** The formation of a volcanic eruption is a dramatic series of events.

_____ **c.** As the plate[3] sinks, friction and the earth's heat cause part of it to melt.

_____ **d.** The magma produces heat, steam, and pressure.

_____ **e.** First of all, most volcanoes are formed where two plates collide.[4]

_____ **f.** Then one of the plates is forced under the other and sinks.

_____ **g.** When the heat, steam, and pressure from the magma finally reach the surface of the Earth, a volcanic eruption occurs.

## The Two Parts of a Topic Sentence

A topic sentence has two essential parts: the topic and the controlling idea. The _topic_ names the subject, or main idea, of the paragraph. The _controlling idea_ makes a specific comment about the topic, which indicates what the rest of the paragraph will say about the topic. It limits or controls the topic to a specific aspect of the topic to be discussed in the space of a single paragraph.

|  TOPIC  |  CONTROLLING IDEA  |
|---|---|

Convenience foods are <u>easy to prepare.</u>

In this example, the topic is named: convenience foods. A specific comment is then made about the topic: They are easy to prepare. From this sentence, the reader immediately knows that the supporting sentences in the remainder of the paragraph will explain or prove how quick and easy it is to prepare convenience foods and perhaps give some examples (frozen dinners, canned soups, etc.).

|  CONTROLLING IDEA  |  TOPIC  |
|---|---|

<u>The native foods of America's immigrant population</u> are reflected in American cooking.

In this example, the topic is American food. The controlling idea of this topic sentence is that Americans eat many foods from other countries. Therefore, the reader should expect the paragraph to give examples of popular ethnic foods such as fried rice (Chinese), tacos (Mexican), sauerbraten (German), sukiyaki (Japanese), spaghetti (Italian), and so on.

|  TOPIC  |  CONTROLLING IDEA  |
|---|---|

The average American teenager consumes <u>enormous quantities of junk food.</u>

In this example, the topic is the average American teenager. The controlling idea about the topic states that the American teenager eats junk food. Thus, the rest of the paragraph should discuss the quantities and types of junk food that American teenagers eat (soft drinks, potato chips, candy bars, etc.).

---

[2] **magma:** melted rock inside the earth
[3] **plate:** rigid section of rock
[4] **collide:** clash

**PRACTICE 2**

*Identifying the Parts of a Topic Sentence*

Circle the topic and underline the controlling idea in each of the following sentences.

**Example**

(Driving on freeways) requires <u>skill and alertness.</u>

1. Driving on freeways requires nerves of steel.[1]
2. Driving on freeways requires an aggressive attitude.
3. The Caribbean island of Trinidad attracts tourists because of its calypso music.
4. Spectacular beaches make Puerto Rico a tourist paradise.
5. Living in an American college dormitory can be a stressful experience for newly arrived international students.
6. Many religious rules developed from the health needs of ancient times.
7. The spread of AIDS can be slowed by educating the public.
8. A major problem for international students is taking essay examinations.
9. Participating in class discussions in English is a problem for international students.
10. In my opinion, many television commercials for cosmetics lie to women.
11. Owning an automobile is a necessity for me.
12. It is an expensive luxury to own an automobile in a large city.

## Writing Topic Sentences

When you write a sentence, remember these two points:

**1.** A topic sentence should be neither too general nor too specific. If it is too general, the reader cannot tell exactly what the paragraph is going to discuss. If it is too specific, the writer may not have anything left to write about in the rest of the paragraph.

Think of a topic sentence as being like the name of a particular course on a restaurant menu. When you order food in a restaurant, you want to know more about a particular course than just "meat" or "soup" or "salad." You want to know *generally* what kind of salad it is. Potato salad? Mixed green salad? Fruit salad? However, you do not necessarily want to know all of its ingredients.

Similarly, the reader of a paragraph wants to know *generally* what to expect in a paragraph, but he/she does not want to learn all of the specific details in the first sentence.

> *Too general:* American food is terrible.
> *Too specific:* American food is tasteless and greasy because Americans use too many canned, frozen, and prepackaged foods and because everything is fried in oil or butter.
> *Good:* American food is tasteless and greasy.

**2.** Do not include too many unrelated ideas in your topic sentence; if you do, your paragraph will not be unified.

> *Too many ideas:* San Francisco is famous for its temperate climate, its many tourist attractions, and its cosmopolitan[2] atmosphere.

The three parts of this controlling idea are too unrelated for a single paragraph. They would require three separate paragraphs.

> *Good:* San Francisco is famous for its cosmopolitan atmosphere.

---

[1] **nerves of steel:** very strong nerves (idiom)      [2] **cosmopolitan:** international

**PRACTICE 3**

*Writing Topic Sentences*

**A.**  Write good topic sentences for the following paragraphs in the spaces provided. Remember to include both a topic and a controlling idea.

**Paragraph 1**

_____

_____

Americans relaxing at home, for example, may put on **kimonos**,[3] which is a Japanese word. Americans who live in a warm climate may take an afternoon **siesta**[4] on an outdoor **patio**[5] without even realizing that these are Spanish words. In their gardens, they may enjoy the fragrance of **jasmine** flowers, a word that came into English from Persian. They may even relax on a **chaise longue**[6] while sipping a drink made with **vodka**, words of French and Russian origin, respectively.

**Paragraph 2**

_____

_____

In European universities, students are not required to attend classes. In fact, professors in Germany generally do not know the names of the students enrolled in their courses. In the United States, however, students are required to attend all classes and may be penalized[7] if they don't. Furthermore, in the European system, there is usually just one comprehensive examination at the end of the students' entire four or five years of study. In the American system, on the other hand, there are usually numerous quizzes, tests, and homework assignments, and there is almost always a final examination in each course at the end of the semester.

**Paragraph 3**

_____

_____

For example, the Eskimos, living in a treeless region of snow and ice, sometimes build temporary homes out of thick blocks of ice. People who live in deserts, on the other hand, use the most available material, mud or clay, which provides good insulation[8] from the heat. In Northern Europe, Russia, and other areas of the world where forests are plentiful, people usually construct their homes out of wood. In the islands of the South Pacific, where there is a plentiful supply of bamboo and palm, people use these tough, fibrous[9] plants to build their homes.

---

[3] **kimono:** lounging robe
[4] **siesta:** afternoon nap
[5] **patio:** courtyard
[6] **chaise longue:** lounge chair

[7] **penalized:** punished
[8] **insulation:** protection
[9] **fibrous:** containing fiber

**B.**  Write two or three topic sentences for each of the following topics. In other words, give two or three controlling ideas for the same topic.

**Example**

*Topic:*              Television's effects on children

*Topic sentences:*    (1) Television is harmful to children because it teaches them violence as a way of solving problems.
                      (2) Television retards[1] a child's reading ability.

Smoking cigarettes              Pollution
Foreign travel                  Touring your hometown
Prejudice

**C.**  With your classmates, choose three topics that interest you as a group. Write a topic sentence for each topic. Be sure to include a controlling idea.

# *The Concluding Sentence*

Now that you know how to write a good topic sentence for a paragraph, you should also learn how to write a good concluding sentence. A concluding sentence is not absolutely necessary; in fact, a concluding sentence is not customary for every paragraph in a multiparagraph essay. However, for single paragraphs, especially long ones, a concluding sentence is helpful to the reader because it signals the end of the paragraph and because it is a reminder of the important points.

A concluding sentence serves three purposes:

**1.**  It signals the end of the paragraph.
**2.**  It summarizes the main points of the paragraph.
**3.**  It gives a final comment on the topic and leaves the reader with the most important ideas to think about.

Use one of the following end-of-paragraph signals to introduce your concluding sentence:

## END-OF-PARAGRAPH SIGNALS

| THESE ARE FOLLOWED BY A COMMA | | THESE ARE NOT FOLLOWED BY A COMMA |
|---|---|---|
| Finally, | As a result, | We can see that . . . |
| In conclusion, | Indeed, | It is clear that . . . |
| In summary, | In brief, | These examples show that . . . |
| Therefore, | In short, | There can be no doubt that . . . |
| Thus, | | The evidence suggests that . . . |

---

[1] **retards:** slows down

The examples that follow demonstrate two different types of concluding sentences. The first one paraphrases the topic sentence; that is, the concluding sentence repeats the main idea of the topic sentence in different words. The second example summarizes the two main points of the paragraph, which were not specifically stated in the topic sentence.

**MODEL**

*Concluding Sentences*

> ### Synonyms
>
> <u>Synonyms, words that have the same basic meaning, do not always have the same emotional meaning.</u> For example, the words *stingy* and *frugal* both mean "careful with money." However, to call a person stingy is an insult, while the word *frugal* has a much more positive connotation. Similarly, a person
> 5  wants to be slender but not skinny, and aggressive but not pushy. <u>Therefore, you should be careful in choosing words because many so-called synonyms are not really synonymous at all.</u>
>
> ### Gold
>
> <u>Gold, a precious metal, is prized for two important characteristics.</u> First of all, gold has a lustrous beauty that is resistant to corrosion. Therefore, it is suitable for jewelry, coins, and ornamental purposes. Gold never needs to be polished and will remain beautiful forever. For example, a Macedonian coin
> 5  remains as untarnished today as the day it was minted twenty-three centuries ago. Another important characteristic of gold is its usefulness to industry and science. For many years, it has been used in hundreds of industrial applications. The most recent use of gold is in astronauts' suits. Astronauts wear gold-plated heat shields for protection outside spaceships. <u>In conclusion, gold is</u>
> 10  <u>treasured not only for its beauty but also for its utility.</u>

**PRACTICE 4**

*Writing Concluding Sentences*

**STEP 1**  Underline the topic sentence in each paragraph.
**STEP 2**  Determine the main idea of each paragraph.
**STEP 3**  Add a good concluding sentence to each. You may either paraphrase the topic sentence or summarize the main points.
**STEP 4**  Begin each concluding sentence with an end-of-paragraph signal.

**Paragraph 1**

You can be a good conversationalist by being a good listener. When you are conversing with someone, pay close attention to the speaker's words while looking at his or her face. Show your interest by smiling and/or nodding. Furthermore, don't interrupt while someone is speaking; it is impolite to
5  do so. If you have a good story, wait until the speaker is finished. Also, watch your body language; it can affect your communication whether you are the speaker or the listener. For instance, don't sit slumped in a chair or make nervous hand and foot movements. Be relaxed and bend your body slightly forward to show interest in the person and the conversation. _____

_____

_____

**Paragraph 2**

    Modern communication technology is driving workers in the corporate world crazy. They feel buried under the large number of messages they receive daily. In addition to telephone calls, office workers receive dozens of E-mail and voice mail messages daily. In one company, in fact, managers
5 receive an average of 100 messages a day. Because they don't have enough time to respond to these messages during office hours, it is common for them to do so in the evenings or on weekends at home. _____

_____

_____

# *Review*

These are the important points you should have learned from this chapter:

**1.** A good topic sentence

- Is a complete sentence with a subject, a verb, and a controlling idea
- Is neither too general nor too specific. It states clearly what the main idea of the paragraph is but does not include specific details
- Is usually the first sentence in the paragraph

**2.** A good concluding sentence

- Signals the end of the paragraph
- Summarizes the important points briefly or restates the topic sentence in different words

**WRITING PRACTICE**

Choose one of the topics from Practice 3B (page 26) and write a paragraph ten to fifteen sentences in length. Remember the steps in the writing process:

**CROSS-REFERENCE**

You may wish to use both coordination and subordination sentence patterns. Refer to *Coordination vs. Subordination* on pages 163–164.

| | |
|---|---|
| **STEP 1** *Prewriting* | Brainstorm for Parallelism: You have already completed this step. |
| **STEP 2** *Planning* | Develop an outline that includes a topic sentence and a concluding sentence (if necessary). Underline them. |
| **STEP 3** *Writing* | Write a rough draft. |
| **STEP 4** *Editing* | Ask a classmate to check your rough draft against the Peer Editing Checklist that follows. |
| **STEP 5** *Rewriting* | Write a second draft, and proofread it for grammar and mechanics. |
| **STEP 6** | Write a final copy to hand in. |

### *Peer Editing*

**Peer editing** is an interactive process of reading and commenting on a classmate's writing. You will exchange rough drafts with a classmate, read each other's paragraphs, and make helpful comments to improve your classmate's content and organization and, therefore, his or her clarity. A peer editor may say that your paragraph is "OK" or "good" but may still offer specific suggestions to improve it. If something is not clear, or if something needs to be explained more completely, he or she will tell you. You should consider his or her suggestions even though you may decide not to use all of them.

This is how to proceed: Exchange copies of your paragraph and textbooks with a classmate. Write your comments and suggestions about his or her paragraph in his or her book. Your classmate will write comments and suggestions about your paragraph in your book.

## PEER EDITING CHECKLIST

|  | PEER EDITOR'S COMMENTS AND SUGGESTIONS |
|---|---|
| **GENERAL** | |
| **1.** What do you like best about this paragraph? | |
| **PAPER FORMAT** | |
| **2.** Is the format (title, indenting, double spacing, margins) correct? Does it look like the model on page 19? | |
| **ORGANIZATION AND CONTENT** | |
| **3. Topic sentence:** Is there a clear topic sentence? Does it have a controlling idea? <br><br> **4. Supporting sentences:** Is the main idea clear? Does the writer need to add more details to explain it? <br><br> **5. Concluding sentence:** Is there a concluding sentence? Does it begin with an appropriate end-of-paragraph signal? | |
| **SENTENCE STRUCTURE** | |
| **6.** Are there any unclear sentences? Can you suggest a way to improve them? | |
| **GRAMMAR AND MECHANICS** | |
| **7.** Are there any errors in grammar and mechanics (spelling, punctuation, and capitalization)? | |

# CHAPTER

# 3 Unity and Outlining

Sumerian tablet

## *Unity*

Another important element of a good paragraph is **unity**. Every good paragraph has unity, which means that only *one* main idea is discussed. For example, if your paragraph is about the advantages of owning a compact car, discuss only that. Do not discuss the disadvantages. Furthermore, it is a good idea for beginning academic writers to discuss only *one* advantage, such as gas economy, in each paragraph. If you begin to discuss another advantage, start a new paragraph. Sometimes it is possible to discuss two or even three aspects[1] of the same idea in one paragraph *if they are closely*

---

[1] **aspects:** ways of thinking about something

*related to each other.* For example, you could discuss gas economy and low maintenance costs in the same paragraph because they are closely related, but you should not discuss both gas economy and easier parking in the same paragraph because they are not closely related.

The second part of unity is that every supporting sentence must directly explain or prove the main idea that is stated in the topic sentence. Do not include any information that does not directly support the topic sentence. Sometimes students write supporting sentences that are "off the topic." These are called irrelevant sentences. For example, if you are writing a paragraph about the high cost of college tuition, you could mention inflation[2] as a factor. However, if you write several sentences about inflation, you are getting off the topic, and your paragraph will not have unity.

Study the three paragraphs that follow. All of them discuss the same topic. In your opinion, which paragraph has unity and which two do not? Which paragraph discusses more than one topic? Which paragraph has irrelevant sentences?

**MODEL**

*Paragraphs with and without Unity*

**Paragraph 1**

The HIV/AIDS epidemic[3] is still growing explosively in most parts of the world. In Central and Eastern Europe, HIV is spreading rapidly in countries that had almost no cases a few years ago. In China, there were an estimated 10,000 HIV-infected persons at the end of 1993, and this total grew ten-fold, to 100,000,
5  by the end of 1995. In the countries of sub-Saharan Africa, the HIV/AIDS epidemic rages on.[4] In Kenya, Malawi, Rwanda, Tanzania, Uganda, Zambia, and Zimbabwe, 10 percent of the women visiting postnatal[5] clinics in urban areas are infected with HIV, and in some areas, the rate is 40 percent. Mothers can give the HIV virus to their children during pregnancy and childbirth or when breast-feeding. The virus is
10  also transmitted through blood and blood products. For example, drug users who share needles may become infected. The main method of transmission is, of course, unprotected sex, which accounts for 75 to 85 percent of infections.

**Paragraph 2**

The HIV/AIDS epidemic is still growing explosively in most parts of the world. In Central and Eastern Europe, HIV is spreading rapidly in countries that had almost no cases a few years ago. In China, there were an estimated 10,000 HIV-infected persons at the end of 1993, and this total grew ten-fold, to 100,000, by the
5  end of 1995. In the countries of sub-Saharan Africa, the HIV/AIDS epidemic rages on. In Kenya, Malawi, Rwanda, Tanzania, Uganda, Zambia, and Zimbabwe, 10 percent of the women visiting postnatal clinics in urban areas are infected with HIV, and in some areas, the rate is 40 percent. Around the world, HIV infection rates are sky-rocketing among sex workers.[6] In Nairobi, Kenya, 80 percent of sex workers are
10  infected, and in Vietnam, the rate of infection climbed from 9 percent to 38 percent between 1992 and 1995. These statistics illustrate with frightening clarity that HIV/AIDS is still a major health problem in most areas of the world.

---

[2] **inflation:** decrease in the value of money
[3] **epidemic:** widespread disease
[4] **rages on:** continues to spread

[5] **postnatal:** after childbirth
[6] **sex workers:** prostitutes, people (usually women) who perform sexual acts for money

**Paragraph 3**

   The HIV/AIDS epidemic is still growing explosively in most parts of the world. In Central and Eastern Europe, HIV is spreading rapidly in countries that had almost no cases a few years ago. In China, there were an estimated 10,000 HIV-infected persons at the end of 1993, and this total grew ten-fold, to 100,000, by the
5  end of 1995. There is evidence that in the United States, the United Kingdom, Australia, and New Zealand, HIV infection rates are declining, at least among males. This is a result of a combination of prevention methods. In the countries of sub-Saharan Africa, the HIV/AIDS epidemic rages on. In Kenya, Malawi, Rwanda, Tanzania, Uganda, Zambia, and Zimbabwe, 10 percent of the women visiting postna-
10 tal clinics in urban areas are infected with HIV, and in some areas, the rate is 40 percent. Although there is no cure for HIV/AIDS, new medicines are available that prolong the lives of people with HIV.

**PRACTICE 1**

*Unity*

**A.** The following short essay has not been divided into paragraphs, but it should contain six: an introductory paragraph, four body paragraphs, and a concluding paragraph.

**STEP 1**   Read the entire essay once or twice.
**STEP 2**   Decide where each new paragraph should begin. (Where does the author begin to discuss a different topic?)
**STEP 3**   Underline the first sentence of each paragraph.

### Culture, Logic,[1] and Rhetoric

   Logic, which is basis of rhetoric, comes from culture; it is not universal. Rhetoric, therefore, is not universal either but varies from culture to culture. The rhetorical system of one language is neither better nor worse than the rhetorical system of another language, but it is different. English logic and
5  English rhetoric, which are based on Anglo-European cultural patterns, are linear[2]—that is, a good English paragraph begins with a general statement of its content and then carefully develops that statement with a series of specific illustrations. A good English paragraph may also use just the reverse sequence: It may state a whole series of examples and then summarize those
10 examples in a single statement at the end of the paragraph. In either case, however, the flow of ideas occurs in a straight line from the opening sentence to the last sentence. Furthermore, a well-structured English paragraph is never digressive.[3] There is nothing that does not belong to the paragraph and nothing that does not support the topic sentence. A type of construction found
15 in Arabic and Persian writing is very different. Whereas English writers use a linear sequence, Arabic and Persian writers tend to construct a paragraph in a parallel sequence using many coordinators[4] such as **and** and **but**. In English, maturity of style is often judged by the degree of subordination[5]

---

[1] **logic:** way of thinking or reasoning
[2] **linear:** in a straight line
[3] **digressive:** wandering away from the main topic

[4] **coordinators:** words that join equal elements
[5] **subordination:** the joining of two unequal elements

20 rather than by the degree of coordination. Therefore, the Arabic and Persian styles of writing, with their emphasis on coordination, seem awkward and immature to an English reader. Some Asian writers, on the other hand, use an indirect approach. In this kind of writing, the topic is viewed from a variety of angles. The topic is never analyzed directly; it is referred to only indirectly. Again, such a development in an English paragraph is awkward and

25 unnecessarily vague[6] to an English reader. Spanish rhetoric differs from English rhetoric in still another way. While the rules of English rhetoric require that every sentence in a paragraph relate directly to the central idea, a Spanish-speaking writer loves to fill a paragraph with interesting digressions. Although a Spanish paragraph may begin and end on the same topic,

30 the writer often digresses into areas that are not directly related to the topic. Spanish rhetoric, therefore, does not follow the English rule of paragraph unity. In summary, a student who has mastered the grammar of English may still write poor papers unless he/she has also mastered the rhetoric of English. Also, the student may have difficulty reading an essay written by

35 the rules of English rhetoric unless he/she understands the "logical" differences from those of his/her own native tongue.

**B.** Both of the following paragraphs break the rule of unity because they contain one or more irrelevant sentences—sentences that do not directly support the topic sentence.

   **STEP 1**   Locate and underline the topic sentence of each paragraph.
   **STEP 2**   Find the irrelevant sentence(s) and cross them out.

### Paragraph 1

   Adventure travel is the hot trend in the tourism industry. Ordinary people are no longer content to spend their two weeks away from the office resting on a sunny beach in Hawaii. More and more often, they are choosing to spend their vacations rafting down wild rivers, hiking through steamy rain forests,
5 climbing the world's highest mountains, or traversing[7] slippery glaciers.[8] People of all ages are choosing educational study tours for their vacations.

### Paragraph 2

   Daredevil[9] sports are also becoming popular. Young people especially are increasingly willing to risk life and limb[10] while mountain biking, backcountry snowboarding, or high-speed skateboarding. Soccer is also becoming popular in the United States, where it was not well known
5 until recently. One of the riskiest new sports is skysurfing, in which people jump out of airplanes with graphite boards attached to their feet. Skysurfing rivals[11] skydiving and bungee jumping for the amount of thrills—and risk.

---

[6] **vague:** unclear
[7] **traversing:** going across
[8] **glaciers:** slowly moving rivers of ice

[9] **daredevil:** high-risk
[10] **risk life and limb:** take a chance of injury or death
[11] **rivals:** competes with

**C.** Both of the following paragraphs have not only two or more topics but also irrelevant sentences.

    **STEP 1**   Decide where each paragraph should be divided into two or more paragraphs. Underline the topic sentence of each.

    **STEP 2**   Find the irrelevant sentence(s) and cross them out.

### Paragraph 1

Because the Internet makes the world a smaller place, the value of having a common language is greatly increased. The question is—which language? Because the Internet grew up in the United States, the largest percentage of its content is now in English. Bill Gates, Microsoft's president, believes

5  that English will remain valuable for a long time as a common language for international communication. His company spends $200 million a year translating software into other languages. He says, "Unless you read English passably well, you miss out on some of the Internet experience." Someday, software may be available to instantly translate both written and spoken lan-

10  guage so well that the need for any common language could decline. That day is decades away, however, because flawless machine translation is a very tough problem. Software that does crude[1] translations already exists. It is useful if all you are trying to do is understand the general idea of something you see on your computer screen. However, if you are trying to negotiate a

15  contract or discuss a scientific subject where details are important, machine translation is totally useless. Computer spelling checkers also exist for various languages.

### Paragraph 2

Even when you try to be polite, it's easy to do the wrong thing inadvertently in a new culture. For example, when someone offers you food or a beverage in America, accept it the first time it is offered. If you say "No, thank you" because it is polite to decline the first one or two offers in your culture,

5  you could become very hungry and thirsty. An American thinks that "no" means "no" and will usually not offer again. American meals are usually more informal than meals in other countries, and the times of meals may be different. Although Americans are usually very direct in social matters, there are a few occasions when they are not. If an American says, "Please drop by

10  sometime," he may or may not want you to visit him in his home. Your clue that this may not be a real invitation is the word "sometime." In some areas of the United States, Americans do not expect you to visit them unless you have an invitation for a specific day and time. In other areas of the United States, however, "dropping by" is a friendly, neighborly gesture. Idioms are

15  often difficult for newcomers to understand.

---

[1] **crude:** rough, without refinement or elegance

# *Paragraph Outlining*

An outline is like an architect's plan for a house. An architect plans a house before it is built to make sure that all the parts will fit. Like an architect, you should plan a paragraph before you write it to make sure that all of your ideas will fit.

Learning to outline will improve your writing for three reasons. First of all, it will help you organize your ideas. Specifically, an outline will ensure that you won't include any irrelevant ideas, that you won't leave out any important points, and that your supporting sentences will be in logical order. Second, learning to outline will help you write more quickly. It may take some practice at first, but once you become used to outlining your ideas before you start to write, you will be surprised at how fast you will actually be able to write. Preparing an outline is 75 percent of the work. The actual writing becomes easier because you don't have to worry about what you are going to say; you already have a well-organized plan to follow. Finally, your grammar will improve because you will be able to concentrate on it, not on your thoughts or organization. Improved organization, speed, and grammar make learning to outline well worth the effort.

There are several different outline forms that can be used. The form used in this book is particularly helpful for students who have never practiced outlining before. However, your instructor may recommend a different form.

A simple outline for a short paragraph might look like this:

**COMPUTER TIP**

Your computer program may have an outlining feature: special commands to help you set up your outline easily.

Topic Sentence ◄─────────────────── | Topic sentence underlined |

*Indent and use capital letters (A, B, C)*

   A.   First Supporting Point
   B.   Second Supporting Point   ◄── | These are equal in importance and written in parallel form |
   C.   Third Supporting Point

*No number or letter*

Concluding Sentence ◄─────────── | Concluding sentence underlined |

Of course, the number of main supporting points (A, B, C) will vary widely from paragraph to paragraph. This particular paragraph has three main supporting points; others may have only two or as many as ten. Also, some paragraphs may not have a concluding sentence, and in others, the topic sentence may not be the first sentence.

Study the simple outline below for the second paragraph above. Then reread the paragraph to see how the writer used this plan to write a well-organized paragraph that is easy to understand.

**MODEL**

*Simple Paragraph Outline*

---

Learning to outline will improve your writing for three reasons.

   A.   It will help you organize your ideas.
   B.   It will help you write more quickly.
   C.   It will help you improve your grammar.

Improved organization, speed, and grammar make learning to outline well worth the effort.

*The "Parallel Form" Rule*

Equal parts of an outline should be written in parallel form. This means that all ideas with the same kind of letter or number should have the same grammatical form; that is, they all should be complete sentences, or all nouns, or all adjectives, or all prepositional phrases, etc. In the first outline that follows, point A is a sentence. What are points B and C?

1. The English language is constantly changing.

*WRONG*
   A. Pronunciation has changed in the past 500 years.
   B. Some grammatical changes.
   C. Vocabulary.

Indeed, English, like all living languages, is continually changing in pronunciation, grammar, and especially vocabulary.

In the next outline, points A, B, and C are all nouns. This outline has parallel form.

2. The English language is constantly changing.

*RIGHT*
   A. Pronunciation.
   B. Grammar.
   C. Vocabulary.

Indeed, English, like all living languages, is continually changing in pronunciation, grammar, and especially vocabulary.

**CROSS-REFERENCE**

Look at *Parallelism* (pages 166–169) for more information.

In the following outline, points A, B, and C are all sentences. This outline also has parallel form.

3. The English language is constantly changing.

*RIGHT*
   A. Pronunciation has changed in the past 500 years.
   B. Some changes in grammar have occurred and are still occurring.
   C. Vocabulary is the area of greatest change.

Indeed, English, like all living languages is continually changing in pronunciation, grammar, and especially vocabulary.

**PRACTICE 2**

*Making Outlines Parallel*

Rewrite each of these outlines to make the support part parallel in form.

1. San Francisco is famous for its tourist attractions.
   A. Golden Gate Park is very famous.
   B. Chinatown.
   C. Fisherman's Wharf attracts hundreds of tourists.
   D. Riding the cable cars.

For these four attractions alone, San Francisco is well worth a visit.

2. Gold, a precious metal, is prized for two important characteristics.
   A. It is beautiful.
   B. Usefulness to science and industry.

In conclusion, gold is treasured not only for its beauty but also for its utility.

3.  Medical researchers will produce some amazing advances in the very near future.

    A.  By the year 2009, a vaccine against the common cold.
    B.  Cloning of the first human in the same year.
    C.  By the year 2014, parents will be able to create designer children.
    D.  By 2020, most diseases diagnosed and treated at home.
    E.  By the year 2030, cancer and heart disease wiped out.

These are just a few examples of medical miracles that are expected in the next few decades.

## The Equivalent Value Rule: Outlines with Details

In an outline, ideas that have the same kind of letter or number must have equal value. This is the "equivalent value" rule. This means that main supporting points all should have the same kind of letter or number. Details should have a different kind of letter or number. Study the detailed outline that follows to see how this system works.

**MODEL**

*Detailed Paragraph Outline*

Learning to outline will improve your writing for three reasons.

    A.  It will help you organize your ideas.
        1.  You won't include irrelevant ideas.
        2.  You won't leave out important points.
        3.  Your supporting sentences will be in logical order.
    B.  It will help you write more quickly.
        1.  It may take practice.
        2.  Seventy-five percent of the work is done.
        3.  You don't worry about what you are going to say.
    C.  It will help you improve your grammar.
        You will be able to concentrate on it.

Improved organization, speed, and grammar make learning to outline well worth the effort.

**Note:** The detail under point C has no number because there is only one detail for it. A further outlining rule states, "If there is no B, there cannot be an A; if there is no 2, there cannot be a 1."

**PRACTICE 3**

*Outlines with Details*

Organize the items in the lists below and on page 38 into outlines. Give the items with equal value the same kind of letter or number. You may follow the system of capital letters and numbers used in the model above, or your instructor may recommend a different system.

**A.  Sports**

surfing     scuba diving     team sports     wrestling
fishing     basketball     soccer     boxing
baseball     skiing     ice skating     American football
individual sports     tennis     hiking     snowboarding
volleyball     marathon running     bicycle racing

**B. Differences between British and American English**

| | |
|---|---|
| bonnet/hood | petrol/gas |
| British people don't always | defence/defense |
|    pronounce *r* | grammar |
| pronunciation | the structure "have got" is not used in |
| colour/color |    American English |
| vocabulary | spelling |
| biscuit/cookie | *schedule:* British say [shed-u-al], |
| *a* is pronounced like *a* in *father* |    Americans say [sked-u-al] |
|    in British English | realise/realize |

# *Review*

These are the important points you should have learned from this chapter:

1. Every good paragraph has unity. Discuss only one idea in each paragraph. All supporting sentences must directly support the topic sentence.
2. An outline is useful as a plan for a paragraph. It organizes the ideas. Outlines should be written in parallel form and follow the equivalent value rule.

Choose one of the suggested topics that follows, and write a paragraph that is ten to fifteen sentences in length. Remember the steps in the writing process:

**CROSS-REFERENCE**

Try to write some compound sentences with conjunctive adverbs instead of coordinating conjunctions. To learn how, see pages 157–159.

| | |
|---|---|
| **STEP 1**<br>*Prewriting* | Brainstorm a topic for ideas, using the listening, freewriting, or clustering techniques you have learned. |
| **STEP 2**<br>*Planning* | Develop an outline that includes a topic sentence and a concluding sentence (if necessary). Underline them. |
| **STEP 3**<br>*Writing* | Write a rough draft. |
| **STEP 4**<br>*Editing* | Have a classmate check your rough draft against the Peer Editing Checklist that follows. Make sure your paragraph has unity. |
| **STEP 5**<br>*Rewriting* | Write a second draft, and proofread it for grammar and mechanics. |
| **STEP 6** | Write a final copy to hand in. |

## *Topic Suggestions*

How have computers changed our lives?

Important skills or qualities of a doctor, veterinarian, engineer, kindergarten teacher, language learner, politician, world leader, businessman or businesswoman, etc.

The source(s) of one type of pollution

## PEER EDITING CHECKLIST

|  | PEER EDITOR'S COMMENTS AND SUGGESTIONS |
|---|---|
| **GENERAL** | |
| 1. What do you like best about this paragraph? | |
| **PAPER FORMAT** | |
| 2. Is the format correct? Does it look like the model on page 19? | |
| **ORGANIZATION AND CONTENT** | |
| 3. **Topic sentence:** Is there a clear topic sentence? Does it have a controlling idea?<br><br>4. **Supporting sentences:** Is the main idea clear? Does the writer need to add more details to explain it?<br><br>5. **Concluding sentence:** Is there a concluding sentence? Does it begin with an appropriate end-of-paragraph signal?<br><br>6. **Unity:** Do all of the sentences support the topic sentence? | |
| **SENTENCE STRUCTURE** | |
| 7. Are there any unclear sentences? Can you suggest a way to improve them? | |
| **GRAMMAR AND MECHANICS** | |
| 8. Are there any errors in grammar and mechanics? | |

# CHAPTER 4
# Coherence

Cuneiform inscription from Persepolis

## Introduction

Another element of a good paragraph is **coherence.** The Latin verb *cohere* means "hold together." In order to have coherence in writing, the sentences must hold together; that is, the movement from one sentence to the next (and in longer essays, from one paragraph to the next) must be logical and smooth. There must be no sudden jumps. Each sentence should flow smoothly into the next one.

There are four ways to achieve coherence. The first two ways involve *repeating key nouns* and *using pronouns* that refer back to key nouns. The third way is to use *transition signals* to show how one idea is related to the next. The fourth way to achieve coherence is to arrange your sentences in *logical order*. You will practice the first three ways to achieve coherence in this chapter, and you will learn about logical order as well.

# Repetition of Key Nouns

The easiest way to achieve coherence is to repeat key nouns frequently in your paragraph. Look at the model paragraph about gold to see how it uses this technique to achieve coherence. The key noun in this paragraph is *gold*. Circle the word *gold* and all pronouns that refer to it.

**MODEL**

*Paragraph with Coherence*

> ### Gold
>
> Gold, a precious metal, is prized for two important characteristics. First of all, gold has a lustrous beauty that is resistant to corrosion. Therefore, it is suitable for jewelry, coins, and ornamental purposes. Gold never needs to be polished and will remain beautiful forever. For example, a Macedonian coin remains as untarnished today as the
> 5 day it was minted twenty-three centuries ago. Another important characteristic of gold is its usefulness to industry and science. For many years, it has been used in hundreds of industrial applications. The most recent use of gold is in astronauts' suits. Astronauts wear gold-plated heat shields for protection outside spaceships. In conclusion, gold is treasured not only for its beauty but also for its utility.

You should have circled the noun *gold* seven times, the pronoun *it* twice, and the pronoun *its* three times. (The word *it* in line 5 refers to *coin*, not *gold*, so you should not have circled it.)

There is no fixed rule about how often to repeat key nouns or when to substitute pronouns. At the very least, you need to repeat a key noun instead of using a pronoun when the meaning is not clear.

Throughout the following paragraph, the word *gold* has been replaced by pronouns, making the paragraph much less coherent.

**MODEL**

*Paragraph without Coherence*

> ### Gold
>
> Gold, a precious metal, is prized for two important characteristics. First of all, it has a lustrous beauty that is resistant to corrosion. Therefore, it is suitable for jewelry, coins, and ornamental purposes. It never needs to be polished and will remain beautiful forever. For example, a Macedonian coin remains as untarnished
> 5 today as the day it was minted twenty-three centuries ago. Another of its important characteristics is its usefulness to industry and science. For many years, it has been used in hundreds of industrial applications. Its most recent use is in astronauts' suits. Astronauts wear heat shields made from it for protection outside spaceships. In conclusion, it is treasured not only for its beauty but also for its utility.

**PRACTICE I**

*Repetition of Key Nouns*

**A.** In the following paragraph, the key noun is never repeated. Replace the pronoun *it* with the key noun *English* wherever you think doing so would make the paragraph more coherent.

### English

English has almost become an international language. Except for Chinese, more people speak it than any other language. Spanish is the official language of more countries in the world, but more countries have it as their official or unofficial second language. More than 70 percent of the world's mail is written
5  in it. It is the primary language on the Internet. In international business, it is used more than any other language, and it is the language of airline pilots and air traffic controllers all over the world. Moreover, although French used to be the language of diplomacy, it has displaced it throughout the world. Therefore, unless you plan to spend your life alone on a desert island in the middle of the
10  Pacific Ocean, it is a useful language to know.

**B.** In the following passage about dolphins, replace some of the pronouns with appropriate singular or plural nouns.

### Dolphins

Dolphins are interesting because they display almost human behavior at times. For example, they display the human emotions of joy and sadness. During training, when they do something correctly, they squeal excitedly and race toward their trainer. When they make a mistake, however, they droop[1]
5  noticeably and mope[2] around their pool. Furthermore, they help each other when they are in trouble. If one is sick, it sends out a message, and others in the area swim to help it. They push it to the surface of the water so that it can breathe. They stay with it for days or weeks—until it recovers or dies. They have also helped trapped or lost whales navigate their way safely out to
10  the open sea. They are so intelligent and helpful, in fact, that the U.S. Navy is training them to become underwater bomb disposal experts.

# Use of Consistent Pronouns

When you use pronouns instead of key nouns, make sure that you use the same person and number throughout your paragraph. Don't change from *you* to *he* or *she* (change of person), or from *he* to *they* (change of number).

---

[1] **droop:** sink down
[2] **mope:** act depressed

**PRACTICE 2**

*Using Consistent Pronouns*

In the following paragraph, the pronouns are not consistent. Correct them to make this paragraph more coherent.

**Olympic Athletes**

Olympic athletes must be strong both physically and mentally. First of all, if you hope to compete in an Olympic sport, you must be physically strong. Furthermore, an aspiring[3] Olympian must train rigorously[4] for many years. For the most demanding sports, they train several hours a day, five or six days a
5 week, for ten or more years. In addition to being physically strong, he or she must also be mentally tough. This means that you have to be totally dedicated to your sport, often giving up a normal school, family, and social life. Being mentally strong also means that he or she must be able to withstand the intense pressure of international competition with its attendant[5] media[6] coverage. Finally, not every-
10 one can win a medal, so they must possess the inner strength to live with defeat.

# Transition Signals

Transition signals are words such as *first, second, next, finally, therefore,* and *however,* or phrases such as *in conclusion, on the other hand,* and *as a result.*

Think of transition signals as traffic signs that tell your reader when to go forward, turn, slow down, and stop. In other words, they tell the reader when you are giving a similar idea (*similarly, moreover, furthermore, in addition*), an opposite idea (*on the other hand, however, in contrast*), an example (*for example*), a result (*as a result*), or a conclusion (*in conclusion*).

Using transition words as a guide makes it easier for your reader to follow your ideas. Transition words give your paragraph coherence.

**PRACTICE 3**

*Transition Signals*

Compare paragraphs 1 and 2 that follow. Both paragraphs give the same information, yet one paragraph is easier to understand than the other because it contains transition signals to lead the reader from one idea to the next.

Which paragraph contains transition signals and is more coherent? Circle all of the transition signals that you can identify.

**Paragraph 1**

A difference among the world's seas and oceans is that the salinity[7] varies in different climate zones. The Baltic Sea in Northern Europe is only one-fourth as saline[8] as the Red Sea in the Middle East. There are reasons for this. In warm climates, water evaporates[9] rapidly. The concentration[10] of salt
5 is greater. The surrounding land is dry and does not contribute much fresh water to dilute[11] the salty sea water. In cold climate zones, water evaporates slowly. The runoff created by melting snow adds a considerable amount of fresh water to dilute the saline sea water.

---

[3] **aspiring:** hopeful
[4] **rigorously:** strictly, without weakness
[5] **attendant:** accompanying
[6] **media:** radio, television, newspapers, and magazines

[7] **salinity:** salt content
[8] **saline:** salty
[9] **evaporates:** dries up
[10] **concentration:** amount
[11] **dilute:** reduce the concentration of

**Paragraph 2**

Another difference among the world's seas and oceans is that the salinity varies in different climate zones. For example, the Baltic Sea in Northern Europe is only one-fourth as saline as the Red Sea in the Middle East. There are two reasons for this. First of all, in warm climate zones, water evaporates rapidly; therefore, the concentration of salt is greater. Second, the surrounding land is dry and, consequently, does not contribute much fresh water to dilute the salty sea water. In cold climate zones, on the other hand, water evaporates slowly. Furthermore, the runoff created by melting snow adds a considerable amount of fresh water to dilute the saline sea water.

Paragraph 2 is more coherent because it contains transition signals. Each transition signal has a special meaning. Each shows how the following sentence relates to the preceding one.

*Another* tells you that this paragraph is part of a longer essay.
*For example* tells you that an example of the preceding idea is coming.
*Two* tells you to look for two different reasons.
*First of all* tells you that this is the first reason.
*Second* and *furthermore* indicate that additional ideas are coming.
*Therefore* and *consequently* indicate that the second statement is a result of the first statement.
*On the other hand* tells you that an opposite idea is coming.

Of course, you should not use a transition signal in front of *every* sentence in a paragraph. Using too many transition signals can be just as confusing as using too few. However, good writing requires that you use enough transition signals to make the relationships among your ideas clear.

On the next page is a chart showing some of the most common transition signals. Learn to use all of them, for they can be used with all kinds of writing. Later on, you will learn about special transition signals that are used with certain types of writing, such as chronological order and comparison/contrast.

## Types of Transition Signals

Transition signals can be categorized into three groups by grammatical function. In the chart shown on page 45, the three groups are *sentence connectors* (including *transition phrases* and *conjunctive adverbs*), *clause connectors* (including *coordinating conjunctions* and *subordinating conjunctions*), and a mixed group called *others*. As you study the chart and the examples that follow it, pay particular attention to the punctuation used with each group.

### Sentence Connectors

*Transition Phrases*

The phrases in this group usually appear at the beginning of sentences. They may also appear in the middle (normally following the subject) or at the end of sentences. They are *always* separated from the rest of the sentence by commas. Hence, these three patterns are possible:

> **For example**, the Baltic Sea in Northern Europe is only one-fourth as saline as the Red Sea in the Middle East.

The Baltic Sea in Northern Europe, **for example**, is only one-fourth as saline as the Red Sea in the Middle East.

The Baltic Sea in Northern Europe is only one-fourth as saline as the Red Sea in the Middle East, **for example**.

## TRANSITION SIGNALS FOR GENERAL USE

| MEANING/ FUNCTION | SENTENCE CONNECTORS | | CLAUSE CONNECTORS | | OTHERS |
|---|---|---|---|---|---|
| | TRANSITION PHRASES | CONJUNCTIVE ADVERBS | COORDINATING CONJUNCTIONS | SUBORDINATING CONJUNCTIONS | |
| To introduce an **additional** idea | in addition | furthermore moreover besides also too | and | | another (+noun) an additional (+noun) |
| To introduce an **opposite** idea | on the other hand in contrast | however nevertheless instead still nonetheless | but yet | although though even though whereas while | in spite of (+ noun) despite (+ noun) |
| To introduce a **choice** or **alternative** | | otherwise | or | if unless | |
| To introduce a **restatement** or **explanation** | in fact indeed | that is | | | |
| To introduce an **example** | for example for instance | | | | an example of (+ noun) such as (+ noun) |
| To introduce a **conclusion** or **summary** | in conclusion in summary in brief in short indeed | | | | |
| To introduce a **result** | accordingly as a result as a consequence | therefore consequently hence thus | so | | |

*Conjunctive Adverbs*

- Conjunctive adverbs (except **too**) may also appear at the beginning, in the middle, or at the end of sentences, and are separated by commas.

    > **Furthermore,** the runoff created by melting snow adds a considerable amount of fresh water to dilute the saline sea water.

    > The runoff created by melting snow, **furthermore,** adds a considerable amount of fresh water to dilute the saline sea water.

    > My parents want me to become an engineer, **however**.

- Conjunctive adverbs are also often used with a semicolon and a comma to join two independent clauses[1] to form a compound sentence.

    > In warm climate zones, water evaporates rapidly; **therefore**, the concentration of salt is greater.

    > The company's sales increased last year; **nevertheless**, its net profit declined.

- Most transition phrases may also follow this pattern.

    > Many societies in the world are matriarchal; **that is**, the mother is head of the family.

    > Some English words do not have exact equivalents in other languages; **for example,** there is no German word for the adjective *fair*, as in *fair play*.

## Clause Connectors

*Coordinating Conjunctions*

- The five coordinating conjunctions in the chart (plus two additional ones, **for** and **nor**) are used with a comma to join two independent clauses to form a compound sentence.

    > In a matriarchy, the mother is the head of the family, **and** all of the children belong to her clan.[2]

    > In warm climate zones, water evaporates rapidly, **so** the concentration of salt is greater.

    > The company's sales increased last year, **yet** its net profit declined.

- **Yet** and **but** have similar meanings: They both signal that an opposite idea is coming. **Yet** is preferred when the second clause is an unexpected or surprising contrast to the first clause. When the two clauses are direct opposites, **but** is preferred.

    > Thomas Edison dropped out of school at age twelve, **yet** he became a famous inventor.

    > I want to study art, **but** my parents want me to become an engineer.

- **Yet** is similar in meaning to **nevertheless**, and **but** is similar to **however**.

**CROSS-REFERENCE**

Look at *Compound Sentences with Coordinators* on pages 155–157 for more examples.

---

[1] **independent clause:** subject + verb + complement that express a complete thought
[2] **clan:** extended family group

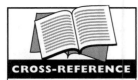

**CROSS-REFERENCE**

You will find a lot of information about subordinating conjunctions in Chapter 12 about adverbial clauses.

## *Subordinating Conjunctions*

These words (and many others including **because, when,** and **so that**) introduce a dependent clause,[3] which is joined to an independent clause to form a complex sentence. There are two possible positions for the dependent clause:

- If the dependent clause comes before the independent clause, use a comma after it.

> **Although** the company's sales increased last year, its net profit declined.

- If the independent clause comes first, do not use a comma.

> The company's net profit declined last year **although** its sales increased.

## *Others*

The transition signals in this group include adjectives such as **additional**, prepositions such as **in spite of**, and nouns such as **example**. There are no special punctuation rules for this group.

> The company's net profit declined last year **in spite of** increased sales.

> **Despite** increased sales, the company's net profit declined last year. (The comma is necessary because the prepositional phrase comes before the subject of the sentence.)

> **An additional** reason for the company's bankruptcy was the lack of competent management.

> **Examples of** vocabulary differences between British and American English include bonnet/hood, petrol/gasoline, windscreen/windshield, and lorry/truck.

**PRACTICE 4**

*Recognizing Transition Signals*

STEP 1   Circle all of the transition signals in the following paragraphs.
STEP 2   Punctuate the transition signals if necessary.

### Genetic[4] Engineering

Genetic research has produced both exciting and frightening possibilities. Scientists are now able to create new forms of life in the laboratory due to the development of gene splicing.[5] On the one hand the ability to create life in the laboratory could greatly benefit humankind. For example it is very
5   expensive to obtain insulin[6] from natural sources, but through genetic research, scientists have now developed a way to manufacture it inexpensively in the laboratory. Another beneficial application of gene splicing is in agriculture. Genetic engineers have created a new tomato that doesn't spoil quickly. Consequently tomato farmers can now let the tomatoes ripen on the plant
10   and develop full flavor and color before they are picked—no more green,

---

[3] **dependent clause:** subordinating conjunction + subject + verb + complement that express an incomplete thought
[4] **genetic:** from *gene,* the unit of heredity
[5] **gene splicing:** gene joining
[6] **insulin:** substance needed by people who have diabetes

flavorless tomatoes in grocery stores! In addition genetic engineers have created larger fish, frost-resistant strawberries, and more productive cows.

       On the other hand not everyone is positive about gene-splicing technology.
Some people feel that it could have terrible consequences. A laboratory acci-

15 dent for example might cause an epidemic of an unknown disease that could
wipe out humanity. Furthermore the ability to clone human beings is a possibility that frightens many people. In 1993, a researcher at George
Washington University Medical Center cloned human embryos[1] by splitting
single embryos into twins and triplets. These embryos did not develop into

20 babies but it is possible that they could do so in the future. Because human
embryos can be frozen and used at a later date, it could be possible for parents to have a child and then, years later, to use a cloned, frozen embryo to
give birth to its identical twin.

**PRACTICE 5**

*Choosing Transition Signals*

**A.** **STEP 1** Choose the transition signal that best shows the relationship between the sentences in each group from the choices given in parentheses. Write the signal in the space.

    **STEP 2** Add punctuation and change capital letters to small letters if necessary.

**Note:** All of the transition signals in this practice are sentence connectors. This is to give you more practice in using and punctuating this type of transition signal correctly.

**Example**

A recent article in *Era* magazine suggested ways to reduce inflation. The article suggested that the president reduce the federal budget; _furthermore_ it suggested that the government reduce federal, state, and local taxes. **(however, in contrast, furthermore)**

1. The same article said that the causes of inflation were easy to find _____ the cure for inflation was not so easy to prescribe. **(however, for example, therefore)**

2. *Era* also suggested that rising wages were one of the primary causes of inflation _____ the government should take action to control wages. **(however, therefore, for example)**

3. In physics, the weight of an object is the gravitational force[2] with which the Earth attracts it _____ if a man weighs 150 pounds, this means that the earth pulls him down with a force of 150 pounds. **(moreover, therefore, for example)**

4. The farther away from the Earth a person is, the less the gravitational force of the Earth _____ a man weighs less when he is 50,000 miles from the Earth than when he is only 5,000 miles away. **(in conclusion, therefore, however)**

---

[1] **embryo:** organism at the very beginning stage of life
[2] **gravitational force:** the force that pulls things toward the Earth

**5.** A **tsunami** is a tidal wave produced by an earthquake on the ocean floor. The waves are very long and low in open water, but when they get close to land, they encounter friction[3] because the water is shallow _____ the waves increase in height and can cause considerable damage when they finally reach land. **(on the other hand, as a result, for example)**

**B.** **STEP 1**    Fill in each blank with an appropriate transition signal from the list provided. Use each only once.

| | | | |
|---|---|---|---|
| for instance | moreover | furthermore | in conclusion |
| however | but | for example | such as |

**STEP 2**    Use correct punctuation.

### Internationalization of Japan

For many years, Japanese consumers have been very slow in accepting foreign goods, mainly because they are very selective and will only purchase high-quality products. Lately _____ the consumer market has been changing. According to a recent article in The Wall Street Journal, **koku-**
5  **saika**, which is defined as "internationalization," is influencing young Japanese consumers, who are very eager to purchase and enjoy products from countries around the world. The greatest access[4] into the Japanese market has been by the food industry. Traditionally, the protein staple[5] in Japan has been fish products, _____ in the last decade or so, the
10  Japanese have been consuming more beef. In fact, annual per capita[6] consumption is expected to be about seven kilos in the next decade.
_____ they have acquired a taste for imported beverages, both of the nonalcohol or low alcohol varieties, like beer drinks and "light" wines imported from England, Germany, Switzerland, the United States, and
15  Australia. _____ young people, especially women who are aware of the importance of health and fitness, are eating Western-style breakfasts. _____ they enjoy fruit, milk, and bran-type cereals imported from the United States.
Not only Western countries but also Asian nations _____
20  South Korea, Taiwan, Singapore, and Thailand have been benefiting from the changing diet of the Japanese consumer. _____ Japan is importing eels (fish) from Taiwan, asparagus (vegetable) from Thailand, and mangoes (fruit) from the Philippines. _____ the Japanese trend toward internationalization should become even greater as we approach
25  the twenty-first century. It will certainly increase international trade, which will definitely be advantageous to many countries of the world.

---

[3] **friction:** resistance
[4] **access:** ease of approach; entrance
[5] **staple:** main food source
[6] **per capita:** per person

**C.** Improve the coherence of the following paragraph by adding transitions at key places.

### Women's Liberation and English

The "women's lib" movement toward greater equality for women has produced some permanent changes in the vocabulary of English. New words have been added. The words **feminist, sexist,** and **male chauvinist** have become common during the past thirty-five years or so. Another new word is the title
5  **Ms.,** which is often used in place of both **Miss** and **Mrs.** A change is that sexist titles of many occupations have been neutralized. A **chairman** is now a **chairperson** (or sometimes simply **chair**), a **waiter/waitress** is now a **waitperson,** and a high school or college **freshman** is now a **first-year student.** A **mailman** is now a **mail carrier,** and an **airline stewardess** is now a **flight**
10  **attendant.** In time, English pronouns may also change as a result of women's desire for equality. Attempts to give equal treatment to masculine and feminine pronouns in English have led to the search for a new pronoun form to replace **he** (such as **he/she** or **s/he**) when referring to neutral nouns like **student** and **manager.** Some of the new words such as **Ms.** are quite useful; you
15  can use **Ms.** to address a woman when you don't know if she is married. The lack of a clear neutral pronoun can lead to awkward sentence construction.

**PRACTICE 6**

*Using Transition Signals*

Choose one of the topic sentences below and write a paragraph that develops it. Use transition signals to connect the supporting sentences smoothly. You may use the transition signals suggested for each topic, or you may use others not listed. Add other sentences without transitions if you need to in order to explain the topic completely.

**1.** The rowdiness[1] of spectators at sports events is getting out of control.

| | |
|---|---|
| two years ago | more recently |
| last year | as a result |

**2.** There are two noticeable differences between British and American English.

| | |
|---|---|
| the first difference | for example |
| for example | in conclusion, although |
| the second difference | |

**3.** Some people enjoy solitude.[2]

| | |
|---|---|
| for instance | on the other hand |
| moreover | therefore |

---

[1] **rowdiness:** rough, disorderly behavior
[2] **solitude:** being alone

# *Logical*³ *Order*

In addition to using transition signals and repeating key nouns and pronouns, a fourth way to achieve coherence is to arrange your sentences in some kind of logical order. Your choice of one kind of logical order over another will, of course, depend on your topic and on your purpose. You may even combine two or more different logical orders in the same paragraph. The important point to remember is to arrange your ideas in some kind of order that is logical to a reader accustomed to the English way of writing.

Some common kinds of logical order in English are *chronological order, logical division of ideas,* and *comparison/contrast.* In this chapter, you will learn to recognize some of the logical orders; in later chapters, you will learn to write them.

Each kind of order has its own special words and phrases to show the relationships among the ideas. For example, in a piece of writing using chronological order, you would expect to find a lot of time expressions:

> first, next, after that, finally, before the last war, after 1990, since then, in 2010, while working on the project, etc.

In a paragraph describing differences (contrast), you would find these expressions:

> the most noticeable difference, larger than, unlike, on the other hand, in contrast, differ from

In a paragraph showing similarities (comparison), you would find these expressions:

> similarity, similarly, as expensive as, just as, just like, compare with, in comparison

Logical division of ideas is another common method of organizing ideas to give a paragraph coherence. Ideas are put into groups, and each group is discussed one after the other. Transition words such as *first, second, third* introduce each group.

**PRACTICE 7**

*Recognizing Kinds of Logical Orders*

Read the following paragraphs and decide which kind of logical order is used in each: comparison/contrast, chronological order, or logical division of ideas. Be able to discuss the reasons for your choice. Circle all transition signals.

**Paragraph 1**

Powerful computers capable of translating documents from one language into another have recently been developed in Japan. The process of machine translation is complex. To translate a document from English into Japanese, for example, the computer first analyzes an English sentence, determining its grammatical
5   structure and identifying the subject, verb, objects, and modifiers. Next, the words are translated by an English-Japanese dictionary. After that, another part of the computer program analyzes the resulting awkward jumble⁴ of words and meanings and produces an intelligible sentence based on the rules of Japanese syntax⁵ and the machine's understanding of what the original English sentence meant. Finally,
10  the computer-produced translation is polished by a human bilingual editor.

Kind of logical order: _____

---

³ **logical:** according to what is reasonable and sensible; having a consistent pattern
⁴ **jumble:** confused mixture
⁵ **syntax:** sentence structure

**Paragraph 2**

French and American business managers have decidedly different man-agement styles. French meetings, for example, are long and rambling[1] and rarely end on time. Furthermore, meetings often end without closure.[2] Americans, on the other hand, make an effort to start and stop a meeting on
5  time, and American business meetings typically end with decisions and action plans. Another difference involves documentation. Americans adore documen-tation; they have a procedure manual for everything. The French, in contrast, think this is childish. French managers find it difficult to stick to a schedule, but American managers are intolerant of delays. In addition, the French pre-
10  fer to work alone, whereas Americans like to work in teams. Another major difference in management style is that in French companies, authority comes from the top; French managers do not share information with subordinates and make decisions with little participation by employees beneath them. In American companies, however, top managers share information and frequent-
15  ly solicit[3] input from subordinates.

Kind of logical order:  _____

**Paragraph 3**

It took more than 2,500 years to develop the calendar used in most Western countries today. In about 700 B.C.E.,[4] the ancient Romans used a cal-endar that had 304 days divided into ten months; March was the beginning of each year. There were more than 60 days missing from the calendar, and so
5  very soon, the calendar didn't match the seasons at all. Spring arrived when the calendar said that it was still winter. A few decades later, the Romans added the months of January and February to the end of the year. This calen-dar lasted about 600 years. Then in 46 B.C.E., Julius Caesar, the Roman ruler, made a new calendar. His calendar had 365 days, with one day added
10  every fourth year. He also moved the beginning of the year to January 1, and he renamed a month for himself: **Julius** (July). In Caesar's calendar, February had 29 days. The very next emperor, Augustus, not only renamed a month for himself (August), but he also took one day from February and added it to August so that "his" month would be just as long as Caesar's. This
15  calendar worked better than the previous ones, but it still wasn't perfect. By 1580, the first calendrical day of spring was ten days too early, so in 1582, Pope Gregory XIII, the leader of the Roman Catholic religion, made a small change to make the calendar more accurate. In the Gregorian calendar, the year is still 26.3 seconds different from the solar year, but it will be a long
20  time before this causes a problem.

Kind of logical order:  _____

---

[1] **rambling:** not focused on a specific goal
[2] **closure:** decisions about points discussed
[3] **solicit:** ask for
[4] **B.C.E.:** Before the Common Era (the Common Era began in the year 1)

**Paragraph 4**

The many different calendars used throughout the world are all based either on the phases of the moon, on the revolution of the Earth around the sun, or on a combination of these. The first kind of calendar is the lunar calendar, which is based on the phases of the moon. A month is calculated as
5  the time between two full moons, 29.5 days, and a year has 354 days. The Islamic calendar used in Muslim countries is a lunar calendar. It has twelve months and a cycle of thirty years in which the 2nd, 5th, 7th, 10th, 13th, 16th, 18th, 21st, 24th, 26th, and 29th years have 355 days, and the others 354 days. A second kind of calendar is the solar calendar, which is based on
10  the revolution of the Earth around the sun. The ancient Egyptians used a solar calendar divided into twelve months of thirty days each, which left five uncounted days at the end of each year. A very accurate calendar developed by the Mayan Indians in North America was also a solar calendar. It had 365 days, 364 of which were divided into 28 weeks of 13 days each. The new
15  year began on the 365th day. Because the solar year is exactly 365 days, 5 hours, 48 minutes, and 46 seconds long, however, a solar calendar is not totally accurate, so many cultures developed a third kind of calendar, the lunisolar calendar. In a lunisolar calendar, extra days are added every so often to reconcile[5] the lunar months with the solar year. The Chinese,
20  Hebrew, and Gregorian calendars used today are lunisolar calendars.

Kind of logical order:  _____

# *Review*

These are the important points you should have learned from this chapter:

**1.** Every good paragraph has coherence. Coherence is achieved by

- Repeating key nouns frequently.
- Using pronouns consistently.
- Using transition signals to show the relationship of one idea to the next.
- Stating your ideas in some kind of logical order.

**2.** Transition signals can be transition phrases, conjunctive adverbs, coordinating conjunctions, subordinating conjunctions, prepositions, adjectives, or nouns. Each type of transition signal is punctuated differently.
**3.** Some common kinds of logical order in English are chronological order, logical division of ideas, and comparison/contrast.

---

[5] **reconcile:** bring together

**WRITING PRACTICE**    Choose one of the suggested topics below and write a paragraph that is ten to fifteen sentences in length. Focus on making your paragraph coherent. The ideas should flow smoothly from beginning to end. Remember the steps in the writing process:

| | |
|---|---|
| **STEP 1** *Prewriting* | Brainstorm a topic for ideas, using the listening, freewriting, or clustering techniques you have learned. Try to end up with at least three major points. |
| **STEP 2** *Planning* | Develop an outline that includes a topic sentence and a concluding sentence (if necessary). Underline them. |
| **STEP 3** *Adding Transitions* | Decide where transition signals would be appropriate and write them in the margin of your outline. |
| **STEP 4** *Writing* | Write a rough draft. Circle your transition signals. |
| **STEP 5** *Editing* | Have a classmate check your draft against the Peer Editing Checklist that follows. Make sure your paragraph has coherence. |
| **STEP 6** *Rewriting* | Write a second draft, and proofread it for grammar and mechanics. |
| **STEP 7** | Write a final copy to hand in. |

## *Topic Suggestions*

| | |
|---|---|
| Drinking laws | New sports |
| The effects of divorce | Your major field of study |
| Working mothers | Current fads or fashions |

## PEER EDITING CHECKLIST

|  | PEER EDITOR'S COMMENTS AND SUGGESTIONS |
|---|---|
| **GENERAL** | |
| **1.** What do you like best about this paragraph? | |
| **PAPER FORMAT** | |
| **2.** Is the format correct? Does it look like the model on page 19? | |
| **ORGANIZATION AND CONTENT** | |
| **3. Topic sentence:** Is there a clear topic sentence? Does it have a controlling idea?<br><br>**4. Supporting sentences:** Is the main idea clear? Does the writer need to add more details to explain it?<br><br>**5. Concluding sentence:** Is there a concluding sentence? Does it begin with an appropriate end-of-paragraph signal?<br><br>**6. Unity:** Do all of the sentences support the topic sentence?<br><br>**7. Coherence:**  Do the sentences flow smoothly? Are there any inconsistent pronouns? Are transition signals used? | |
| **SENTENCE STRUCTURE** | |
| **8.** Are there any unclear sentences? Can you suggest a way to improve them? | |
| **GRAMMAR AND MECHANICS** | |
| **9.** Are there any errors in grammar and mechanics? | |

# CHAPTER

# Kinds of Logical Order

Ancient Greek tablet

## *Introduction*

In Chapter 4, you learned that writing your ideas in some kind of **logical order** is necessary to achieve coherence. You also learned to recognize three of the common kinds of logical orders in English—chronological order, logical division of ideas, and comparison/contrast. In this chapter, you will practice using them in paragraphs.

# *Chronological Order*

Chronological order is one of the easiest methods of organization to master. *Chronos* is a Greek word meaning time. Chronological order, therefore, is a way of organizing the ideas in a paragraph in the order of their occurrence in time.

Chronological order is used for something as simple as a recipe and for something as complex as a history book. In academic writing, chronological order has many uses. One of the primary ways you might use it is to write a historical narrative about the subject of a term paper. For example, you might review the history of labor unions before you discuss the current situation.

However, chronological order is not just used for historical narratives; it is also used in business, science, and engineering to explain processes and procedures. For example, chronological order would be used to explain how to take a photograph, how to perform a chemistry experiment, or how to set up an accounting system. Such paragraphs are called "how to" or "process" paragraphs.

There are two keys to writing a good chronological paragraph:

1. Discuss the events (in a narrative) or the steps (in a process) in the order in which they occur.
2. Use chronological transition signals to indicate the sequence of events or steps.

Analyze the following model paragraphs for their organization by time. Circle any words or expressions that indicate time order (*first, next, after that, in 1971,* etc.). The first model reviews very briefly the history of computers. The second model is an example of a process paragraph. It explains the process of cloning.

**MODEL**

*Chronological Order: Narration*

---

### The Evolution[1] of Computers

In the relatively short span of sixty years, there has been an incredible evolution in the size and capabilities of computers. Today, computer chips smaller than the tip of your fingernail have the same capabilities as the room-sized machines of years ago. The first computers were developed around 1945. They were so large that they
5   required special air-conditioned rooms. About twenty years later, in the 1960s, desk-sized computers were developed. This represented a gigantic advance. Before the end of that same decade, however, a third generation of computers, which used simple integrated circuits and which were even smaller and faster, had appeared. In 1971, the first microprocessor, less than one square centimeter in size, was
10   developed. Today, modern microprocessors contain as many as 10 million transistors, and the number of transistors and the computational speed of microprocessors doubles every eighteen months.

---

[1] **evolution:** development

**MODEL**

*Chronological Order: Process*

**Cloning Technology**

*Background information: In 1997, a lamb born in Scotland became an instant celebrity. An exact duplicate of her six-year-old mother, Dolly was the first animal cloned from the cells of an adult. Other animals had previously been cloned from the cells of embryos, but Dolly was the first animal to come from an adult. Her birth represented a giant step in cloning technology.*

The cloning of Dolly involved several steps. First, cells that had previously been taken from Dolly's mother were starved for five days, which caused them to stop dividing. This interruption of the cells' division cycle made it easier for them to reprogram themselves to start growing a new organism.[1] After five days, the nuclei[2]
5  of these cells were removed and transferred into an unfertilized sheep egg, from which the natural nucleus had previously been removed. In the next step, the egg was grown in the laboratory for a period of time. Then the egg was implanted into a different sheep, where it grew normally. When the sheep finally gave birth, the lamb was an exact genetic copy, or clone, of the sheep that had provided the
10  transferred nucleus, not of the sheep that had provided the egg.

## Writing Technique Questions

1. What are the two uses of chronological order that the two model paragraphs exemplify?
2. What are the main time divisions in the paragraph about computers? How would you outline it?
3. What transition signals and time expressions are used in the first model to show chronological order?
4. What transition signals and time expressions are used in the second model to show the steps in the process?

**Topic Sentences for Chronological Order**

Notice that the topic sentence of a chronological paragraph in some way indicates the time order. In paragraphs such as the one on computers, phrases such as *in the relatively short span of sixty years* and *evolution* give the reader a hint that this is a chronological paragraph.

In a "how to," or process, paragraph such as the one about cloning technology, the process to be described is named in the topic sentence and tells the reader to expect a chronological paragraph.

**PRACTICE 1**

*Chronological Topic Sentences*

**STEP 1**  Put a check in the space to the left of every topic sentence suggesting that a chronological paragraph will follow.
**STEP 2**  In the sentences you have checked, circle the word or words that indicate chronological order.

---

[1] **organism:** any form of life
[2] **nuclei:** plural of *nucleus*, the part of a cell that contains its hereditary material and controls its metabolism, growth, and reproduction

**Example**

_____ ✔   (In the past sixty years) (developments) in the field of electronics have revolutionized the computer industry.

_____ **1.** A person's intelligence is the product of both heredity[3] and environment.

_____ **2.** The tensions[4] that led to last year's student riots had been building for several years.

_____ **3.** The life cycle of the Pacific salmon is a fascinating phenomenon.[5]

_____ **4.** There are two main reasons I believe women in the army should not be allowed in a war zone along with men.

_____ **5.** Surviving a major earthquake is possible if you follow certain procedures.

_____ **6.** The worst day in my life was the day I left my family and my friends to come to the United States.

_____ **7.** American directness often conflicts with Asian modesty.

_____ **8.** The two most publicized holidays in the United States are first, Christmas and second, Thanksgiving.

_____ **9.** The traditions of Christmas originated in several different countries.

_____ **10.** Every year, our family celebrates the Muslim holiday Ramadan in the same way.

_____ **11.** The preparation of the poisonous puffer fish for eating is not for amateur chefs.

_____ **12.** You can avoid jet lag after a long flight if you follow these suggestions.

## Transition Signals for Chronological Order

Transition signals are especially important in a chronological paragraph. You have to be very clear about the sequence of events: Did one event happen before, at the same time as, or after another event?

Chronological transition signals include the following:

**CROSS-REFERENCE**

For more on time clauses to help show time order, see pages 196–197.

| TRANSITION WORDS AND PHRASES | | | SUBORDINATORS | | OTHERS |
|---|---|---|---|---|---|
| first, | first of all, | soon, | after | since | the first step . . . |
| second, | after that, | gradually, | as | until | in the second step . . . |
| next, | finally, | meanwhile, | as soon as | when | on the third day . . . |
| now | last, | | before | while | during the night . . . |
| then | | | | | |

Keep in mind that *any* time expression can serve as a chronological transition signal. Here are some examples:

Later that morning,         In the next fifteen years,
Twenty-five years ago,      From June through August,
In 2001,                    Before the invention of the fax machine,

---

[3] **heredity:** characteristics received from one's parents (hair color, eye color, height, etc.)
[4] **tensions:** stresses
[5] **phenomenon:** an unusual or scientific fact or event

*Chronological
Transition Signals*

Add appropriate chronological transition signals to the following essay and punctuate them. Use the signals listed in the chart or others you know.

### How to Reduce the Danger of Smoking

The Department of Health, Education and Welfare (HEW) has outlined
some steps to take some of the danger out of smoking for those people who
are unable to quit smoking outright.[1] _____ choose a cigarette
with less tar and nicotine to reduce your intake of these pollutants.

5   _____ don't smoke your cigarette all the way down. Smoke
halfway, and you will inhale only about 40 percent of the total tar and nicotine. Remember, 60 percent of these substances[2] is contained in the last half
of the cigarette. _____ take fewer draws on each cigarette;
that is, reduce the number of puffs on each cigarette. This will cut down on

10  your smoking. _____ reduce your inhaling. Don't open your
lungs by inhaling deeply. Take short, shallow puffs. _____
smoke fewer cigarettes each day. This may be the most difficult step of all.
_____ think about the terrible diseases you are opening yourself up to each time you smoke a cigarette. _____ if you follow

15  each of these steps without cheating, you should be able to at least control
the number of cigarettes you smoke daily. Who knows, this might be the
beginning of the end—of your smoking, that is.[3]

**PRACTICE 3**

*Writing a Chronological
Paragraph*

Choose one of the suggested topics and follow the steps listed below to write a paragraph using chronological order. Both narrative and process topics are suggested.

**STEP 1**   Make a simple outline that lists the events (in a narrative) or the steps (in a
process) in the order of their occurrence.
**STEP 2**   Add transition signals at appropriate points in the left margin of your outline.
**STEP 3**   Write a topic sentence that names the event or the process.
**STEP 4**   Write your paragraph, following your outline. Add enough details to make
the chain of events or steps in the process very clear.
**STEP 5**   Ask a classmate to check your paragraph using the Peer Editing Checklist at
the end of the chapter (page 70) before you hand it in.

---

[1] **outright:** all at once
[2] **substances:** materials
[3] DHEW Publication No. (CDC) 78-8705, U.S. Government Printing Office, 1978, 0-252-573.

### *Topic Suggestions*

#### A. Process Topics

| | |
|---|---|
| How to get a driver's license | How to get an F |
| How to break a bad habit | How to jump-start a car |
| How to make someone you know angry or happy | How to cook a special dish from your culture |
| How to flirt | How to buy a used car |
| How to get an A | How to soothe a crying baby |

#### B. Narrative Topics

A brief autobiography (You may write more than one paragraph.)

A brief biography of a well-known person

A recent journey

A wedding ceremony

An important event in your life

An important decision you have made

The historical development of _____ (automobiles, air travel, a sport, a type of music, telecommunications—any topic you have information about)

# *Logical Division of Ideas/Order of Importance*

Logical division is one of the most common ways to organize ideas in English. When you use logical division, you group related ideas together and discuss each group, one after the other. In everyday life, things are divided into groups. Grocery stores separate items into groups: produce (fresh fruits and vegetables) is in one section, milk products (milk, butter, cheese) are in another section, meats in another, and so on. Similarly, corporations divide themselves into departments: marketing, research, accounting, etc., and authors divide books into chapters.

There is usually more than one way to divide things. Suppose, for example, you are asked to divide the members of your class into groups. How many different ways could you divide them? Make a list:

| | |
|---|---|
| By gender (male, females) | By _____ |
| By age | By _____ |

If the groups are all more or less equally important in the mind of the writer, they can be discussed in any order. However, each group should be unified within itself. In other words, you shouldn't put meat in the produce section.

Read the model paragraph on the next page and then answer the questions that follow.

**MODEL**

*Logical Division of Ideas*

### Life in Space

Living aboard a space station in orbit around the Earth for months at a time poses problems for astronauts' bodies as well as for their minds. One major problem is maintaining astronauts' physical health. Medical treatment may be days or even weeks away, as there may not be a doctor on board. Illnesses such as
5   appendicitis or ulcers, routinely treated on Earth, could be fatal in space because of the delay in getting to a doctor. Furthermore, surgery may be impossible because blood would float around inside the operating room. Another health problem is the potential for bone deterioration.[1] In a weightless environment, the body produces less calcium. Astronauts must exercise at least three hours a day to
10  prevent bone loss. A second major problem is maintaining astronauts' mental health. Being confined for long periods of time in dark and hostile[2] space undoubtedly produces anxiety.[3] Loneliness and boredom are other psychological concerns. Finally, how can astronauts "let off steam"[4] when interpersonal conflicts develop? It is clear that space-station duty will require astronauts who are not only
15  physically but also mentally strong.

### Writing Technique Questions

1. How many main groups is the topic of this paragraph divided into? What are they?
2. Does the topic sentence of the paragraph tell you the topics of these groups? Does the concluding sentence?
3. What transition signals indicate the divisions? Where else are transition signals used?
4. In your opinion, would it make any difference if mental health were discussed before physical health? Do you think that one is more important than the other, or are they approximately equal in importance?

*Transition Signals for Logical Division of Ideas*

Transition signals used in logical division include many that you already know.

| SENTENCE CONNECTORS | OTHERS |
| --- | --- |
| first, second, third, etc.<br>next, last, finally<br>in addition, moreover<br>furthermore<br>also | the first (+ noun)<br>the/a second (+ noun)<br>one (+ noun)<br>another (+ noun)<br>an additional (+ noun) |

---

[1] **deterioration:** reduction in amount
[2] **hostile:** unfriendly

[3] **anxiety:** fear; worry
[4] **"let off steam":** get rid of anger, frustration (idiom)

**Examples**

> **First**, maintaining astronauts' physical health is a concern.
>
> **In addition**, sanitation[5] is a problem in weightless space.
>
> **A second** concern is maintaining astronauts' mental health.

*Transition Signals for Order of Importance*

If some of your points are more important than others, you can indicate their relative importance by using these transition signals:

| SENTENCE CONNECTORS | OTHERS |
|---|---|
| more importantly<br>most significantly<br>above all<br>primarily | a more important (+ noun)<br>the most important (+ noun)<br>the second most significant (+ noun)<br>the primary (+ noun) |

> Astronauts in space experience loneliness and boredom; **more importantly,** they can suffer from anxiety.

**PRACTICE 4**

*Transition Signals for Logical Division/Order of Importance*

A. Reread the model paragraph "Life in Space" on page 62 and circle all of the transition signals used to show logical division.

B. Suggest changes in the transition signals to show that one group of problems (physical or psychological) is more important than the other.

*Topic Sentences for Logical Division/Order of Importance*

The topic sentence of logical division and order of importance paragraphs often indicates the number of groups the topic is divided into.

> Gold, a precious metal, is prized for two important characteristics.
>
> Inflation has three causes.

The topic sentence may even tell what the groups are.

> Gold, a precious metal, is prized not only for its beauty but also for its utility.
>
> Inflation has three causes: an increase in the supply of paper money, excessive government spending, and unrestrained consumer borrowing.

The topic sentence for order of importance differs only in that it may contain an order of importance transition signal.

> Gold, a precious metal, is prized not only for its beauty but, **more importantly,** for its utility.

---

[5] **sanitation:** cleanliness

**PRACTICE 5**

*Topic Sentences for
Logical Division/Order
of Importance*

**A.** Put a check (✔) in the space to the left of every topic sentence that suggests
logical division as a method of organization. Put a double check (✔✔) if the
sentence suggests order of importance. Some are neither, so leave these
unchecked.

_____  **1.** My eighteenth birthday was a day I will never forget.

_____  **2.** On their eighteenth birthdays, Americans receive two important
rights/responsibilities: they can vote, and they can sign legal contracts.

_____  **3.** In most occupations, women are still unequal to men in three areas:
salary, power, and status.

_____  **4.** Living in a dormitory offers several advantages to a newly arrived
international student.

_____  **5.** Photosynthesis is the process by which plants manufacture their own
food.

_____  **6.** Television game shows are boring for the educated viewer because they
are poorly disguised commercials but more importantly, because they
require such a minimal level of knowledge.

_____  **7.** Earthquake prediction is still an inexact science although seismologists[1]
learn more each time they monitor[2] a quake.

_____  **8.** A college degree in international business today requires first, a
knowledge of business procedures and second, a knowledge of cultural
differences in business methods.

_____  **9.** A computer is both faster and more accurate than a human.

_____  **10.** Teenagers demonstrate their independence in several ways.

**B.** Suggest changes to the topic sentence of the model paragraph "Life in Space" on
page 62 to show that one group of problems (physical or psychological) is more
important than the other.

# Two Topic Sentence Tips[3]

Here are two tips to help you write topic sentences for logical division and order of
importance paragraphs:

**1.** Use a colon [:] in front of the names of the groups. (For more information about
the use of colons, see Appendix A, page 251.)

> In one shocking week of 1997, the world lost two remarkable women who,
> although they lived very different lives, shared a common compassion for the
> sick and injured: Princess Diana of Britain and Mother Teresa of India.

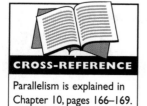

**CROSS-REFERENCE**

Parallelism is explained in
Chapter 10, pages 166–169.

**2.** Use paired (correlative) conjunctions when there are only two groups. Paired
conjunctions are *both . . . and . . . ; not only . . . but also . . . ; either . . . or . . . ; neither
. . . nor. . . .*

Remember that paired (correlative) conjunctions follow the rule of parallelism. If
you put a noun after the word *both,* you **must** put a noun after the word *and.* If
you use a prepositional phrase after *not only,* you **must** use one after *but also.*

---

[1] **seismologists:** scientists who study earthquakes     [3] **tip:** helpful advice
[2] **monitor:** observe; check with instruments

Here are some examples of logical division topic sentences with these special conjunctions.

Gold, a precious metal, is prized **not only** *for its beauty* **but also** *for its utility.* *(prepositional phrases)*

To stay healthy, you should **both** *eat nutritious food* **and** *exercise daily.* *(verbs)*

In my opinion, **neither** *wealth* **nor** *beauty* guarantees happiness. *(nouns)*

Most people buying a personal computer for the first time will consider **either** *a PC* **or** *a Macintosh.* *(nouns)*

# Comparison/Contrast

Comparison/contrast involves analyzing the similarities and differences between two or more items. Almost every decision you make involves weighing similarities and differences. Every time you decide which jacket to buy or which apartment to rent, you compare and contrast features and prices. In the business world, employers compare job applicants, proposals from different advertising agencies, and employee health insurance policies from competing companies. Job applicants compare job offers in terms of salary, responsibilities, and benefit packages. In college classes, professors frequently test students' understanding of material by asking them to compare and contrast two theories, two methods, two economic policies, two historical periods, or two characters in a play or film.

As with the other kinds of paragraphs, the keys to writing a comparison/contrast paragraph are to put the ideas in some kind of order and to use appropriate transition signals.

The content of a comparison/contrast paragraph can vary. Some paragraphs emphasize similarities, while others emphasize differences. You can also discuss both similarities and differences in one paragraph if you don't have many points to discuss. Study the model paragraphs that follow and determine whether they discuss similarities, differences, or both.

**MODEL**

*Comparison/Contrast*

### PCs versus Macs

**Paragraph 1**

If you are planning to buy a personal computer, you should know some of the basic similarities and differences between PCs and Macs. First of all, both PCs and Macs are composed of the same elements: a CPU,[4] the electronic circuitry to run the computer; memory (hard and/or floppy disk drives) for storing information;
5  input devices such as a keyboard or mouse for putting information into the computer; and output devices such as a monitor, printer, and audio speakers for conveying information. They also have the same uses: PCs are used to communicate on computer networks, to write (with the help of word processing and desktop publishing software), to track finances, and to play games. Macs are likewise used to
10 communicate, write, calculate, and entertain.

---

[4] **CPU:** central processing unit

**Paragraph 2**

There are some differences, however. Whereas you will find more PCs in business offices, you will find more Macs in classrooms. Although Macs are the computers of choice of people who do a lot of art and graphic design in their work, PCs seem to be the choice of people who do a lot of "number crunching."[1]
5  Finally, there is a difference in the availability of software, vendors, and service for the two computers. In general, there is a lot of PC-compatible[2] software, but relatively little Mac software. Furthermore, for a Mac, you must purchase your machine and get service from a Macintosh-authorized dealer, whereas many different computer stores sell and service PCs.

## *Writing Technique Questions*

**1.** Which paragraph shows comparison? Which paragraph shows contrast? Turn back to the paragraph about French and American management styles on page 52. Which type of paragraph is it?
**2.** On how many points are the two computers compared? On how many points are they contrasted?
**3.** What transition signals are used to show similarities? To show differences? (Refer to the following charts.)

*Transition Signals for Comparison/ Contrast*

## COMPARISON TRANSITION SIGNALS

| SENTENCE CONNECTORS | CONJUNCTIONS | OTHERS |
| --- | --- | --- |
| similarly<br>likewise<br>also<br>too | and<br>both . . . and<br>not only . . . but also<br>as<br>just as | like<br>just like<br>alike<br>as . . . as<br>(be) similar<br>similar to<br>the same (as)<br>compare to/with |

---

[1] **number crunching:** mathematical calculations
[2] **PC-compatible:** can be used in PC computers

## CONTRAST TRANSITION SIGNALS

| SENTENCE CONNECTORS | CONJUNCTIONS | OTHERS |
|---|---|---|
| however<br>on the other hand<br>on the contrary<br>in contrast<br>in (by) comparison | but<br>yet<br>although<br>though<br>even though<br>while<br>whereas | unlike<br>differ from<br>(be) dissimilar<br>compare to<br>compare with |

**PRACTICE 6**

*Comparison/Contrast*

**A.** Circle all of the comparison/contrast transition signals in the two paragraphs about PCs versus Macs on pages 65–66 and in the paragraph about French and American management styles on page 52.

**B.** Review the topic sentence practice (Practice 5) on page 64. Find two topic sentences that could indicate comparison/contrast order.

# Review

These are the important points you should have learned from this chapter:

**1.** You can achieve coherence in writing by stating your ideas in logical order. There are several kinds of logical order: chronological order, logical division of ideas/order of importance, and comparison/contrast.
**2.** Each kind of logical order has special words and expressions, or transition signals, that will support your logic.

**PREWRITING PRACTICE**

*Brainstorming Essay Exam Questions*

Below is a list of fifteen possible essay questions that might be asked on a typical college examination. The first five are general questions that might be asked on a college writing test. The last ten are specific to a field of study. Get together with a group of one or two other students and brainstorm: Which logical order might you use to answer each question—chronological order, logical division of ideas/order of importance, or comparison/contrast?

_____     **1.** What do you hope to gain from your college education?
_____     **2.** Evaluate a significant experience or achievement that has meaning for you.
_____     **3.** Discuss some issue of personal, local, national, or international concern and its importance to you.
_____     **4.** Write about your idea of a perfect day.
_____     **5.** How do you think the world will be different fifty years from now? What changes do you expect to witness?

_____   **6.** Compare and contrast the relationship between the two pairs of lovers in Shakespeare's <u>Much Ado about Nothing</u>.

_____   **7.** In James Joyce's novel <u>Portrait of the Artist as a Young Man</u>, identify the three major incidents that affect Stephen Dedalus emotionally in Chapter 1. Which incident do you think changes him most? Why?

_____   **8.** Explain the electrical conductivity of an electrolyte solution. Use an example to illustrate.

_____   **9.** Consider a mixture of 10 million $O_2$ molecules and 20 million $H_2$ molecules. In what way is this mixture similar to 20 million water molecules? In what way is it dissimilar?

_____   **10.** Describe the steps necessary for a proposed bill to become a law in the United States.

_____   **11.** Explain the cash and accrual methods of accounting.

_____   **12.** Describe the procedure for taking a year-end inventory in a small retail business.

_____   **13.** Discuss the goals of American foreign policy before and after the fall of the Berlin Wall.

_____   **14.** Explain the differences between a sole proprietorship, a partnership, and a corporation.

_____   **15.** Explain how a hurricane forms.

**WRITING PRACTICE**

Choose one of the suggested topics that follow and write a paragraph that is ten to fifteen sentences in length. Use logical division of ideas, order of importance, or comparison and/or contrast to organize your ideas. Your instructor may wish to limit your choice in order to give you practice in a specific type of paragraph.

Remember the steps in the writing process:

**STEP 1**
*Prewriting*
Brainstorm a topic for ideas, using the listening, freewriting, or clustering techniques you have learned.

**STEP 2**
*Planning*
Develop an outline that includes a topic sentence and a concluding sentence (if necessary). Underline them.

**STEP 3**
*Writing*
Write a rough draft. Be sure to use transition signals.

**STEP 4**
*Editing*
Have a classmate check your draft against the Peer Editing Checklist.

**STEP 5**
*Rewriting*
Write a second draft, and proofread it for grammar and mechanics.

**STEP 6**
Write a final copy to hand in.

## *Topic Suggestions*

Ways to improve your English speaking skills

Important lessons you have learned in life

Three pieces of advice you might give to a friend who plans to study abroad

Eating customs in your country and another country

Two automobile models, two music styles, two sports stars, two airlines, two restaurants, two well-known people

Reasons you are learning English

Reasons you want to become a _____ (doctor, musician, interior designer, computer programmer, etc.)

## PEER EDITING CHECKLIST

| | PEER EDITOR'S COMMENTS AND SUGGESTIONS |
|---|---|
| **GENERAL** | |
| 1. What do you like best about this paragraph? | |
| **PAPER FORMAT** | |
| 2. Is the format correct? Does it look like the model on page 19? | |
| **ORGANIZATION AND CONTENT** | |
| 3. **Topic sentence:** Is there a clear topic sentence? Does it have a controlling idea? <br><br> 4. **Supporting sentences:** Is the main idea clear? Does the writer need to add more details to explain it? <br><br> 5. **Concluding sentence:** Is there a concluding sentence? Does it begin with an appropriate end-of-paragraph signal? <br><br> 6. **Unity:** Do all of the sentences support the topic sentence? <br><br> 7. **Coherence:** Do the sentences flow smoothly? Are there any inconsistent pronouns? Are there enough transition signals? What kind of logical order is used? | |
| **SENTENCE STRUCTURE** | |
| 8. Are there any unclear sentences? Can you suggest a way to improve them? | |
| **GRAMMAR AND MECHANICS** | |
| 9. Are there any errors in grammar and mechanics? | |

# CHAPTER

**6**

# Concrete Support I

Latin inscription from a Roman temple

## *Introduction*

One of the biggest problems in student writing is that student writers often fail to prove their points. They fail because they do not support their points with concrete details. Their papers are too often full of opinions and generalizations without the factual details needed to support them.

A successful paragraph contains **concrete[1] support** for the topic sentence. Support your topic sentence by using specific and factual details.

---

[1] **concrete:** specific; definite

# *Facts versus Opinions*

**Facts** are objective statements of truths.

> At sea level, water boils at 100 degrees Celsius.
> Women live longer than men.
> Lung cancer among women is increasing.

**Opinions** are subjective statements based on a person's beliefs or attitudes.

> Men are better drivers than women.
> Engineering students do not need to take a lot of English courses.
> Americans are only superficially[1] friendly.

It is certainly acceptable to express opinions in academic writing. In fact, most professors want you to express your own ideas. However, you must support your opinions with factual details. The more specific you are, the better.

In very formal academic writing, even some statements that are considered facts need further support. In other words, they need specific supporting details in order to be completely convincing.

Here are some examples of statements that need further support to be acceptable in formal academic writing and of additional necessary concrete supporting details.

| UNSUPPORTED "FACTS" | CONCRETE SUPPORTING DETAILS |
| --- | --- |
| Teenage smoking is on the rise. | In 1995, the U.S. surgeon general reported that more than three million teenagers smoked cigarettes. |
| Smoking can cause lung cancer. | The American Cancer Society reports that the number one cause of lung cancer among men and women is smoking. |

**PRACTICE 1**

*Facts versus Opinions*

**STEP 1**    Decide whether each of the following statements is a fact or an opinion. Write F for fact, O for opinion.

**STEP 2**    Decide if the facts need additional supporting details. Write NFS for "needs further support" next to those that do.

**STEP 3**    Discuss with your classmates what specific supporting details you might use to support the sentences you marked O (opinion) or F-NFS.

_____  **1.** Smoking is relaxing and, therefore, enjoyable.

_____  **2.** Dr. Kathleen Parker, a well-known cancer specialist, recently admitted in an interview, "Although I see the harmful effects of smoking nearly every day in my work, I still enjoy relaxing with a cigarette after dinner."

_____  **3.** Early in the next decade, more women than men will die of lung cancer, according to the American Cancer Society.

_____  **4.** Smoking is attracting more and more adults.

---

[1] **superficially:** on the surface

    **5.** According to a recent <u>New York Times</u> article, cigarette smoking is increasing among adults in their forties as well as among the college educated and those earning more than $35,000 annually.

    **6.** Red-light runners[2] must take a driver's education class. Then they will become safer drivers.

    **7.** Red-light runners cause scores of[3] accidents, including deaths and injuries as well as millions of dollars in damages.

    **8.** Red-light runners should have their driver's licenses suspended for a period of time.

    **9.** Nationwide, the number of red-light running accidents increased 18 percent from 1991 through 1995. In 1991, 2,425 deaths resulted, and in 1995, the number rose to 2,866.

## Concrete Supporting Details

**COMPUTER TIP**

Look in on-line newspapers for current quotations and other support for your topic.

There are several kinds of concrete supporting details that you can use to support or prove your topic sentence. Among the most common are examples, statistics, and quotations.

    Read the following article about the changing American family, as more married women with children are going to work and more fathers are staying at home. Notice how the different kinds of concrete details support the writer's main ideas.

**MODEL**

*Concrete Supporting Details*

*Extended example*

*Statistic*

*Statistic*

### Dad's New Role

    Dr. Elizabeth Lee is the medical director in charge of communicable diseases in the county[4] where she lives. She enjoys her challenging career and prefers it to staying at home with her two young children. Both she and her husband, Jack, realize the importance of parents' active participation in their children's lives.
5 Therefore, they decided that one of them should stay at home to be a full-time parent. Jack became the primary caregiver because staying home would enable him to spend time developing his graphic design business.

    Jack Lee is one of a growing number of stay-at-home dads. According to a 1996 survey by the *Los Angeles Times,* 39 percent of the men who responded to the
10 survey indicated that they would be willing to quit their jobs to take care of their children, while their wives became the primary breadwinners.[5] Furthermore, the U.S. Census Bureau reported in 1997 that approximately two million men across the United States have primary responsibility for their children.

---

[2] **red-light runners:** drivers who speed through red traffic signal lights
[3] **scores of:** many
[4] **county:** administrative subdivision of a state in the United States
[5] **breadwinners:** family members who earn money

*Example*

15    Other fathers are telecommuting[1] or have part-time jobs that allow them to spend more time with their kids. For example, telecommuting gives advertising executive Ron Stemple time to take his children to school and pick them up. He can also drive them to their after-school activities. A 1997 study by job placement

*Statistic*

agency Executive Search, Inc. reported that between 57 and 78 percent of men would be willing to reduce their work hours and their salaries to spend more time

20    with their children.

        According to the experts, Dad does just as well as Mom at parenting. As Joan

*Quotation*

Grant of the New York Department of Social Services stated, "Men are just as capable as women of taking care of their children's needs, including preparing nutritious meals; dispensing love, discipline, and Band-Aids; and providing a happy

25    home environment."

## Writing Technique Questions

**1.** What main idea does the first paragraph about Dr. Lee illustrate?
**2.** What is the main idea of the second paragraph? What statistics are given?
**3.** What is the main idea of the third paragraph? How is it supported?
**4.** What is the main idea of the last paragraph? What kind of concrete supporting detail is used to prove it?

In the following sections, you will practice using each kind of concrete supporting detail.

## Examples/ Extended Examples

Examples and extended examples, which are anecdotes or short stories, are perhaps the easiest kind of supporting details to use. You don't have to search in the library for information; you can often take examples from your own knowledge and personal experiences. Furthermore, examples are usually interesting and make your writing enjoyable to read. Finally, since it is easy to remember a striking example or a good story, your reader is more likely to remember your point.

However, there are two cautions you should keep in mind if you use examples and extended examples for support. First, remember that in formal academic writing— research papers, theses, and the like—personal examples are considered weak support, so use them sparingly.[2] Second, be sure that your examples really prove your point. For instance, if you are trying to prove that, on the average, men are better drivers than women, don't use famous racing car drivers as examples of male drivers because professional drivers aren't average men.

Study the two models to see how examples and extended examples can be used to support a topic sentence.

---

[1] **telecommuting:** working at home and using a computer to communicate with one's office and customers
[2] **sparingly:** infrequently

## Language and Perception

Although we all possess the same physical organs for sensing the world—eyes for seeing, ears for hearing, noses for smelling, skin for feeling, and mouths for tasting—our perception of the world depends to a great extent on the language we speak. Scholars have discovered that we cannot perceive things that we have
5   not named. Each language is like a pair of eyeglasses through which we "see" the world in a particular way. A classic example of the relationship between language and perception is the word *snow*. In the English language, there is only that one word to describe all of the possible kinds of snow. In Eskimo languages, however, there are as many as thirty-two different words for snow. For instance, the
10   Eskimos have different words for falling snow, snow on the ground, snow packed as hard as ice, slushy snow, wind-driven show, and what we might call "cornmeal" snow. In contrast, cultures that rarely experience cold weather and snow may have only one word to express several concepts that are differentiated in English. The ancient Aztec languages of Mexico, for example, used only one word to mean
15   snow, cold, and ice.

## Nonverbal Communication[3]

Nonverbal communication, or "body language," is communication by facial expressions, head or eye movements, hand signals, and body postures. It can be just as important to understanding as words are. Misunderstandings—often amusing but sometimes serious—can arise between people from different cultures if they misin-
5   terpret nonverbal signals. Take, for example, the differences in meaning of a gesture[4] very common in the United States: a circle made with the thumb and index finger.[5] To an American, it means that everything is OK. To a Japanese, it means that you are talking about money. In France, it means that something is worthless, and in Greece, it is an obscene[6] gesture. Therefore, an American could unknowingly offend
10   a Greek by using that particular hand signal.

That following incident illustrates how conflicting nonverbal signals can cause serious misunderstandings. While lecturing to his poetry class at Ain Shams University in Cairo, a British professor became so relaxed that he leaned back in his chair and revealed the bottom of his foot to the astonished class. Making such a
15   gesture in Muslim society is the worst kind of insult. The next day, the Cairo newspapers carried headlines about the student demonstration that resulted, and they denounced British arrogance[7] and demanded that the professor be sent home.

---

[3] **nonverbal communication:** communication without words
[4] **gesture:** hand signal
[5] **index finger:** the finger next to the thumb
[6] **obscene:** indecent, disgusting
[7] **arrogance:** too much pride

## Writing Technique Questions

**1.** What is the main idea of each paragraph? (There are three paragraphs, one paragraph in the first model and two paragraphs in the second model.) Underline the topic sentence in each paragraph.

**2.** What examples are used to support each topic sentence? Which paragraph has an extended example?

**3.** What words and phrases are used to introduce the examples? To introduce the extended example?

## Tips for Using Examples and Extended Examples

**1.** Make sure that your example really supports your point.

**2.** Introduce examples with appropriate transition signals.

### TRANSITION SIGNALS FOR EXAMPLES

| SENTENCE CONNECTORS | OTHERS |
|---|---|
| for example<br><br>for instance | such as<br><br>The following example (story/incident) illustrates (shows/demonstrates) . . . |

The ancient Aztec languages of Mexico, **for example,** used only one word to mean snow, cold, and ice.

**For instance,** the Eskimos have different words for falling snow, snow on the ground, snow packed as hard as ice . . . and "cornmeal" snow.

Job titles **such as** *stewardess, waitress,* and *mailman* are today considered sexist[1] and have been replaced by nongender-specific job titles **such as** *flight attendant, waitperson,* and *mail carrier.*

**WRITING PRACTICE**

*Writing with Examples*

Choose either A or B below and write a paragraph using an example and/or an extended example to support your topic sentence. Ask a classmate to check your paragraph against the Peer Editing Checklist at the end of the chapter before you hand it in.

**A.** Describe a body language signal from your own culture that is different from a body language signal used in the United States. Explain the confusion that can result when people misunderstand the signal.

**B.** Explain a proverb[2] from your first language by using examples. Some proverbs in English are

> Don't count your chickens before they hatch.
> A bird in the hand is worth two in the bush.
> People who live in glass houses shouldn't throw stones.

---

[1] **sexist:** discriminatory based on gender (male/female)
[2] **proverb:** wise saying that gives a practical rule for living

***Statistics***

In business, engineering, and the sciences, statistics are often used for support. In this section, you will practice using statistics from charts and graphs to support your writing ideas.

Study the chart below, and then read the paragraph that explains it. Notice that the source of the information is given in the sentence that begins "According to. . . ."

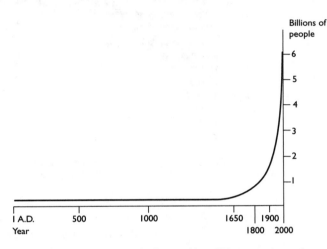

World population growth. (Source: United Nations estimates.)

**MODEL**

*Figures and Statistics*

### World Population Growth

The world's population has been increasing dramatically. According to a United Nations chart of world population growth, the world's population suddenly multiplied in the nineteenth and twentieth centuries. At the beginning of the Christian era, the estimated world population was 200 to 300 million. It took more
5  than 1,800 years for the population to reach one billion. Then in less than one hundred years, the figure doubled to two billion by 1930. By 1975, when it reached four billion, it had doubled again in less than fifty years. The United Nations has projected an increase to more than six billion by the year 2000.

### *Writing Technique Questions*

1. What is the main idea of the paragraph?
2. What five statistics are used to support this idea? What is the source of these numbers?
3. Turn back to the model "Dad's New Role" on pages 73–74. What statistics are used there? What are their sources?

**PRACTICE 2**

*Using Figures and
Statistics*

Study the graph below, which shows how the world's largest economies dominate global energy use. Then use the information in the graph to complete the paragraph that follows.

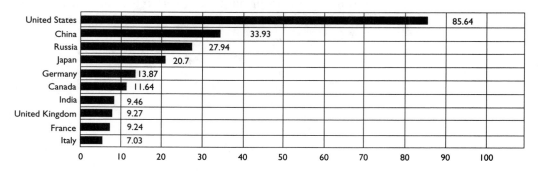

World's major consumers of primary energy, 1994. [Source: Energy Information Administration, U.S. Department of Energy, International Database, August 1996. Figures represent quadrillion Btu (British thermal units).]

### World's Major Consumers of Primary Energy

According to statistics published by the U.S. Department of Energy, the world's consumption of primary energy continued to increase in 1994 in quadrillion Btu's. The three top consumers included the United States, _____ . However, the largest consumer was

5  _____ . It used _____ . Japan consumed _____ , whereas Germany consumed _____ . The countries that consumed less than 10 quadrillion Btu included _____

_____ .

**WRITING
PRACTICE**

*Statistics*

Two sets of graphs follow: one on the topic of credit, the other on working women in Japan and the United States. Choose either set of graphs and write a paragraph explaining its significance.

**STEP 1**  Decide what main idea the graphs illustrate, and write this idea as a topic sentence.

**STEP 2**  Write five to eight supporting statements, using the statistical information shown in the graphs. Be sure to mention the source of your statistics in your paragraph.

**STEP 3**  Ask a classmate to check your paragraph against the Peer Editing Checklist at the end of the chapter before you hand it in.

## A. Hooked on[1] Credit

The graphs below are the results of a *USA Today* survey of 2,300 readers.

**1.** Survey question: Are you concerned about the amount of debt you have on credit cards?

Results:

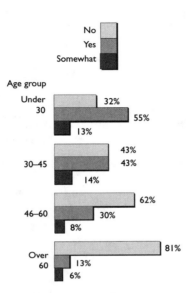

Source: *USA Today* survey, analyzed by Barbara Pearson.

**2.** Survey question: Do you pay off all credit card bills every month?

Results:

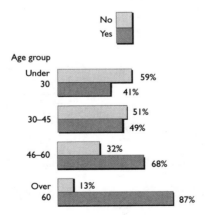

Source: *USA Today* survey, analyzed by Barbara Pearson.

[1] **hooked on:** addicted to something

## B. Working Women in Japan and the United States

The following graphs from the *New York Times* compare working women in Japan and the United States.

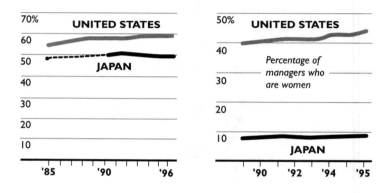

1.  **While the share of women in Japan who work is not substantially smaller than in the United States . . .**

. . . **women in Japan hold fewer positions of responsibility in the workplace . . .**

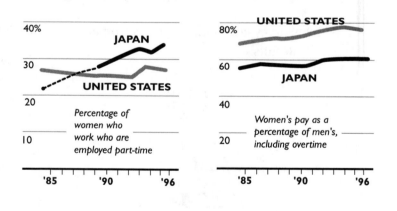

2.  . . . **are more likely to have a part-time job . . .**

. . . **and experience a larger wage gap with men . . .**

# *Review*

These are the important points you should have learned from this chapter:

**1.** Use concrete supporting details to prove your points.

**2.** Do not use opinions for support.

**3.** Use examples, extended examples, or statistics as support.

## PEER EDITING CHECKLIST

| | PEER EDITOR'S COMMENTS AND SUGGESTIONS |
|---|---|
| **GENERAL** | |
| **1.** What do you like best about this paragraph? | |
| **PAPER FORMAT** | |
| **2.** Is the format correct? Does it look like the model on page 19? | |
| **ORGANIZATION AND CONTENT** | |
| **3. Topic sentence:** Is there a clear topic sentence? Does it have a controlling idea? <br><br> **4. Supporting sentences:** What kind of concrete support is used? Are the statistics or examples incorporated smoothly into the paragraph? <br><br> **5. Concluding sentence:** Is there a concluding sentence? Does it begin with an appropriate end-of-paragraph signal? <br><br> **6. Unity:** Do all of the sentences support the topic sentence? <br><br> **7. Coherence:** Do the sentences flow smoothly? Are there any inconsistent pronouns? Are there enough transition signals used? | |
| **SENTENCE STRUCTURE** | |
| **8.** Are there any unclear sentences? Can you suggest a way to improve them? | |
| **GRAMMAR AND MECHANICS** | |
| **9.** Are there any errors in grammar and mechanics? | |

# Concrete Support II

Runic writing from eleventh-century Sweden

## *Quotations, Paraphrases, and Summaries*

In addition to the examples, extended examples, and statistics that you studied in the previous chapter, you may also need to use other kinds of concrete information to support your ideas. Using quotations and writing paraphrases and summaries of information from outside sources are important tools in academic writing. In some college classes, instructors ask their students to write research papers (also called term papers). To write a term paper, you must find information about your topic in books, newspapers, periodicals,[1] encyclopedias, and similar sources. Then you include this information in the body of your paper.

It is important to learn how to use information from outside sources without committing plagiarism.[2] Plagiarism is a serious offense. It occurs in two situations. It occurs when you use another person's words or ideas without acknowledging that the person is your source. Plagiarism also occurs even when you acknowledge the other person *if your rewritten version is too similar to the other person's*. In this chapter, you will learn how to use other people's words and ideas without plagiarizing them.

When you borrow another person's words or ideas by quoting, paraphrasing, or summarizing them, you must show where you got the ideas by putting certain information in parentheses immediately after the material you have borrowed. As you study this chapter, look for the ways this information is given. At the end of the chapter, you will learn how to prepare such in-text citations.

## Quotations

There are two kinds of quotations: direct and indirect. In a direct quotation, another person's exact words are repeated and are enclosed in quotation marks. In an indirect quotation, the speaker's words are reported without quotation marks. You should learn to use both kinds of quotations in your writing.

### Direct Quotations

Read the following model and study how direct quotations are used to support the topic sentence.

**MODEL**

*Direct Quotations*

**Drugs and the Olympic Games**

It is no secret that performance-enhancing[3] drugs have been used by Olympic athletes for decades. In 1993, the head of the International Olympic Committee's medical commission, Prince Alexandre de Merode of Belgium, stated, "I believe that as many as 10% of all Olympic athletes are regular users of performance-enhancing
5   drugs" (qtd. in Bamberger and Yaeger 63).[4] Despite rigorous[5] drug testing of Olympic athletes, the use of banned performance-enhancing substances has become more widespread than ever. It is clear that if athletes want to win, they must consider using drugs. In a 1997 article in *Sports Illustrated* magazine, Dutch physician Michel Karsten is quoted as saying, "There may be some sportsmen who can win
10   gold medals without taking drugs, but there are very few." According to Dr. Karsten, who says he has prescribed anabolic steroids[6] to hundreds of world-class athletes over the last twenty-five years, "If you are especially gifted, you may win once, but from my experience you can't continue to win without drugs. The field is just too filled with drug users" (qtd. in Bamberger and Yaeger 62).

---

[1] **periodicals:** magazines
[2] **plagiarism:** the use of someone else's words or ideas as your own
[3] **enhancing:** improving
[4] **qtd. in Bamberger and Yaeger 63:** This form of in-text citation means that the words in quotation marks were spoken by Prince Alexandre de Merode and were quoted on page 63 of an article written by two people named Bamberger and Yaeger.
[5] **rigorous:** strict
[6] **anabolic steroids:** drugs that increase muscle

## Reporting Verbs and Phrases

Reporting verbs and phrases are used to introduce a quotation or other borrowed information (such as statistics). Some of the more common reporting terms are as follows:

| | | | |
|---|---|---|---|
| according to | insist | report | suggest |
| claim | maintain | say | write |
| declare | mention | state | |

Here are some rules for their use:

**1.** Reporting verbs can appear before, in the middle of, or after a quotation.

Dr. Karsten **said**, "_____ ."

"_____ ," the doctor **stated**, "_____ ."

"_____ ," **declared** the president of the International Olympic Committee (IOC).

**2.** Reporting verbs can be used with or without the subordinator *as*.

**As** a spokesperson for the IOC **suggested**, "_____ ."

A spokesperson for the IOC **suggested**, "_____ ."

**3.** Reporting verbs may be in any tense.

As the IOC **stated** in its report after the 1996 games in Atlanta, "_____
_____ ."

The IOC **states** in its report after the 1996 games in Atlanta, "_____
_____ ."

As the IOC **has** always **insisted**, "_____ ."

**4.** The reporting phrase *according to* can be used in place of a reporting verb. Use quotation marks if you are quoting someone's words exactly.

**According to** the IOC, "_____ ."

**5.** It is a good idea to include the source of the quotation in your sentence.

**According to a report published by the IOC**, "_____ ."

## Punctuating Direct Quotations

The rules for punctuating direct quotations can become very complex. For general purposes, the rules are as follows:

**1.** Quotation marks are always used in pairs. Place a comma between the reporting phrase and the quotation. Put quotation marks before and after the actual words quoted. Normally, place commas (and periods) before the first mark and also before the second mark in a pair.

According to *Sports Illustrated*, "The use of steroids—and other, more exotic substances such as human growth hormone (hGH)—has spread to almost every sport, from major league baseball to college basketball to high school football."

"The use of steroids—and other, more exotic substances such as human growth hormone (hGH)—has spread to almost every sport, from major league baseball to college basketball to high school football," according to *Sports Illustrated*.

**CROSS-REFERENCE**

For more examples showing the use of quotation marks, see pages 252–253 in Appendix A.

There is an important exception to this rule: When you add an in-text citation after a quotation, the period goes at the very end, after the closing parenthesis:

Prince Alexandre de Merode of Belgium stated, "I believe that as many as 10% of all Olympic athletes are regular users of performance-enhancing drugs" (qtd. in Bamberger and Yaeger 63).

**2.** Capitalize the first word of the quotation as well as the first word of the sentence.

Dr. Donald Catlin, director of a drug-testing lab at UCLA, stated, "The sophisticated athlete who wants to take drugs has switched to things we can't test for."

**3.** If you break a quotation into two parts, enclose both parts in quotation marks and separate the parts with commas. Capitalize only the first word of the sentence.

"The use of steroids—and other, more exotic substances such as human growth hormone (hGH)—has spread," according to *Sports Illustrated*, "to almost every sport, from major league baseball to college basketball to high school football."

**4.** If you omit part of a direct quotation, use an ellipsis ( . . . ).

According to *Sports Illustrated*, "The use of steroids . . . has spread to almost every sport, from major league baseball to college basketball to high school football."

**5.** If you have a good reason to add words of your own to the original, put brackets[ ] around the words that you have added.

Commenting on the difficulty of detecting drug use among Olympic athletes, the director of drug testing for the U.S. Olympic Committee at the 1984 and 1988 games declared, "The testers know that the [drug] gurus[1] are smarter than they are."

**PRACTICE 1**

*Direct Quotations*

**A.** Turn back to the model paragraph about drug use among Olympic athletes on page 83 and answer the following questions.

**1.** How many direct quotations are used in the model paragraph?
**2.** What reporting verbs and phrases are used to introduce the direct quotations?

**B.** Add punctuation to the following direct quotations. Change the capitalization if necessary. (The sentences in this practice are about black holes, which are invisible masses in space larger than giant stars.)

**1.** Dr. Yixuan Ma, a well-known astrophysicist who has been studying black holes, said it is one of the most interesting phenomena we astrophysicists have ever studied.
**2.** As she explained in black holes the laws of nature do not seem to apply.
**3.** A black hole is a tiny point with the mass 25 times the mass of our sun explained Ma's associate, Chun-Yi Su. Black holes are created by the death of a very large star she stated.

---

[1] **gurus:** advisors

4. It is an invisible vacuum cleaner in space she added with tremendous gravitational pull.

5. According to Dr. Su, if a person falls into a black hole, he will eventually be crushed due to the tremendous gravitational forces.

6. Time will slow down for him as he approaches the event horizon[1] she said and when he reaches the event horizon, time will stand still for him.

## Indirect Quotations

In indirect quotations, the speaker's (or writer's) words are reported indirectly. For this reason, indirect quotations are sometimes called reported speech. Indirect quotations are introduced by the same reporting verbs used for direct quotations, often with the added word *that*. Do not use quotation marks. Also, the tense of verbs in indirect quotations is affected by the tense of the reporting verb. Study the model and observe how indirect quotations support the main ideas. Notice also the verb tenses.

**MODEL**

*Indirect Quotations*

**CROSS-REFERENCE**

For additional information about indirect quotations, you may also want to look at Chapter 11, Noun Clauses, pages 178–182.

### Seeking a Spouse on the Web

The global reach of the Internet is helping expatriate[2] citizens of India find marriage partners. Most Indians prefer their partners to come from the same region of India as they and to have similar religious and socioeconomic backgrounds. For young Indians who live abroad, searching for a suitable wife or
5  husband becomes quite difficult. They often must depend on their families back home in India to find them mates. However, computer scientist Raj Baronia, who lives and works in Silicon Valley in California, has developed a site on the World Wide Web to help called Indolink. In an interview, Baronia said that he had developed Indolink to allow Indians living abroad to take responsibility for finding
10  their own marriage partners rather than having their parents do it for them. He estimated that about half of Indolink ads were placed by marriage seekers themselves, rather than by family. Baronia also said Indolink allowed them to search not only in India but also in expatriate communities around the world (qtd. in Bentley).[3] For example, Sandeep Gupta, a young computer programmer from
15  Toronto, is seeking a wife through Indolink. He is looking for intellectual women, and, according to Gupta, anyone he meets on the Internet will probably be professional and educated. He added, "I am planning to fly to New York soon to meet a young woman I met through Indolink" (qtd. in Bentley).

## Changing Direct Quotations to Indirect Quotations

Good writers use both direct and indirect quotations. In certain situations, you may find it easier to use one kind or the other, and using both adds variety to your writing. In the following examples, notice what changes occur when a direct quotation is rewritten as an indirect quotation.

---

[1] **event horizon:** the point of no return in a black hole
[2] **expatriate:** living in a foreign country
[3] This in-text citation means that the words were spoken by Mr. Baronia and were indirectly quoted in a one-page article written by Bentley.

| DIRECT QUOTATION | INDIRECT QUOTATION |
|---|---|
| He declared, "I am looking for intellectual women." | He declared that he was looking for intellectual women. |
| My father told me, "I want you to do your best." | My father told me that he wanted me to do my best. |
| The teacher told us, "You can take another test to try to improve your grades." | The teacher told us we could take another test to try to improve our grades. |
| The students confessed, "We didn't study." | The students confessed that they hadn't studied. |

To change a direct quotation to an indirect quotation:

1. Omit the quotation marks.
2. Add the subordinator *that*. (You may omit *that* if the meaning is clear.)
3. Change the verb tense if necessary. Follow the sequence of tenses rules provided here.
4. Change pronouns as necessary.

### *Sequence of Tenses Rules*

1. If the reporting verb is in a past tense, the verbs in an indirect quotation may change tense according to the following rules:

|  | DIRECT QUOTATION | INDIRECT QUOTATION |
|---|---|---|
| Simple present changes to simple past | Susan said, "The exam **is** at eight o'clock." | Susan said (that) the exam **was** at eight o'clock. |
| Simple past and present perfect change to past perfect | She said, "We **didn't have** time to eat breakfast." <br><br> He said, "The exam **has** just **started**." | She said (that) they **hadn't had** time to eat breakfast. <br><br> He said (that) the exam **had** just **started**. |
| *Will* changes to *would,* can to *could,* and *may* to *might.* | Pedro mentioned, "Today I **will eat** Chinese food, and tomorrow I'**ll eat** French food if I **can find** a good restaurant." | Pedro mentioned that today he **would eat** Chinese food and that tomorrow he'**d eat** French food if he **could find** a good restaurant. |

**2.** When the quoted information is a fact or a general truth, the verb tense in the quotation does not change.

> He said, "Water **boils** at a lower temperature in the mountains."
> He said that water **boils** at a lower temperature in the mountains.

**3.** When the reporting verb is simple present, present perfect, or future, the verb tense in the quotation does not change.

> He says, "I **can finish** it today."
> He says that he **can finish** it today.

**4.** When the reporting phrase is *according to*, the verb tense does not change.

> Gupta said, "Anyone I **meet** on the Internet **will** probably **be** professional and educated."
> According to Gupta, anyone he **meets** on the Internet **will** probably **be** professional and educated.

## PRACTICE 2

*Changing Direct Quotations to Indirect Quotations*

**A.** Turn back to the model paragraph "Seeking a Spouse on the Web" on page 86 and answer these questions:

1. How many indirect quotations does the paragraph contain?
2. What reporting verbs or phrases introduce the indirect quotations? Which one(s) do not contain the word *that*?

**B.** Look at the model paragraph "Drugs and the Olympic Games" on page 83 and find the one indirect quotation. Does it follow the sequence of tenses rules?

**C.** Rewrite the following direct quotations as indirect quotations.

1. Television channel KSA General Manager Jim Burns said, "Everyone cannot attend college in the traditional way. Therefore, taking courses via television will offer many more students the chance to earn a college degree." _____ _____ _____

2. Pre-med student Alma Rodriguez said, "I miss being on campus, but I have to work and take care of my family." _____ _____ _____

3. Other students said, "Last year, we spent several hours a day commuting to and from school. Now we don't have to do that." _____ _____ _____

4. Computer engineering student Amir Mehdizadeh stated, "I can choose when to study and how to study without pressure." He also said, "I will take two more telecourses[1] in the fall." _____ _____ _____

---

[1] **telecourses:** college courses taken using telecommunication technology

**D.** Change all of the direct quotations in the model paragraph on drugs and Olympic athletes (page 83) into indirect quotations.

*Writing with Quotations*

Write a short paragraph that develops the topic you are given below. Use the quotations for support. You may use them either as direct or as indirect quotations. Include some additional supporting sentences and transition signals to connect the ideas and make your paragraph flow smoothly.

**STEP 1**    Copy the topic sentence exactly as it is given.

**STEP 2**    Write several supporting sentences, using the main points and quotations supplied. Add supporting details such as examples if you can. Use the techniques and rules you have learned for direct and/or indirect quotations. Be sure to mention somewhere in your paragraph the book or article that is the source of the quotations.

**STEP 3**    Document the source further by putting the author's name and a page number in parentheses at the end of your paragraph. (Refer to Documenting Sources of Information on pages 95–97.)

**STEP 4**    Before you hand in your paragraph, ask a classmate to check it against the Peer Editing Checklist on page 98.

**Example**

*Topic Sentence*    The increased use of computers in business has been accompanied by a costly increase in computer crime.

*Main point*    Computer criminals cost business a lot of money.

*Quotation*    "The financial losses to business from computer thefts will exceed $15 billion in 1998."

*Main point*    Computer criminals steal not only money but also information.

*Quotation*    "It is not just the money they steal; they steal data, and data is power."

*Source*    A book by Meredith Bruce, *Cybercrime*, page 185.

*Completed paragraph*    The increased use of computers in business has been accompanied by a costly increase in computer crime. The losses to victims of computer crimes are very high. In her book, *Cybercrime*, author Meredith Bruce claimed that the financial losses to business from computer thefts would exceed $15 billion in 1998. Computer criminals steal not only money but also information. For example, they steal confidential business records, customer lists, and corporate plans. As Bruce stated, "It is not just the money they steal; they steal data, and data is power" (Bruce 185).

**COMPUTER TIP**

Computers allow you to use various fonts or type styles. When you quote books or articles, you may use a special font to write the titles of your sources.

**Topic for Your Writing**

*Topic sentence*    Computers cannot be compared to human brains.

*Main point*    The human brain is more powerful than any computer.

*Quotation*    "It has been estimated that the information processing capacity of even the most powerful supercomputer is equal to the nervous system of a snail—a tiny fraction of the power available to the supercomputer inside the human skull."[2]

---

[2] **skull:** head

| | |
|---|---|
| *Main point* | The kinds of processing are different, too. |
| *Quotation* | "Computers find it easy to remember a 25-digit number but find it hard to summarize the gist[1] of [children's story] *Little Red Riding Hood*, and humans find it hard to remember the number but easy to summarize the story." |
| *Main point* | Human brains also have the advantage of being inside humans. |
| *Quotation* | "They [human brains] can soak up terabytes[2] of information over the years as the humans interact with other humans and with the environment." |
| *Source* | An article by Steven Pinker in *U.S. News & World Report*, August 18–25, 1997, page 64. |

## *Paraphrases*

In the preceding section, you learned how to use someone else's ideas for support by quoting his/her words directly or indirectly. Now you will learn two other ways to use ideas from outside sources: by paraphrasing and by summarizing.

Paraphrasing is a writing skill in which you "rephrase" (rewrite) information from an outside source in your own words without changing its meaning. Because you include in your rewriting all, or nearly all, of the content of the original passage, a paraphrase is almost as long. A summary, by contrast, is much shorter than the original. A summary includes only the main ideas of someone else's writing, restated in your own words. In summarizing and paraphrasing, however, you must not change the meaning of the original.

When paraphrasing, it is important to avoid plagiarizing; that is, writing a paraphrase that is too similar to the original. A paraphrase is unacceptable when it contains the same vocabulary and sentence structure as the original. The following model shows unacceptable and acceptable paraphrases.

## MODEL
*Paraphrase*

### Original Passage

Language is the main means of communication between peoples.[3] But so many different languages have developed that language has often been a barrier rather than an aid to understanding among peoples. For many years, people have dreamed of setting up an international, universal language which all people could speak and
5  understand. The arguments in favor of a universal language are simple and obvious. If all peoples spoke the same tongue, cultural and economic ties might be much closer, and good will might increase between countries (Kispert).

### Unacceptable Paraphrase

Language is the principal means of communication between peoples. However, because there are numerous languages, language itself has frequently been a barrier rather than an aid to understanding among the world population. For many years, people have envisioned a common universal language that everyone in the world
5  could communicate in. The reasons for having a universal language are clearly understandable. If the same tongue were spoken by all countries, they would undoubtedly become closer culturally and economically. It would probably also create good will among nations (Kispert).

---

[1] **gist:** main ideas
[2] **terabytes:** trillions of bytes
[3] **peoples:** groups of people that share a common culture, religion, language, etc.

> **Acceptable Paraphrase**
>
> Humans communicate through language. However, because there are so many languages in the world, language is an obstacle rather than an aid to communication. For a long time, people have wished for an international language that speakers all over the world could understand. A universal language would certainly build cultural and economic bonds. It would also create better feelings among countries (Kispert).

The first paraphrase is plagiarism. Even though the writer has changed many of the words, the sentence structure is very similar to the original. In the second paraphrase, both the vocabulary and sentence structure are different.

You can write a good paraphrase if you follow these steps:

**STEP 1**   Read the original passage several times until you understand it fully. Look up unfamiliar words, and find synonyms for them. If you need to take notes, write down only one or two words for each idea—not complete sentences. For example, here are one writer's notes on the original passage about universal language:

> language—people use to communicate—but too many—obstacle—dream—international language—reasons: cultural, economic bonds, good feelings between countries

It may be helpful to make a brief outline like the following:

A.   Language—main means of communication

   1. Too many languages—barrier to understanding

   2. Universal language needed

B.   Reasons for a universal language

   1. Increase cultural, economic bonds

   2. Increase good feelings between countries

**STEP 2**   Write your paraphrase from memory. Include as much of the information as you remember. Don't look at the original while you are writing.

**STEP 3**   Check your paraphrase against the original for accuracy and completeness. If necessary, add points you have missed.

**STEP 4**   Name the source of the original passage in parentheses at the end of your paraphrase. (Refer to Documenting Sources of Information on pages 95–97.)

**PRACTICE 3**

*Writing a Paraphrase*

**A.** Follow the preceding four steps and write paraphrases of the following passages. Write your notes and paraphrases in the spaces provided. Work with a partner or in a group if you wish.

**1.**                              **Artificial Languages**

Since the time of Descartes,[1] it is estimated that no fewer than five hundred attempts have been made to create artificial languages for international use. The most successful by far has been Esperanto, a language constructed around the end of the nineteenth century by Dr. Zamenhof of Poland.
5   Esperanto is a language that is extremely easy to learn and speak, with its words drawn mainly from English, German, the Romance languages,[2] Latin, and Greek.

A more recent arrival on the international scene is Interlingua, scientifically constructed by a group of language experts out of Latin, the Romance
10   languages, and English. But whereas Esperanto has a large body of people who actually speak it scattered throughout the world, Interlingua has not yet achieved much popularity (Pei 175–176).

**Notes:**

_____
_____
_____
_____
_____
_____

**Paraphrase:**

_____
_____
_____
_____
_____
_____
_____
_____
_____
_____

**2.**                    **Artificial Languages—Objections**

The main objection to constructed languages, like Esperanto or Interlingua, is that they have not developed all the thought-carrying machinery and shades of meaning that natural languages have had a chance to work out for themselves over a period of many centuries; also, the artificial lan-
5   guages presented so far lean too heavily in the direction of the western European and American nations, and carry too little in the way of Slavic, Asiatic, and African words and habits of thought (Pei 176).

---

[1] **Descartes:** seventeenth-century French mathematician and philosopher
[2] **Romance languages:** languages that developed from Latin

**Notes:**

_____

_____

_____

_____

_____

_____

**Paraphrase:**

_____

_____

_____

_____

_____

_____

_____

_____

_____

_____

**B.** Follow the same four steps and write paraphrases of these two paragraphs on
your own. Write your notes and paraphrases on a separate sheet of paper.

**1.** **Americans**

Despite its ethnic diversity,[3] the United States has managed to absorb bits
and pieces of many cultures and weave them into a unique culture that is
strikingly consistent and distinct. You can pick out Americans anyplace in the
world, often very quickly, because of their behavior. Among their most
5  observable traits are openness, friendliness, informality, optimism, creativity,
loudness, and vitality (Hall and Hall 140).

**2.** **The Work Ethic[4] of Americans and Europeans**

Europeans often observe that Americans schedule everything
except time for relaxation. This is particularly true of American executives, who drive themselves hard, often at the expense of their families
and their health. Americans have fewer holidays and take shorter
5  vacations than do Europeans. In the opinion of many German and
French executives, American executives are obsessed with work;
they're workaholics. Most Europeans do not accept working on weekends or holidays; they reserve these times for themselves and their
families (Hall and Hall 145).

_____

[3] **ethnic diversity:** cultural differences
[4] **work ethic:** beliefs about and behavior reflecting the value of hard work

*Summaries*

A summary is similar to a paraphrase except that a summary is shorter. When you summarize, you compress[1] large amounts of information into the fewest possible sentences. In order to do this, you include only the main points and main supporting points, leaving out the details. However, just as when you paraphrase, you must not change the meaning of the original.

The original passage used in the model on page 90 is repeated here in order to show you clearly the difference between a paraphrase and a summary.

**MODEL**

*Summary*

**Original Passage**

Language is the main means of communication between peoples. But so many different languages have developed that language has often been a barrier rather than an aid to understanding among peoples. For many years, people have dreamed of setting up an international, universal language which all people
5   could speak and understand. The arguments in favor of a universal language are simple and obvious. If all peoples spoke the same tongue, cultural and economic ties might be much closer, and good will might increase between countries (Kispert).

**Summary**

People communicate mainly through language; however, having so many different languages creates communication barriers. Some think that one universal language would bring countries together culturally and economically and also increase good feelings among them (Kispert).

Compare this summary with the acceptable paraphrase on page 91. Notice that some details are omitted from the summary that were included in the paraphrase:

that people have dreamed of setting up an international, universal language
the arguments are simple and obvious

However, the meaning of the original has not been changed.

The steps for writing a summary are the same as for writing a paraphrase.

**STEP 1**   Read the original passage several times until you understand it fully. Look up unfamiliar words, and find synonyms for them. If you need to take notes, write down only one or two words for each idea—not complete sentences.

**STEP 2**   Write your summary from memory. Include important points and omit unnecessary details. Don't look at the original while you are writing. Remember that your goal in writing a summary is to restate the main ideas in as few words as possible.

**STEP 3**   Check your summary against the original for accuracy.

**STEP 4**   Put the source of the original passage in parentheses at the end of your summary. (See Documenting Sources of Information on pages 95–97.)

---

[1] **compress:** squeeze; press together

**PRACTICE 4**

*Writing a Summary*

**A.** Write a summary of each of the four passages from Practice 3 (pages 91–93), which you previously paraphrased.

**B.** Write a separate summary of each of the following paragraphs.

---

### A Less Social Society Becoming Shy

Growing numbers of those people standing silently in line at the automatic teller machine (ATM) or pumping their own self-service gas are probably victims of America's silent, anonymous epidemic. They're shy—and the rapid technological and social changes rippling[2] through
5  America are increasing their numbers rapidly, says the world's pioneering researcher into shyness. . . . The increasing numbers of shy people mean Americans are lonelier, more alienated,[3] and in worse shape, both mentally and physically. That is hardly a prescription for a healthy society (Epstein A1).
10  Stanford University professor Philip G. Zimbardo places the blame for the rising tide of shyness on three factors. First, automation, as exemplified[4] by ATMs and self-service gas pumps that take credit cards, "robs many of us of one more small opportunity for social contact." Second, the revolution in personal computers and home electronic entertainment
15  means couch potatoes[5] and cyber-surfers[6] have less reason for social interaction. "E-mail means you don't have to talk to people, even over the telephone," Zimbardo commented. Third, the changing nature of family life and rising fear of crime are shutting people off from each other. "You don't see kids in the streets anymore. All play is organized for them, so
20  they don't develop the give-and-take and the leadership skills of the playground," he warned. With some 50 percent of marriages ending in divorce and with most parents working, children are robbed of the nurturing communication they once enjoyed with their parents and extended families (qtd. in Epstein A10).

---

# Documenting Sources of Information

You have now learned how to use other people's words and ideas by quoting, paraphrasing, and summarizing. Remember that whenever you use the ideas of others, you must give proper credit to the originator of those ideas even when you do not use his or her exact words, or you will be guilty of plagiarism.

There are two steps to documenting your sources. The first step is to put a reference to each source within the text of your essay or term paper. This is called an in-text citation. The second step is to prepare a list that fully describes all of your sources to attach to the end of your paper.

---

[2] **rippling:** moving with a gentle waving motion
[3] **alienated:** feeling isolated; separated from others
[4] **exemplify:** give an example
[5] **couch potatoes:** people who watch TV a lot
[6] **cyber-surfers:** people who spend a lot of time on the Internet

This section will introduce you only to the basics of documentation. Any good English language handbook or style manual will give you more details about the correct ways to document different sources of information.

## In-Text Citations

There are several possible ways to write an in-text citation. One way is to put a brief reference in parentheses immediately following the quoted, paraphrased, or summarized material. Remember, when you add an in-text citation, the period goes at the very end, after the closing parenthesis.

Usually, you will need to give the last name of the author of your source and a page number (or numbers, if the borrowed information is on more than one page):

(Pei 175–176).

If there are two authors, give both names:

(Hall and Hall 140).

Do not give any more information than is necessary for your reader to identify the source of the material when he or she looks at your list of works cited. For example, leave out page numbers if the article from which you are borrowing information is only one page long.

(Bentley).

If you have already mentioned the author's name in the text, do not repeat the name in your citation. For example, if you began your paraphrase of the paragraph "Americans" on page 93 with the phrase *According to Hall and Hall,* give only the page number:

(140).

If you use material from an encyclopedia, use the author's name if it is given. If no author is named, put the title of the article in quotation marks. You do not need a page number since encyclopedia articles are arranged alphabetically and your reader will be able to find the source easily.

("Rock Music").

If you use someone's words that are quoted in a source written by a different person, begin the in-text citation with the abbreviation *qtd. in.* (for *quoted in*):

(qtd. in Bamberger and Yaeger 63).

## A List of Works Cited

The second step in documentation is to list all of your sources in alphabetical order by the author's family name or by the first word of the article if there is no author. This list is entitled "Works Cited." Include publishing information about each source.

<table>
<tr><td>Magazine article with 2<br>authors on more<br>than 1 page</td><td>**Works Cited**</td></tr>
</table>

|  |  |
|---|---|
| *Magazine article with 2 authors on more than 1 page* | Bamberger, Michael, and Don Yaeger. "Over the Edge." *Sports Illustrated* 14 April 1997:60+. |
| *Newspaper article on 1 page* | Bentley, Cheryl. "Net Finds Mates for Indian Expatriates." *San Francisco Chronicle* 8 April 1997:C4. |
| *Newspaper article on more than 1 page* | Epstein, Edward. "A Less Social Society Is Becoming Shy." *San Francisco Chronicle* 14 Sept. 1995:A-1+. |
| *Book with 2 authors* | Hall, Edward T., and Mildred Reed Hall. *Understanding Cultural Differences.* Yarmouth, Maine: Intercultural Press, 1990. |
| *Book with 1 author* | Pei, Mario A. *All About Language.* Philadelphia: Lippincott, 1954. |
| *Encyclopedia article with author named* | Kispert, Robert J. "Universal Language." *World Book Encyclopedia.* 1997. |
| *Encyclopedia article on CD-ROM with no author named* | "Company." *Microsoft Encarta 97 Encyclopedia.* 1997. |

# Review

These are the important points you should have learned from this chapter:

**1.** In academic writing, you are expected to use information from outside sources to support your ideas. When you include in an academic paper information from a book, newspaper, magazine, encyclopedia, dictionary, or nonprint sources such as television programs, CD-ROMs, or the Internet, use any of the following methods:

- Direct quotations: Repeat the author's or speaker's exact words, and place them within quotation marks.
- Indirect quotations: Report the author's words, making changes in pronouns and verb tenses as necessary. Do not use quotation marks.
- Paraphrase: Rewrite the author's meaning in your own words. Include all, or almost all, of the ideas that are in the original. Change the sentence structure and substitute synonyms where possible to avoid plagiarizing.
- Summary: Condense a writer's words and summarize the main ideas in as few of your own words as possible.

**2.** Document your sources to avoid plagiarizing and to help your reader find the sources of your information.

- Use in-text citations.
- Prepare an alphabetical list of works cited.

## PEER EDITING CHECKLIST

| | PEER EDITOR'S COMMENTS AND SUGGESTIONS |
|---|---|
| **GENERAL** | |
| **1.** What do you like best about this paragraph? | |
| **PAPER FORMAT** | |
| **2.** Is the format correct? Does it look like the model on page 19? | |
| **ORGANIZATION AND CONTENT** | |
| **3. Topic sentence:** Is there a clear topic sentence? Does it have a controlling idea?<br><br>**4. Supporting sentences:** Are the quotations incorporated smoothly into the paragraph? Did the writer follow the rules for using direct and indirect quotations? Are there enough supporting details?<br><br>**5. Coherence:** Do the ideas and sentences flow smoothly? Are transition signals used where they are needed? | |
| **SENTENCE STRUCTURE** | |
| **6.** Are there any unclear sentences? Can you suggest a way to improve them? | |
| **GRAMMAR AND MECHANICS** | |
| **7.** Are there any errors in grammar and mechanics? | |

# PART II

# Writing an Essay

# CHAPTER

# 8 The Essay

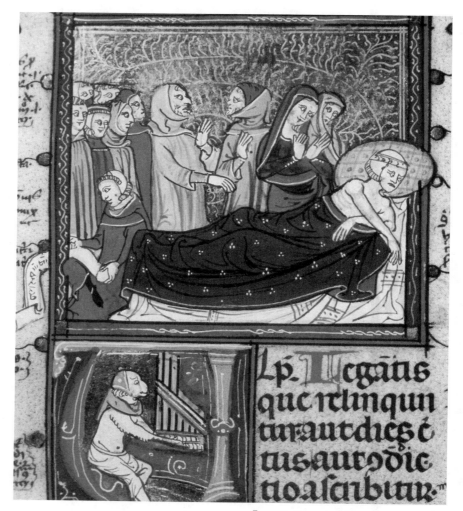

Fourteenth-century European manuscript

## *Writing an Essay*

An **essay** is a piece of writing several paragraphs long instead of just one or two paragraphs. It is written about one topic, just as a paragraph is. However, the topic of an essay is too complex to discuss in one paragraph. Therefore, you must divide the topic into several paragraphs, one for each major point. Then you must tie all of the separate paragraphs together by adding an introduction and a conclusion.

Writing an essay is no more difficult than writing a paragraph except that an essay is longer. The principles of organization are the same for both, so if you can write a good paragraph, you can write a good essay.

An essay has three main parts:

**1.** An *introductory paragraph*
**2.** A *body* (at least one, but usually two or more paragraphs)
**3.** A *concluding paragraph*

The **introductory paragraph** consists of two parts: a few *general statements* about your subject to attract your reader's attention and a *thesis statement* to state the specific subdivisions of your topic and/or the "plan" of your paper. A thesis statement for an essay is just like a topic sentence for a paragraph: It names the specific topic and the controlling ideas or major subdivisions of the topic.

The **body** consists of one or more paragraphs. Each paragraph develops a subdivision of your topic, so the number of paragraphs in the body will vary with the number of subdivisions or subtopics. The body is the longest part of the essay and can contain as many paragraphs as necessary to support the controlling ideas of your thesis statement. The paragraphs of the body of the essay are like the main supporting points in a single paragraph. Furthermore, you can organize the paragraphs in an essay just as you organize the ideas in a paragraph, by chronological order, logical division of ideas, comparison and contrast, etc.

The **conclusion** in an essay, like the concluding sentence in a paragraph, is a summary or review of the main points discussed in the body.

The only additional element in an essay is the linking expressions between the paragraphs of the body. These are just like transitions within a paragraph. You use transitions *within* a paragraph to connect the ideas between two sentences. Similarly, you use transitions *between* paragraphs to connect the ideas between them.

You can see that writing an essay is essentially the same as writing a paragraph; an essay is just longer. The chart on the next page shows you how the parts of a paragraph correspond to the parts of an essay.

## The Introductory Paragraph

All writers (even professionals) complain that the most difficult part of writing is getting started. Getting started, or writing an introductory paragraph,[1] can be easy if you remember that an introduction has four purposes:

**1.** It introduces the topic of the essay.
**2.** It gives a general background of the topic.
**3.** It often indicates the overall "plan" of the essay.
**4.** It should arouse the reader's interest in the topic.

The introduction has two parts:

• General statements
• A thesis statement

---

[1] A writer doesn't always have to write the general statements in the introductory paragraph first; it can be written even after the other paragraphs have been completed. However, the writer must have a thesis statement to focus his or her thinking.

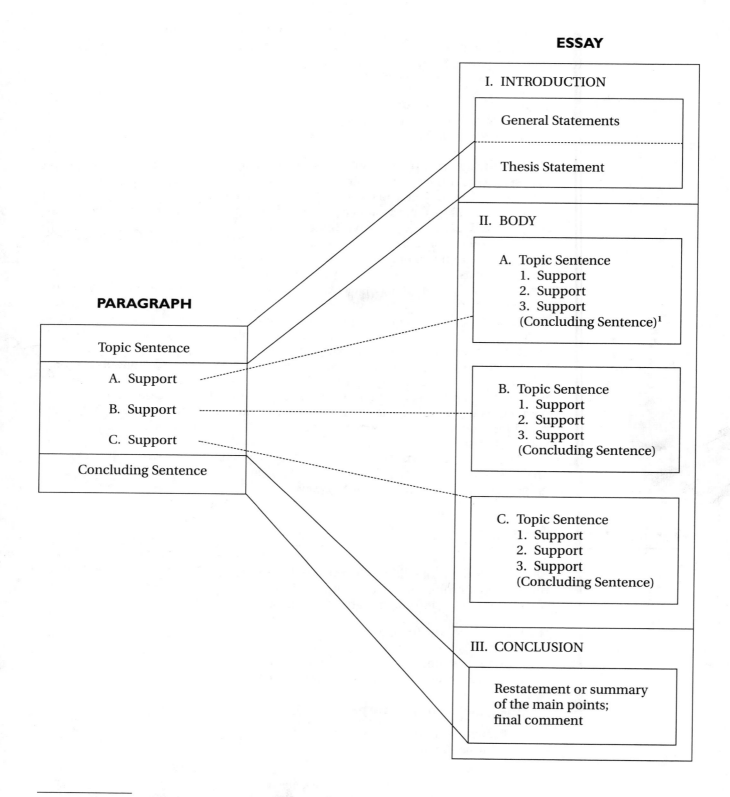

**PARAGRAPH**

Topic Sentence

   A. Support

   B. Support

   C. Support

Concluding Sentence

**ESSAY**

I. INTRODUCTION

   General Statements

   Thesis Statement

II. BODY

   A. Topic Sentence
     1. Support
     2. Support
     3. Support
     (Concluding Sentence)[1]

   B. Topic Sentence
     1. Support
     2. Support
     3. Support
     (Concluding Sentence)

   C. Topic Sentence
     1. Support
     2. Support
     3. Support
     (Concluding Sentence)

III. CONCLUSION

   Restatement or summary
   of the main points;
   final comment

---

[1] Concluding sentences for body paragraphs in an essay are not always necessary.

Notice the two parts of the introductory paragraph in the following model.

**MODEL**

*Introductory Paragraph*

*General statements*


*Thesis statement*

> Any person who has lived in the twentieth century has seen a lot of changes take place in almost all areas of human existence. Some people are excited by the challenges that these changes offer; others want to return to the simpler life-style of the past. The twentieth century has certain advantages such as a higher standard of living for many, but it also has some disadvantages such as a polluted environment, the depersonalization of human relationships, and the weakening of spiritual values.

### General statements

- Introduce the topic of the essay
- Give background information on the topic

The first sentence in an introductory paragraph should be a very general comment about the subject. Its purpose is to attract the reader's attention and to give background information on the topic. Each subsequent sentence should become more specific than the previous one and finally lead into the thesis statement.

### The thesis statement

- States the main topic
- Often lists the subdivisions of the topic or subtopics
- May indicate the method of organization of the entire paper
- Is usually the last sentence in the introductory paragraph

The thesis statement is the most important sentence in the introduction. It states the specific topic and often lists the major subtopics that will be discussed in the body of the essay. Furthermore, it may indicate the method of organization such as chronological order or order of importance.

Here are three examples of thesis statements with no subtopics mentioned:

> Being the oldest son has more disadvantages than advantages.
> Young people in my culture have less freedom than young people in the United States.
> The large movement of people from rural to urban areas has major effects on cities.

In the following thesis statement, the subtopics are named:

> The large movement of people from rural to urban areas has major effects on a city's ability to provide housing, employment, and adequate sanitation services.

When listing two or more subtopics in a thesis statement, a colon (:) is often useful:

> Prejudice arises from three basic causes: childhood conditioning, ignorance, and fear.

**CROSS-REFERENCE**

See Colons, page 251, and Correlative Conjunctions, page 168.

Correlative conjunctions *(both . . . and, not only . . . but also, neither . . . nor, either . . . or)* are also useful in thesis statements listing two subtopics:

> Young people in my culture have less freedom than young people in the United States **not only** in their choice of life-style **but also** in their choice of careers.

> Puppies, like children, need **both** love **and** discipline to become responsible citizens.

To sum up, an introductory paragraph is like a funnel: very wide at the top, increasingly narrow in the middle, and very small at the neck or bottom.

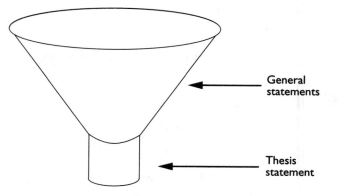

General statements

Thesis statement

**PRACTICE 1**

*Recognizing the Parts of an Introduction*

**STEP 1**    Read the following introductory paragraphs, each of which is in scrambled order.

**STEP 2**    Rewrite each paragraph, beginning with the most general statement first. Then add each sentence in the correct order until the introduction becomes more specific. Write the thesis statement last.

### Paragraph 1

(1) If done properly, a handshake gives the impression of strength and honesty, and if done improperly, it conveys weakness and dishonesty. (2) In some cultures, people bow, and in others, they shake hands. (3) In English-speaking countries, shaking hands is the custom. (4) A proper handshake has four ingredients: pressure, pumps,[1] eye contact, and verbal message. (5) The way people greet each other when they meet for the first time varies from culture to culture. (6) How one shakes hands sends an important message about one's character.

### Paragraph 2

(1) However, in others, the nuclear family is the norm, with only the parents and young children sharing the same house. (2) People in different cultures all over the world have different systems for family life. (3) In most cultures, people live in extended families, in which several generations share the same house. (4) If this new system becomes widespread, it could have enormous effects on American society. (5) On the positive side, living together might reduce the divorce rate in the United States; on the negative side, it might lead to the eventual disintegration[2] of the traditional family unit

---

[1] **pumps:** movements up and down
[2] **disintegration:** falling apart

altogether. (6) In the United States, some couples are experimenting with still another system of family life: living together without marriage.

**Paragraph 3**

(1) Although scientists have experimented with different methods of prediction, from observing animal behavior to measuring radio signals from quasars,[3] no method has proven successful. (2) Earthquakes are the most destructive natural disasters known to humans, in terms of the millions of deaths and billions of dollars in property loss that they cause. (3) Despite these heavy losses, scientists are still unable to predict earthquakes. (4) This paper will review the history of the science of earthquake prediction, then discuss each of the prediction methods in more detail, and finally present data indicating the success-failure ratios of each method.

**PRACTICE 2**

*Thesis Statements I*

**A.** Study these thesis statements from two different essays on the topic of the status of women in Xanadu, an imaginary country. Which method of organization (chronological order or comparison and contrast) does each one indicate?

   **1.** Beginning in World War II and continuing through the period of economic boom,[4] the status of women in Xanadu has changed remarkably.

   Method of organization: _____

   **2.** Although the status of women in Xanadu has improved remarkably in recent years, it is still very low when compared to the status of women in the countries of the industrial world.

   Method of organization: _____

**B.** In each of the following two thesis statements, both the method of organization and the major subdivisions of the topic are indicated. Each subdivision will itself become the topic of a separate paragraph in the body of the essay. How many paragraphs will the body of each essay probably contain? Underline the topics of each paragraph.

   **1.** The status of women in Xanadu has changed remarkably in recent years due to increased educational opportunities and changes in the country's laws.

   Probable number of paragraphs: _____

   **2.** The status of women in Xanadu has improved remarkably in recent years in the areas of economic independence, political rights, educational opportunities, and social status.

   Probable number of paragraphs: _____

**C.** Analyze the following thesis statements.

   **STEP 1**   Locate the main topic and the subtopics in each of the following thesis statements.
   **STEP 2**   Underline the subtopics.
   **STEP 3**   Draw a circle around the words or punctuation marks that are used to introduce the subtopics.

---

[3] **quasars:** starlike objects in space
[4] **boom:** rapid development

**Example**

Capital punishment should be abolished (not only) because it deprives another person
of life (but also) because it does not stop crime.

1. Women generally live longer than men for two main reasons: they tend to take better care of their health, and they have better resistance to stress.
2. Drug and alcohol abuse among teenagers can be traced to the following causes: lack of parental supervision, lax¹ enforcement of drug laws, and the social and psychological problems of teenagers themselves.
3. In choosing a major, a student has to consider various factors, such as personal interest, job opportunities, and the availability of training institutions.
4. An architect should be both an artist and an engineer.
5. The purpose of this report is to analyze the influence of the Spanish language on American English.

**PRACTICE 3**

*Thesis Statements II*

**A.  STEP 1**   Complete the following thesis statements by adding subtopics to them.
**STEP 2**   Circle your subtopics. If you use correlative conjunctions, be sure your structures are parallel.

1. A computer is necessary for college students for three reasons: _____

2. International students have a difficult time taking notes in class due to

3. Successful students have the following qualities: _____

4. A generation gap² exists in my home because of _____

5. To survive a major disaster such as an earthquake requires _____

6. Poverty creates negative consequences for society such as _____

7. My two sisters are as different as day and night not only in _____ but also in _____

8. Living in a city has certain advantages over living in the suburbs: _____

**B.**  Write a clear thesis statement for an essay on each of the following topics:

Leaving home        Choosing a career
Foreign travel       A personal bad habit

---
¹ **lax:** not strict
² **generation gap:** difference in attitudes and values between generations, especially between parents and children

# The Concluding Paragraph

The final paragraph in an essay is the conclusion, which tells the reader that you have completed an essay. First, you write a summary of the main points discussed in the body of the essay or rewrite the thesis statement in different words. Then you add your final comments on the subject—food for thought.[3] Take this opportunity to make a strong, effective message that the reader will remember.

The concluding paragraph consists of

**CROSS-REFERENCE**

See Conclusion Transition Signals in Appendix B, page 257.

**1.** A summary of the main points, or a restatement of your thesis in different words
**2.** Your final comment on the subject, based on the information you have provided

Be sure to introduce the concluding paragraph with a conclusion transition signal.

Turn back to page 103 and reread the model introductory paragraph. Then study the following concluding paragraph for the same essay. Is the concluding paragraph a summary of the main points of the essay, or is it a paraphrase of the thesis statement? Is there a final message for the reader?

**MODEL**

*Concluding Paragraph*

> In short, although the twentieth century has indeed given some of us a lot of advantages by making us richer, healthier, and freer to enjoy our lives, it has, in my opinion, not made us wiser. The twentieth century has also made our earth dirtier, our people less humane, and our spiritual lives poorer. We wish to continue to enjoy
> 5   the benefits of technological advancement because they free us to pursue our other interests and goals. However, we must make a concerted[4] effort to preserve our natural environment for future generations. Moreover, we should take the time now to make our lives more meaningful in our increasingly impersonal, mechanized world.

**PRACTICE 4**

*Concluding Paragraphs*

**A.** Write concluding paragraphs for the following introductions.

**STEP 1**    Summarize the main points or paraphrase the thesis statement. Be sure to begin with an expression signaling conclusion.

**STEP 2**    Add your own comments as a final message to the reader.

**Introductory Paragraph 1**

The busy schedules that most adults face from day to day have created a growing health problem in the modern world. Stress affects almost everyone, from the highly pressured executive to the busy homemaker or student. It can cause a variety of physical disorders, ranging from headaches to stomach
5   ulcers and even alcoholism. Stress, like a common cold, is a problem that can't be cured; however, it can be controlled. A person can learn to control stress by setting realistic goals, by enjoying a hobby and/or physical exercise, and by maintaining good, warm relationships with family and friends.

---

[3] **food for thought:** something to think about
[4] **concerted:** joint; united

**Introductory Paragraph 2**

New technology creates new opportunities for good and for ill.[1] Anyone with a computer, access to the Internet, and an E-mail address has probably received unsolicited, unwanted E-mail at least. There seems to be no way to avoid "spam," as junk E-mail is now called. Worse, the anonymity[2] of cyber-
5   space[3] has created opportunities for E-mailers to send rude, even abusive messages without having to take responsibility for their words. In my opinion, there is a need to develop some rules of etiquette[4] especially for this new means of communication.

**B.** Write concluding paragraphs for introductory paragraphs 1, 2, and 3 that you reorganized in Practice 1, pages 104–105.

# The Essay Body: Outlining

Because an essay is longer and more complex than a paragraph, it is even more important to organize your thoughts and to plan the body of your essay before you begin to write. The best way to do this is to make an outline.

The principles and techniques that you have already learned for paragraph outlining can be applied to essays. You may be required during the course of your academic writing career to produce a formal outline. The number/letter system for a formal outline is illustrated in the model outline that follows.

Notice that subtopics that form the body of the essay are indented to the right. As you move to the right, the ideas become more and more specific.

Study the following model outline for an essay on modern technology. In this outline, the introduction contains only the thesis statement, and the conclusion is abbreviated. The body of the essay, however, is developed in detail.

**MODEL**

*Essay Outline*

**Modern Technology**

**I. Introduction**

Thesis statement: The most recent significant discoveries to benefit humankind in modern times are in the fields of television and computer technology.

**II. Body**

A. A popular form of instant communication all over the world is television.

   1. Witnessing important events

     a. Destruction of Berlin Wall

     b. Launching of spacecraft

   2. Long-distance medicine by two-way video

     a. Patient and doctor conferences

     b. Special equipment to monitor[5] patient

---

[1] **ill:** bad
[2] **anonymity:** being unknown or unidentified
[3] **cyberspace:** the "world" of computers
[4] **etiquette:** polite behavior
[5] **monitor:** watch; observe

B. In the last few decades, computer technology has made tremendous progress in the world of communication to benefit humankind.
   1. Long-distance communication
   2. Information superhighway
   3. Global computer networks
      Electronic mail
C. Technology has contributed enormously to advances in computer medicine, which has benefited both doctors and patients.
   1. Rural[6] doctors and medical information
      a. Less access in past
      b. Immediate access today
   2. Rural doctors and urban medical centers
      Use of computer to prescribe treatment
   3. X-ray pictures of body parts
      a. Diagnoses of diseases and disorders
      b. Necessary treatments
   4. Computer-aided diagnosis
      Example of woman with headaches

**III. Conclusion**
   To conclude, scientific research and experiments have certainly opened the doors to faster, more easily accessible information worldwide on television and the computer. Many of these discoveries have changed our lives for the better and have made the peoples of the world closer.

**PRACTICE 5**

*Essay Outlining*

Prepare an outline of the essay "Culture, Logic, and Rhetoric" in Chapter 3, pages 32–33. Use the system of indenting, numbering, and lettering illustrated in the preceding model outline.

# Transition Signals between Paragraphs

Transition signals are important not only *within* paragraphs but also *between* paragraphs. If you write two or more paragraphs, you need to show the relationship between your first and second paragraph, between your second and third paragraph, and so on.

Think of transitions between paragraphs as the links of a chain. The links of a chain connect the chain; they hold it together. Similarly, a transition signal between two paragraphs links your ideas together.

Two paragraphs are linked by adding a transition signal to the topic sentence of the second paragraph. This transition signal may be a single word, a phrase, or a dependent clause that repeats or summarizes the main idea in the first paragraph.

Study the following model, and notice how the paragraphs are linked by a single word, a phrase, or a clause.

---

[6] **rural:** country or village

**MODEL**

*Paragraph Transitions*

*Introductory paragraph*

*Body paragraph 1*

*Body paragraph 2*

*Body paragraph 3*

*Body paragraph 4*

*Concluding paragraph*

### Aggressive Drivers

The number of vehicles on freeways and streets is increasing at an alarming rate. This influx[1] of motor vehicles is creating hazardous conditions. Moreover, drivers are in such a rush to get to their destinations that many become angry or impatient with other motorists who are too slow or who are in their way. Aggressive drivers react foolishly toward others in several dangerous ways.

TRANSITION WORDS

**One way** an angry driver may react is to cut off[2] another motorist. (+ supporting sentences) _____

_____

_____

TRANSITION WORDS

**Another way** is to tailgate[3] the other car. (+ supporting sentences)

_____

_____

_____

TRANSITION PHRASE

**In addition to cutting off and tailgating other cars,** aggressive drivers often use rude language or gestures to show their anger. (+ supporting sentences)

_____

_____

_____

TRANSITION CLAUSE

**Although law enforcement authorities warn motorists against aggressive driving,** the number who act out their angry impulses has not declined. (+ supporting sentences) _____

_____

_____

**To conclude,** aggressive drivers are endangering everyone because they create hazardous conditions by acting and driving foolishly. They should control their anger and learn to drive safely. After all, the lives they save could be their own.

**PRACTICE 6**

*Transitions between Paragraphs*

**A.** Connect the ideas in the following paragraphs by adding a transition word, phrase, or clause to the topic sentences of the third, fourth, and fifth paragraphs. Try to vary the transitional linking expressions that you use. You may rewrite the topic sentences if necessary.

---

[1] **influx:** increase
[2] **cut off:** drive in front of
[3] **tailgate:** drive closely behind

**Icebergs—A Potential Source of Water**

The supply of fresh water has not been a major problem for most countries in the world because a rainy season is part of their yearly climatic conditions. However, in countries where the rainfall is very sparse[4] scientists must constantly seek ways to increase supplies of this precious element.

5 Government planners in South America and the Middle East have been trying to devise new ways of increasing their nations' supplies of fresh water. The first method being considered is the use of desalinization plants, which would remove salt from sea water. Another method being considered is the towing of icebergs. According to this method, large icebergs from Antarctica would be

10 wrapped in cloth or plastic, tied to powerful tugboats by strong ropes, and towed to the countries needing fresh water. While this plan may have some potential, there are certain practical problems that must be solved.
<u>The first problem</u>_____ is the expense. According to estimates, it would cost between $50 and $100 million

15 to tow a single 100-million-ton iceberg from Antarctica to, for example, the coast of Saudi Arabia.

_____ is the possibility that the iceberg would melt en route.[5] No one knows if an iceberg could be effectively insulated during such a long journey. At the very least,

20 there is the possibility that it would break up into smaller pieces, which would create still other problems.

_____ there is the danger that a huge block of ice floating off an arid[6] coast could have unexpected environmental effects. The ice could drastically[7] change the

25 weather along the coast, and it would probably affect the fish population.

_____ the cost of providing fresh water from icebergs would be less than the cost of providing water by desalinization, according to most estimates. It would cost between 50¢ and 60¢ per cubic meter to get water from an iceberg, as opposed to the

30 80¢ per cubic meter it costs to get the same amount by desalinization.

In conclusion, before icebergs can become a source of fresh water in the future, problems involving cost, overall practicality, and most importantly, environmental impact[8] must be solved.

**B.** Add transition words, phrases, or clauses to the topic sentences of the paragraphs in this essay. Rewrite the topic sentences if necessary.

**Medicine and Ethics[9]**

Recent advances in the fields of medicine and biotechnology have brought about situations that could scarcely be imagined only a generation ago. Battery-operated plastic hearts can be implanted into[10] people. People can be kept alive indefinitely by machines. Exact duplicates of animals can be made.

---

[4] **sparse:** small in amount
[5] **en route:** during the journey
[6] **arid:** dry
[7] **drastically:** in an extreme way

[8] **impact:** effect
[9] **ethics:** the study of right and wrong
[10] **implanted into:** put in

5    While such scientific achievements may ultimately benefit humankind, they
     have also created complex legal and ethical issues.
     _____ involves
     doctors' ability to intervene in human reproduction. A well-known example is
     the case of Baby M. A man paid a woman to bear a child for him and his
10   wife, who could not have children. They signed a contract, but after the baby
     was born, the woman wanted to keep the baby. The father said the baby was
     his, but the woman said it was hers. It took the courts many months to
     decide who was right.

     _____ ,
15   another ethical dilemma[1] has arisen because doctors are now able to keep
     people who are in comas[2] alive for years by attaching their bodies to
     machines. This gives great power and great responsibility to the people who
     control the machines. How does a person decide whether another person
     whose heart cannot beat on its own and whose lungs are pumped by a
20   machine is still alive or not? As a result of this power, society has had to
     develop a new definition of death.

     _____ is the abil-
     ity to transplant[3] organs from one person into another. Doctors are now able
     to transplant hearts, lungs, livers, and kidneys from one human to another.
25   Should doctors also be allowed to transplant organs from animals to humans?
     Such an operation was actually performed in 1987, when doctors transplant-
     ed a baboon's heart into a dying human baby. The ethics of this experiment is
     still being debated.

     _____ , the ability
30   of biotechnologists to produce new forms of life in their laboratories is anoth-
     er area with profound[4] ethical consequences. Isn't a scientist who creates, for
     example, a new bacterium "playing God"? Furthermore, is it even safe to
     introduce new life forms into the earth's atmosphere? Is there a risk that
     such life forms could get out of control? Some people fear so.
35   _____ , scientists
     are now able to duplicate living organisms, cell by cell, through a process
     called cloning. Recently, the world was stunned by the successful cloning of an
     adult sheep. How long will it be before biotechnologists can clone people?
     Should they be allowed to? Who should control this?
40   _____ revolutions—
     political or technological—cause upheaval[5] and force change. Our new ability
     to create and prolong life is raising questions and forcing changes in our
     very concept of life, an issue involving not only legal but also profound moral
     considerations.

---

[1] **dilemma:** difficult problem
[2] **comas:** states of unconsciousness (being unable to see, hear, or speak)
[3] **transplant:** take out of one person and put into another
[4] **profound:** important; serious
[5] **upheaval:** social disturbance

# The Writing Process

**Writing and Revising an Essay**

In Chapter 1, on pages 3–15, you were introduced to the steps of planning, writing, and revising drafts of a single paragraph. You went through each of these steps as you studied the model paragraph "Culture Shock." As part of her planning process, the writer of the paragraph first brainstormed for ideas. Next, she organized the ideas into an outline. Then she began the writing and editing process. She wrote a first rough draft, edited it for organization and content, and then wrote a second draft. She proofread the second draft to correct sentence structure, grammar, mechanics, and vocabulary. At last, she wrote the final copy.

The process of writing an essay is exactly the same as writing a single-paragraph composition; that is, you brainstorm for ideas, make an outline, and write several drafts until you have produced a final copy that you can be proud of.

The following models show how one student worked through the process of writing and revising drafts of his essay on modern technology. He has already completed the first two steps, brainstorming and planning, and he has already developed the essay outline on pages 108–109. He is now ready to write a first rough draft and then to edit it for organization and content. Notice that he doesn't begin with the introductory paragraph. He begins, rather, with the body paragraphs. Many writers find it easier to get started if they begin with the body.

**MODEL**

*The First Rough Draft*

---

### Modern Technology

~~A~~ *The most* popular form of instant communication is television. It has a big impact on viewers because they can instantly see important events that are happening all over *(add "for example")* the world. In 1992 viewers worldwide were spectators to the amazing destruction of the Berlin Wall. It had separated East and West Berliners since August 1961. ~~Some people said that they felt like they were right there as the wall crumbled.~~ *(delete)* They were also able to watch the joyous celebrations that erupted[6] all citizens of Berlin were reunited. Another interesting event *that* ~~the~~ world is able to watch is the *(on* television *)* launching of space shuttles. For instance, on March 4, 1994 the shuttle Columbia, was sent on a research mission. It successfully soared[7] from the launch pad and went into orbit from the Kennedy Space Center in Cape Canaveral, Florida. When the flight of Columbia finished on March 18, 1994, aerial television *(delete)* showed its successful landing. ~~It was the result of great teamwork.~~ *(new ¶)* Not only does television technology allows us to be eyewitnesses to worldwide events. It has played a big role in long-distance medicine around the world. For instance, by using *(add more details)* special equipment, doctors can monitor[8] a patients heart and lungs or examine his throat. They can diagnose the problem and recommended for treatment, because of *(write more clearly)* long-distance television technology. These are only two examples of modern medical miracles that telemedicine has created.

---

[6] **erupted:** started up    [7] **soar:** fly; go upward    [8] **monitor:** listen to

*(handwritten note: move prep. phrase)* ^Computer technology has also made tremendous progress in the world of communication to benefit the mankind (in the last few decades.) The computer has the ability to communicate across long distances. In addition, an information supahighway has been created for the computer huge amounts of data can be transmitted around the world at high speed. Computer technology also makes *it*^ possible for computer networks to link academic, research, government and business organisations globally. *(handwritten note: add example)* ^Using Electronik mail, or E-mail, allows scholars, researchers, and businesses, as well as families and friends to communicate quickly and easily by typing a document into one computer then it appears on another one perhaps across the country or in another nation in a short time. *(handwritten note: new ¶)* Furthermore, technology has contributed enormously to advance in computer medicine. It has benefits both doctors and patients. In the *(handwritten note: add more details)* past, doctors in rural hospitals did not have immediate access to the latest medical information. The computer can also convert x-ray data into picture images of a body part. *There*^Images can help the rural doctor because the specialist can help to diagnose diseases and disorders and prescribe the best treatment. A recent development is the computer's ability to pinpoint[1] an exact cause of a medical condition. For instance, a patient with chronic[2] headaches had not been treated successfully by several doctors. A new doctor had her fill out a lengthy questionnaire about her medical history. When the answers were fed into the computer, it produced list of 100 causes of headaches. The computer then highlighted exact cause of the patient's headaches, she is now being treated successfully.

To conclude, scientific research and experiments have certainly opened the doors to faster, more easily accessible information worldwide on television and the computer. Many of these discoveries have changed our lives for the better and have made the peoples of the world closer. *(handwritten note: add a final comment)*

### The Writer's Changes to the First Draft

After writing the first draft, the writer edits it for organization and content. To begin with, he designates television as "the most popular form of instant communication. . . ." He also deletes several unnecessary sentences and words. The writer divides the long paragraph about television into two paragraphs. In the first paragraph about computer technology, he adds an example. The writer adds more details to "long-distance medicine" in the television section and "the latest medical information" in the computer technology part of the essay. In the concluding paragraph, the writer makes a note to himself to add a final comment. Finally, he writes the introductory paragraph.

---

[1] **pinpoint:** find; locate
[2] **chronic:** continual; long-lasting

## Modern Technology

People living in modern times have benefited from many discoveries and inventions that have enriched the world. Dedicated scientists spend years and even a lifetime searching for new scientific knowledge and discovering new ways to improve our lives. The most recent significant discoveries to benefit humankind in
5  modern times are in the fields of television and computer technology.

The most popular form of instant communication is television. It has a ~~big~~ *tremendous* impact on viewers because they can instantly ~~see~~ *witness* important events that are happening all over the world. For example, in 1992, viewers worldwide were spectators to the ~~amazing~~ *stunning* destruction of the Berlin Wall, ~~It~~ *which* had separated East and
10  West Berliners since August, 1961. They were also able to watch the joyous *(add comma)* celebrations that erupted *when* all citizens of Berlin were reunited. Another ~~interesting~~ *historic* event that the world is able to watch is the launching of space shuttles on television. For instance, on March 4, 1994, the shuttle Columbia was sent on a research mission. It successfully soared from the launch pad and went into orbit
15  from the Kennedy Space Center in Cape Canaveral, Florida. When the flight of Columbia ~~finished~~ *ended* on March 18, 1994, aerial television showed its successful landing.

*Moreover,* Not only does television technology ~~allows~~ allow us to be eyewitnesses to worldwide events, ~~It~~ *but* has also played a ~~big~~ *significant* role in long-distance medicine around the world. Telemedicine allows patients and their doctors to conference with medical
20  staff at a distant facility via a two-way video. For instance, by using special equipment, doctors can monitor a patient's heart and lungs or examine *(add apostrophe)* his throat. They can diagnose the problem and make recommendations for treatment, all via long-distance television technology. These are only two examples of modern medical miracles that telemedicine has created.
25      In the last few decades, computer technology has also made tremendous progress in the world of communication to benefit humankind. The computer has the ~~ability~~ *capability* to communicate across long distances. Furthermore, an information ~~supahighway~~ *superhighway* has been created for the computer, *in which* huge amounts of data can be transmitted around the world at high speed. Computer technology also makes it
30  possible for computer networks to link academic, research, government and business organizations globally. For example, a primary means of communication using the computer is through the Internet. It enables scientists and scholars as well

as educators and students ~to~ connect with worldwide research institutions and
libraries. They can also access publications in their specific fields. Using Electronic ~Besides,~
35  mail, or E-mail, allows scholars, researchers, and businesses~,~ as well as families and
friends to communicate quickly and easily by typing a document into one computer
~which~ then ~it~ appears on another one perhaps across the country or in another nation in
a short time.

Furthermore, technology has contributed enormously to advance~s~ in computer
40  medicine, ~which~ ~it~ has benefit~ed~ both doctors and patients. ~Also,~ ~As~ in ~the~ past, doctors in rural
hospitals did not have immediate access to the latest medical information. However,
today they can contact specialists in urban medical centers even hundreds of miles
away through the computer to get the latest methods of treating their patients. The
computer can also convert x-ray data into picture images of a body part. The~se~
45  images can help the rural doctor because the specialist can help to diagnose
diseases and disorders and prescribe the best treatment. ~Another~ A recent development is
the computer's ability to pinpoint an exact cause of a medical condition~s~. For
instance, a patient with chronic headaches had not been treated successfully by
several doctors. A new doctor had her fill out a lengthy questionnaire about her
50  medical history. When the answers were fed into the computer, it produced ~a~ list of
100 causes of headaches. The computer then highlighted ~the~ exact cause of the
patient's headaches, ~and~ she is now being treated successfully.

To conclude, scientific research and experiments have certainly opened the
doors to faster, more easily accessible information worldwide on television and the
55  computer. Many of these discover~e~is have changed our lives for the better and have
made the world closer. It will be interesting to see what developments will occur in
the future, not only in television and computer technology but also in other fields.

**The Writer's Changes to the Second Draft**

Working with his second draft, the writer corrects punctuation, spelling, and other errors in mechanics as well as changing some vocabulary words. He also corrects the grammar and improves the sentence structure. If the writer is completely satisfied with the second draft, he is ready to make the final copy.

## Modern Technology

People living in modern times have benefited from many discoveries and inventions that have enriched the world. Dedicated scientists spend years and even a lifetime searching for new scientific knowledge and discovering new ways to improve our lives. The most recent significant discoveries to benefit humankind in
5    modern times are in the fields of television and computer technology.

The most popular form of instant communication is television. It has a tremendous impact on viewers because they can instantly witness important events that are happening all over the world. For example, in 1992, viewers worldwide were spectators to the stunning destruction of the Berlin Wall, which had
10    separated East and West Berliners since August 1961. They were also able to watch the joyous celebrations that erupted when all citizens of Berlin were reunited. Another historic event that the world is able to watch on television is the launching of space shuttles. For instance, on March 4, 1994, the shuttle Columbia was sent on a research mission. It successfully soared from the launch pad and
15    went into orbit from the Kennedy Space Center in Cape Canaveral, Florida. When the flight of Columbia ended on March 18, 1994, aerial television showed its successful landing.

Moreover, not only does television technology allow us to be eyewitnesses to worldwide events, but it has also played a significant role in long-distance medicine
20    around the world. Telemedicine allows patients and their doctors to confer with medical staff at a distant facility via a two-way video. For instance, by using special equipment, doctors can monitor a patient's heart and lungs or examine his throat. They can diagnose the problem and make recommendations for treatment, all via long-distance television technology. These are only two examples of modern
25    medical miracles that telemedicine has created.

In the last few decades, computer technology has also made tremendous progress in the world of communication to benefit humankind. The computer has the capability to communicate across long distances. Furthermore, an information superhighway has been created for the computer, in which huge amounts of data
30    can be transmitted around the world at high speed. Computer technology also makes it possible for computer networks to link academic, research, and government organizations globally. For example, a primary means of communication using the computer is through the Internet. It enables scientists and scholars as well as educators and students to connect with worldwide research institutions and
35    libraries. They can also access publications in their specific fields. Besides, using Electronic mail, or E-mail, allows scholars, researchers, and businesses as well as families and friends to communicate quickly and easily by typing a document into one computer, which then appears on another one perhaps across the country or to another nation in a short time.
40    Furthermore, technology has contributed enormously to advances in computer medicine, which has benefited both doctors and patients. In the past, doctors in rural hospitals did not have immediate access to the latest medical information.

However, today they can contact specialists in urban medical centers even hundreds of miles away through the computer to get the latest methods of treating their
45   patients. The computer can also convert x-ray data into picture images of a body part. These images can help the rural doctor because the specialist can help to diagnose diseases and disorders and prescribe the best treatment. Another recent development is the computer's ability to pinpoint an exact cause of a medical condition. For instance, a patient with chronic headaches had not been treated
50   successfully by several doctors. A new doctor had her fill out a lengthy questionnaire about her medical history. When the answers were fed into a computer, it produced a list of 100 causes of headaches. The computer then highlighted the exact cause of the patient's headaches, and she is now being treated successfully.

To conclude, scientific research and experiments have certainly opened the
55   doors to faster, more easily accessible information worldwide on television and the computer. Many of these discoveries have changed our lives for the better and have made the world closer. It will be interesting to see what developments will occur in the future, not only in television and computer technology but also in other fields.

## Writing Technique Questions

1. What are the two parts of the introductory paragraph?
2. Underline the thesis statement of the model essay.
3. How many body paragraphs are there? Underline each of the topic sentences.
4. Is each body paragraph unified? Do all the supporting sentences for each body paragraph clearly and adequately explain the main idea of that paragraph?
5. Circle the transition signals that introduce each of the body paragraphs.
6. Is the conclusion a summary of the main points of the essay or a restatement of the thesis statement?
7. Underline the writer's final comments.

As you can see, you must go through several stages of writing and rewriting if you want to produce a good piece of writing. The major part of the revision process includes not only checking the content and focus of the entire essay but also adding or deleting whole paragraphs, checking the development and ordering of ideas within each paragraph, adding transitions, examples, and other concrete supporting details. Then only after all of the major changes have been made should you check the more specific problems like sentence structure, spelling, and mechanics such as punctuation and capitalization. Just remember that each time you write, revise, and rewrite again, you have improved your paper.

# Review

These are the important points you should have learned from this chapter.

## Main Parts of an Essay

An essay has three main parts: an introduction, a body, and a conclusion.

1. The introductory paragraph attracts the reader's attention and informs the reader what your main topic of discussion will be. An introductory paragraph has two parts:
   a. Several general sentences that give background information on your subject and gradually lead your reader into your specific topic.
   b. A thesis statement that states the subdivisions (topics of each paragraph). It may also indicate your method of development.
2. The body of an essay discusses your subdivided topics, one by one. It contains as many paragraphs as necessary to explain the controlling ideas in the thesis statement.
3. The concluding paragraph reminds your reader of what you have said. Remember to use a "conclusion" transition signal. Your concluding paragraph has a summary of the main ideas or a restatement of the thesis in different words and your final comment on the topic.

## Transitions between Paragraphs

Remember to show the relationship *between* paragraphs by using appropriate linking words, phrases, or clauses.

## Outlining an Essay

Always make an outline of an essay before you begin to write. Follow the model in this chapter, pages 108–109.

## Writing and Revising the Essay

1. Write the first rough draft of your essay from the outline. Skip lines in order to have enough space to make changes.
2. Revise the first draft for content and organization, and write a second draft.
3. Proofread the second draft for grammar, sentence structure, and mechanics. Write as many drafts as necessary before the final copy.

## PEER EDITING CHECKLIST

|  | PEER EDITOR'S COMMENTS AND SUGGESTIONS |
|---|---|
| **ESSAY ORGANIZATION** | |
| 1. **Introduction:** Does the introductory paragraph have both general sentences and a clear thesis statement? | |
| 2. **Body:** Is the method of organization (chronological order, comparison/ contrast, etc.) appropriate for the topic? | |
| 3. **Conclusion:** Is there a concluding sentence that is either a paraphrase of the thesis or a summary of the main points? Is there a final comment (if one is appropriate)? | |
| **PARAGRAPH ORGANIZATION** | |
| 4. **Topic sentences:** Does each paragraph have a topic sentence? Does each topic sentence have a controlling idea? | |
| 5. **Supporting sentences:** Do the supporting sentences flow smoothly? Are there sufficient concrete details to support each point? Are transition signals used effectively both within and between paragraphs? Does each paragraph have unity? | |
| 6. **Concluding sentences:** Are concluding sentences used (if they are necessary)? | |
| **SENTENCE STRUCTURE** | |
| 7. Are there any unclear sentences? Can you suggest a way to improve them? | |
| **GRAMMAR AND MECHANICS** | |
| 8. Are there any errors in grammar and mechanics? | |

# CHAPTER

## 9 Patterns of Essay Organization

Arabic script from a Turkish Album of Calligraphy

## *Introduction*

Organizing an **essay** is essentially the same as organizing a paragraph; the only difference is that instead of working with single sentences, you are working with paragraphs. You can use the same patterns (or combination of patterns) for essays as you use for paragraphs. You simply decide what information belongs in each paragraph, and then in what order you should arrange the paragraphs.

You already know three patterns of organization in English: chronological order, logical division/order of importance, and comparison/contrast as ways of sequencing ideas. So far, however, you have studied these different orders only within a paragraph.

In this chapter, you will practice writing essays using these three kinds of organization, as well as a fourth one, cause and effect.

## *Chronological Order*

As you already know, chronological order is order by time. It is used in almost all academic fields. One of its primary uses is to explain processes such as how to plan a community meeting, how to perform a physics experiment, or how to play a game. Even when giving directions for someone to come to your house or when you write a recipe, you use chronological order: *First, preheat the oven to* 350°F. *Next, mix together.* . . . In addition to explaining processes, chronological order is also used to describe events over a period of time. Biography, autobiography, history, and narrative ("story") writing all use chronological order.

The model essay on pages 123–124 uses chronological order to explain two scientific processes involving nuclear energy. As you read the model, look for these two processes.

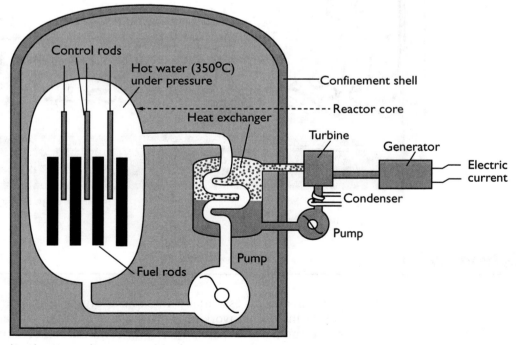

A nuclear power plant.

**MODEL**

*Chronological Order
Essay*

## Understanding Chernobyl

Clouds of radioactive steam shoot into the sky. Fires burn unstoppably, sending radioactive smoke and particles into the atmosphere. Men dressed in protective clothing work feverishly[1] to extinguish the fires and contain the contamination.[2] Hundreds of residents hastily grab their possessions and flee their homes.

5    Roadblocks are erected to keep strangers away. This was the scene at the Chernobyl nuclear power plant in the former U.S.S.R. in April 1986. The plant's nuclear reactor had exploded, spreading radioactive contamination over an area that stretched as far away as Norway and Sweden. This catastrophic[3] accident renewed fears about the safety of nuclear reactors around the world. Are such fears justified?[4] In order to

10   understand how the accident at Chernobyl happened, it is necessary to understand how a nuclear power plant is constructed and how one operates.

A nuclear power plant contains a nuclear reactor that uses controlled nuclear fission[5] to produce electricity. The reactor consists of fuel rods alternating with control rods inside a very large container called the reactor core. The fuel rods

15   contain radioactive fuel such as uranium-235, and the control rods contain neutron[6]-absorbing[7] substances such as boron and cadmium. By varying the depth of the control rods within the core, one can increase or decrease the absorption of neutrons, thereby speeding up or slowing down the fission process. If necessary, these rods can be dropped all the way into the core to stop the reaction completely. A

20   high-pressure water bath surrounds the rods. The water acts as a coolant by slowing down the neutrons. In some reactors, graphite[8] is added to the water because graphite also slows down neutrons. A confinement shell usually surrounds the parts containing radioactive material so that radioactivity cannot escape.

How do nuclear reactors produce electricity? First, a series of nuclear fissions

25   are produced by bombarding the nuclei[9] of uranium-235 with neutrons. When a neutron strikes a nucleus, the nucleus splits,[10] releasing energy. The released energy then heats the water surrounding the rods. After that, the hot water is pumped to a heat exchanger, where steam is produced. Finally, the steam passes to a turbine that drives a generator to produce electricity.

30   How did the accident at Chernobyl happen? It happened because on the day of the accident, the safety system on the reactor had been disabled[11] while operators performed an experimental test. During the test, the reactor cooled excessively and threatened to shut down. If this happened, the operators would not be able to restart the reactor for a long period of time. To avoid such a situation, they

35   removed most of the control rods, which was against all safety rules. Soon, the reactor began to overheat. When the reactor overheated, the fuel rods melted and spilled their radioactive contents into the superheated water, which then flashed[12]

---

[1] **feverishly:** very quickly
[2] **contamination:** pollution
[3] **catastrophic:** terrible; disastrous
[4] **justified:** appropriate; right
[5] **nuclear fission:** nuclear reaction resulting from splitting a nucleus
[6] **neutron:** electrically neutral particle inside an atom

[7] **absorbing:** taking inside itself, as a sponge absorbs water
[8] **graphite:** gray substance used in lead pencils
[9] **nuclei:** plural of *nucleus,* the central part of an atom
[10] **splits:** divides into two parts
[11] **disabled:** made unable to function
[12] **flashed:** instantly became

into steam. Next, the increased pressure from the steam blew the top off the reactor, and because there was no confinement shell around the reactor,
40  radioactive material blew into the sky. At the same time, hot steam reacted with the zirconium shells of the fuel rods and with the graphite in the coolant water to produce hydrogen gas, which then ignited.[1] The graphite burned for a long time, spreading even more radioactivity into the atmosphere.

   In the end, the cost of the Chernobyl accident was enormous. Thirty-one
45  people died, and several hundred were hospitalized. Thousands had to be evacuated and resettled. The soil around Chernobyl will remain contaminated for years. The lesson from Chernobyl is this: A well-designed nuclear power plant using normal fuel is not dangerous as long as proper safety procedures are followed. However, poor design and/or disregard for safety regulations can lead to catastrophe.

## Writing Technique Questions

**1.** What is the thesis statement? How does it indicate that at least part of this essay will use chronological order?
**2.** Which two paragraphs explain processes (how something works or how something happened)? What two processes are explained?
**3.** Which paragraph describes the design of nuclear power plants?

## Organization for Chronological Order

The organization of the model essay follows a typical plan for a chronological process type of essay. The first paragraph is, of course, the introduction. It captures the reader's interest and names the topic. The first paragraph of the body describes the tools, equipment, or ingredients needed for the process, and the remaining body paragraphs explain the steps in the process. The final paragraph concludes the essay by mentioning the process result and making a final comment. You could follow this same plan to write up a lab experiment for a science class or even to write cooking instructions for your favorite recipe.

## Transition Signals for Chronological Order

The transition signals used in chronological order essays are the same as those used in time order paragraphs. You might want to review them in Chapter 5, page 59. In addition, chronological order essays frequently contain **time clauses** (such as *after the liquid has evaporated* and *as soon as we entered the icy water*) to show the sequence of events. They also contain **time phrases** (such as *before the earthquake, while stirring the soup,* and *before adding the liquid,* etc.).

**PRACTICE 1**

*Transition Signals for Chronological Order*

Review the chart of transition signals on page 59. Then complete the chart on page 125 with expressions from the model essay "Understanding Chernobyl" showing order in time.

---

[1] **ignited:** began to burn

| TIME WORDS | TIME CLAUSES | TIME PHRASES |
|---|---|---|
| first | after that happens | during the test |
|  |  |  |

## *Dramatic Introductory Paragraphs*

Perhaps you noticed that the essay about Chernobyl did not have a "funnel" intro-ductory paragraph. Instead, it used a dramatic description of the scene around Chernobyl minutes and days after the accident. This type of introduction is called a **dramatic introductory paragraph.** The thesis statement is in its normal position at the end of the paragraph, and the words "how the accident at Chernobyl happened" and "how one operates" both point to chronological development.

This type of introduction is effective because it captures the reader's interest and attention. If you wish, you could narrate a dramatic story instead of describing a dra-matic scene. For example, in an essay about a social problem such as youth gangs, your introduction could be a dramatic introductory paragraph telling the story of a young person's violent encounter with a gang.

## *Thesis Statements for Chronological Order*

A thesis statement for a chronological order essay should do two things: (1) it should name the topic, and (2) it should indicate that the essay will be organized in chrono-logical order. Words such as *the process of, the procedure of, the development of, the evolution of, five stages, two steps, several phases,* etc. indicate that chronological order will be used. Here are some examples:

The field of genetic engineering has developed rapidly in the past ten years.

My passion for physics evolved slowly during my high school years.

The process of taking inventory in a small retail business has become much easier since the development of bar coding technology.

The process of heating water by using the sun's rays is a simple process.

Sometimes, the number of steps in a process or procedure is mentioned:

> The process of heating water by using the sun's rays involves three main steps.

The thesis statement may even name the steps:

> The main steps in the process of heating water by using the sun's rays are (1) trapping the sun's energy, (2) heating and storing the hot water, and (3) distributing the hot water to its points of use.

**PRACTICE 2**

*Dramatic Introductory Paragraphs*

**STEP 1**   With a partner or small group, orally brainstorm dramatic introductions to essays on all six of the topics below.

**STEP 2**   For the three chronological order topics *only*, write out dramatic introductory paragraphs, including thesis statements.

| General Topics | Chronological Order Topics |
|---|---|
| Automobile safety | How to travel safely |
| Corruption in politics | Saving a life: How to administer CPR[1] |
| Intercultural marriages | Earthquake survival |

**WRITING PRACTICE**

Choose one of the three chronological order topics given above and write an essay using chronological order as a method of organization. Follow these steps to success:

1. Brainstorm by freewriting, listing, or clustering all the steps in the process that you are going to explain.
2. Draw a simple diagram or flowchart that shows the steps.
3. Develop an outline from your flowchart.
4. Write your first draft.
   - Write a funnel or a dramatic introduction paragraph, as you prefer.
   - Be sure to use chronological transition signals.
5. Revise your first draft as you have learned. Ask a classmate to review your essay using the Peer Editing Checklist on page 120.

**Alternate Topic Suggestions**

How to make _____
   (batik, a ceramic sculpture, or any other interesting object that involves a several-step process)

How a special holiday is celebrated in your culture

How to overcome a fear

How to repair a broken heart

How to learn a foreign language

How to cook a special dish from your culture

How to get a driver's license

---

[1] **CPR:** cardiopulmonary resuscitation

# Logical Division of Ideas

Logical division of ideas is a form of essay organization that is used to group related items according to some quality they have in common. Logical division can be useful in planning an academic paper because it will help you divide a broad subject into several categories or groups and in that way focus the topics for discussion. Then each subtopic can be discussed in order.

For instance, as an engineer, you might write a paper in which you classify the various options available to students in the field of engineering. You might divide the main field into the following subclasses: civil engineering, electrical engineering, mechanical engineering, space engineering, and electronic engineering. By dividing the field into subclasses, you can discuss each one separately, which simplifies the task of explaining such a broad subject.

Review logical division organization in Chapter 5, pages 61–65. Then study the model essay, which discusses some of the influences of Native Americans[2] on modern American culture. Notice that the same techniques used for logical division paragraphs can also be used for whole essays.

**MODEL**

*Logical Division Essay*

### Native American Influences on Modern American Culture

When the first Europeans came to the North American continent, they encountered[3] the completely new cultures of the Native American peoples of North America. Native Americans, who had highly developed cultures in many respects, must have been as curious about the strange European manners and customs as the
5   Europeans were curious about them. As always happens when two or more cultures come into contact, there was a cultural exchange. Native Americans adopted[4] some of the Europeans' ways, and the Europeans adopted some of their ways. As a result, Native Americans have made many valuable contributions to American culture, particularly in the areas of language, art, food, and government.
10  First of all, Native Americans left a permanent imprint[5] on the English language. The early English-speaking settlers borrowed from several different Native American languages words for the new places and new objects that they had found in this new land. All across the country, one can find cities, towns, rivers, and states with Native American names. For example, the states of Delaware, Iowa, Illinois, and
15  Alabama are named after Native American tribes,[6] as are the cities of Chicago, Miami, and Spokane. In addition to place names, English adopted from various Native American languages the words for animals and plants that were to be found only in the Americas and no place else. *Chipmunk, moose, raccoon, skunk, tobacco,* and *potato* are just a few examples.
20  Although the vocabulary of English is the area that shows the most Native American influence, it is not the only area of American culture that was shaped by contact with Native Americans. Art is another area of important Native American contributions. Wool rugs woven by women of the Navajo tribe in Arizona and New

---

[2] **Native Americans:** American Indians
[3] **encountered:** met unexpectedly
[4] **adopted:** took and used as their own

[5] **imprint:** mark left on
[6] **tribes:** groups of native people

25    Mexico are highly valued works of art in the United States. Also, Native American jewelry made from silver and turquoise is very popular and very expensive. Especially in the western and southwestern regions of the United States, native crafts such as pottery, handcrafted leather products, and beadwork can be found in many homes. Indeed, native art and handicrafts are a treasured part of American culture.

30    In addition to language and art, agriculture is another area in which Native Americans had a great and lasting influence on the peoples who arrived here from Europe, Africa, and Asia. Being skilled farmers, the Native Americans of North America taught the newcomers many things about farming techniques and crops. Every American schoolchild has heard the story of how Native Americans taught the first settlers to place a dead fish in a planting hole to provide fertilizer for the

35    growing plant. Furthermore, they taught the settlers irrigation methods and crop rotation. In addition, many of the foods Americans eat today were introduced to the Europeans by Native Americans. For example, potatoes, corn, chocolate, and peanuts were unknown in Europe. Now they are staples in the American diet.

Finally, it may surprise some people to learn that Americans are also indebted[1]

40    to the native people for our form of government. The Iroquois, who were an extremely large tribe with many branches called "nations," had developed a highly sophisticated[2] system of government to settle disputes that arose between the various branches. Five of the nations had joined together in a confederation called "The League of the Iroquois." Under the League, each nation was autonomous[3] in

45    running its own internal affairs, but the nations acted as a unit when dealing with outsiders. The League kept the Iroquois from fighting among themselves and was also valuable in diplomatic relations with other tribes. When the thirteen American colonies were considering what kind of government to establish after they won their independence from Britain, someone suggested that they use a system similar

50    to that of the League of the Iroquois. Under this system, each colony or future state would be autonomous in managing its own affairs but would join forces with the other states to deal with matters that concerned them all. This is exactly what happened. As a result, the present form of government of the United States can be traced directly back to a Native American model.

55    In conclusion, we can easily see from these few examples the extent of Native American influence on our language, our art forms, our eating habits, and our government. Modern Americans are deeply indebted to Native Americans for their contributions to United States culture.

## Writing Technique Questions

**1.** Is the introductory paragraph of the model essay a "funnel" or a "dramatic" introduction? What is the thesis statement? How many subtopics does it list?

**2.** How many paragraphs are in the body of the model essay? Underline the topic sentence of each body paragraph once. (**Note:** The topic sentence is not necessarily the first sentence in every paragraph.)

**3.** Locate the main sentence in the concluding paragraph and underline it twice. Is it a paraphrase of the thesis statement?

---

[1] **indebted:** owing gratitude    [3] **autonomous:** independent, self-governing
[2] **sophisticated:** highly developed

***Organization for Logical Division of Ideas***

A logical division essay is organized just like a logical division paragraph, which you studied in Chapter 5. In an essay, a large topic is divided up into smaller subtopics, each of which can be discussed in a separate paragraph. The introductory paragraph introduces the main topic, and the thesis statement may give the number of subtopics, or it may name them. Each body paragraph discusses one subtopic. The concluding paragraph brings the essay to a close by reminding the reader of the essay's main points.

### *Transition Signals and Thesis Statements*

Transition signals are the same for logical division paragraphs and logical division essays, and thesis statements for logical division essays are similar to topic sentences for logical division paragraphs. A thesis statement may name the subtopics or simply indicate that there are a certain number of subtopics, as in these examples:

Subtopics not named:

A college education is a necessity in today's competitive world for two main reasons.

Subtopics named:

A college education is a necessity in today's competitive world not only because of the knowledge you gain but also because of the social contacts you make.

**PRACTICE 3**

*Logical Division of Ideas Organization*

**A. Outlining**
Working alone or in a group, make an outline of the model essay about Native American influences on American culture. Make your outline as detailed as possible. Follow the model outline on pages 108–109. If you work in a group, assign one paragraph to each student to outline. When you are finished, combine all of the group's outlines on one paper.

**B. Transition Signals**
Circle the transition signals in the model essay. Count the number of signals that you circled and compare your total with your classmates' totals.

**C. Transitions between Paragraphs**
Copy the words, phrases, and clauses that serve as links between the six paragraphs.

Between 1 and 2:  _____
Between 2 and 3:  _____
Between 3 and 4:  _____
Between 4 and 5:  _____
Between 5 and 6:  _____

**WRITING PRACTICE**

Choose either topic A or B, and write an essay using logical division of ideas as a means of organization.

A. Explain the influence of one culture on another. Choose two cultures with which you are familiar. For example, if you are from Mexico, you could write about Spain's influence on Mexican culture, or about Mexico's influence on the United States (or vice versa), or about the influence of Mayan or Aztec culture on Mexico.

B. Discuss the customs and traditions of your culture that you wish to preserve as a part of your life-style today.

Follow these steps to success:

1. Brainstorm by freewriting, clustering, or listing all of the ideas that come into your mind. Think about different areas of culture such as language, religion, food, clothing, music, dating and marriage customs, family structure (husband-wife roles, parent-child relationships, etc.), business methods, shopping habits, educational systems, and so on.
2. Choose two to four areas that you wish to write about. These will be your subtopics. Brainstorm for specific supporting details for each subtopic.
3. Make an outline. Use the outline on pages 108–109 as a model.
4. Write your first rough draft from your outline. Be sure to use transition signals both *within* and *between* paragraphs.
5. Revise your rough draft as you have learned to do with paragraphs. Ask a classmate to edit your work using the Peer Editing Checklist on page 120.

### *Alternate Topic Suggestions*

Kinds of students, teachers, shoppers, automobile drivers, etc.

The various submajors in your major field of study (engineering, business, or biology, for example)

The various career options that are available to graduates in your field of study

Breeds of dogs (or cats)

Clothing styles among your peers

# *Cause and Effect Order*

Another common method of organizing an essay is by cause and effect. In a cause and effect essay, you discuss the reasons or causes for something, and then you discuss the results.

The following are examples of typical cause and effect essay examination questions.

Sociology: Discuss the causes of the rising divorce rate in modern society.
Environmental Studies: Discuss the causes of global warming.
Business and Economics: Discuss NAFTA[1] and its effects on the U.S. economy.
History: Discuss the reasons behind the fall of communism in Eastern Europe.
Psychology: Explain the high suicide rate in Scandinavia.

Indeed, cause and effect (which can also be called reason and result) is one of the most-used forms of organization in academic writing. In this section, you will learn about two different ways to write about causes and effects.

## *Organization for Cause and Effect Order*

There are basically two main ways to organize a cause and effect essay: "block" organization and "chain" organization. In *block organization,* you first discuss all of the causes as a block (in one, two, three, or more paragraphs, depending on the number of causes). Then you discuss all of the effects together as a block. In *chain organization,* you discuss a first cause and its effect, a second cause and its effect, and a third cause and its effect. Usually, each new cause is the result of the preceding effect. Discussion of each new cause and its effect begins with a new paragraph. All the paragraphs are linked in a "chain."

---

[1] **NAFTA:** North American Free Trade Agreement, a trade agreement among Canada, Mexico, and the United States.

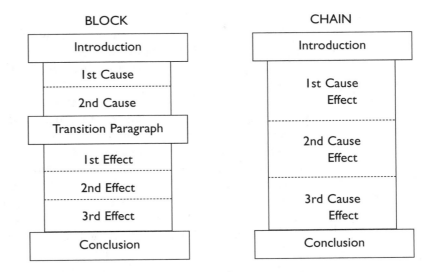

The type of cause and effect organization you choose will depend on your topic. Some topics are more easily organized one way, and some the other way. A chain pattern is usually easier if the causes and effects are very closely interrelated. The chain pattern also works better with smaller topics. With larger topics, and when there is no *direct* cause and effect relationship, the block style is usually easier. Some topics require a combination of block and chain organization, as in the model essay below..

**Block Organization with Transition Paragraphs**

In block organization, there is often a short paragraph that separates the "causes" part from the "effects" part. This is called a transition paragraph. The purpose of a transition paragraphs is to conclude the first part of the essay and introduce the second part. It is not always necessary to write a transition paragraph, but it is helpful when your topic is long and complex. If the transition paragraph is only one sentence, as in the following model, that sentence could be the end of one paragraph or the beginning of the next paragraph.

As you read the model essay, pay attention to its organization. Notice that the essay as a whole is block style, but that individual paragraphs use chain organization.

**MODEL**

*Cause and Effect Essay (Block Organization)*

### Women's Liberation

Since the middle of this century, women around the world have been seeking greater independence and recognition. No longer content with their traditional roles as housewives and mothers, women have joined together to create the women's liberation movement. While the forces behind this international
5   movement vary from culture to culture and from individual to individual, the basic causes in the United States can be traced to three events: the development of effective birth-control methods, the invention of labor-saving devices for the home, and the advent[2] of World War II.

---

[2] **advent:** arrival

The first cause of the liberation of women was the development of effective
10  birth-control methods, freeing women from the endless cycle of childbearing and
rearing. As a result of having a choice as to *when* and *if* to bear children, women
acquired the freedom and the time to pursue interests outside of the home.
Because of the development of birth control, women could delay having children or
avoid having them altogether; consequently, women had the opportunity to acquire
15  an education and/or pursue a career.

Another event was the development of mechanized labor-saving devices
for the home, resulting in more leisure time and freedom for women. For
example, fifty years ago, a housewife spent an average of twelve to fourteen
hours per day doing housework. Due to the invention of machines such as
20  vacuum cleaners, washing machines, and dishwashers, a housewife can now take
care of her daily housework in about five hours.

The final event that, at least in the United States, gave impetus[1] to the
liberation of women was World War II. During the war, most men were serving in
the military. Consequently, women had to fill the vacancies in the labor force.
25  Women by the thousands went to work in factories and took over businesses for
their absent husbands. This was a great change for the majority of American
women, for they discovered that they could weld[2] airplane parts and manage
businesses as well change diapers and bake bread.

These three events planted the seeds of great change in society, and the effects
30  of this change are being felt at all levels: in the family, in business, and in government.

One of the biggest effects of the greater independence of women today is
being felt in the home. The traditional husband-wife relationship is undergoing a
radical transformation.[3] Because so many women are working, men are learning to
share the household tasks of cooking, cleaning, and caring for children. In most
35  American families, the husband still earns most of the money, and the wife still does
most of the housework. Nevertheless, the child-rearing system in the United States
is changing as a result of women's increasing participation in the away-from-home
work force. The number of mothers going out to jobs tripled from 1950 to 1987 to
more than twelve million; as a result, millions of children are being reared by paid
40  childcare workers in infant, preschool, and after-school daycare programs instead of
by their mothers at home.

The effects of women's liberation are being felt not only in the home but also
at the job site. In 1986, almost 48 million women age 16 and over were employed.
This number represents 44 percent of the total paid work force in the United
45  States. Most women still work in low-paying, low-status occupations as secretaries,
salesclerks, elementary school teachers, and healthcare workers. However, in the
last two decades, more women have entered the new high-technology industries;
by 1986, for example, 34 percent of all computer programmers were women.
There has also been a slow but steady increase in the number of women who have
50  risen to executive and managerial positions in business and who have entered the
traditionally male professions of architecture, engineering, medicine, and law.

---

[1] **impetus:** stimulation
[2] **weld:** join metal parts using heat

[3] **radical transformation:** extreme change

Politics and government are still other areas that are feeling the effects of the women's movement. Although the United States doesn't appear ready to accept a woman president as have some other nations around the world, American women
55  are being elected and appointed to high public office in increasing numbers. The United States has women cabinet[4] members, women senators and congresswomen, women governors[5] and women mayors. In 1984, Geraldine Ferraro was the Democratic party's nominee[6] for the office of vice president, the first woman so nominated, but she was not elected.
60      In conclusion, women in the United States are acquiring greater independence, which is causing sweeping changes at home, at work, and in government. Although American women do not yet have the equality with men that women in some Western countries like Sweden enjoy, they are making steady gains. The full impact of this process on society remains to be seen.

## Writing Technique Questions

**1.** Which paragraphs discuss the causes of the liberation of women in the United States? Which paragraphs discuss the effects?
**2.** What is the function of the paragraph that begins on line 29?
**3.** Does the thesis statement list both causes and effects, or just causes?
**4.** Does the conclusion review both causes and effects, or just effects?

**PRACTICE 4**

*Block Organization for Cause and Effect Order*

Taking causes and effects from the model essay on women's liberation, fill in the boxes below to show the "block" organizational pattern of the essay.

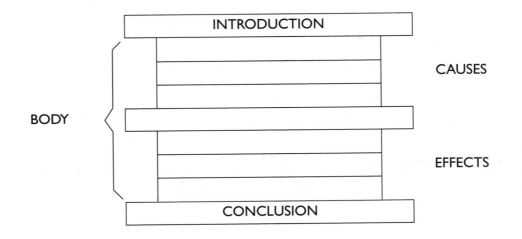

<sup></sup>—

[4] **cabinet:** group of people who are heads of departments of the government and who advise the president or prime minister
[5] **governor:** highest official in a state
[6] **nominee:** person chosen to stand for election

## *Chain Organization*

The other organizational pattern that you might use to write about causes and effects is "chain" organization, described on pages 130–131. Using special structure words, causes and effects are linked to each other in a logical chain. One event causes a second event, which in turn causes a third event, which in turn causes a fourth event, and so on. The following short essay describes a simple chain reaction.

described on pages 130–131.

**MODEL**

*Cause and Effect Essay
(Chain Organization)*

---

### SAD

When winter arrives, some people get sad, even suicidal.

Doctors have recently started to study the causes of a medical disorder that they have appropriately named SAD, or **s**easonal **a**ffective **d**isorder. People who suffer from SAD become very depressed during the winter months. Their
5   depression appears to be the result of a decrease in the amount of sunlight they are exposed to. Doctors theorize that decreased sunlight affects the production of melatonin, a hormone manufactured in the brain, and serotonin, a chemical that helps transmit nerve impulses. Depression may result from the ensuing[1] imbalance of these two substances in the body. Also, doctors believe that a decrease in the
10   amount of sunlight the body receives may cause a disturbance in the body's natural clock[2] which could, in turn, result in symptoms such as lethargy,[3] oversleeping, weight gain, anxiety, and irritability—all signs of depression.

Since absence of light seems to be the cause of this disorder, a daily dose of light appears to be the cure. Doctors advise patients to sit in front of a special light
15   box that simulates[4] natural light for a few hours every day.

In conclusion, the depressive effect of low sunlight levels may help explain the high suicide rate in the Scandinavian countries, and more importantly, it may suggest a remedy:[5] When the days grow short, turn on the lights.

---

## *Writing Technique Questions*

**1.** What causes the days to grow shorter?
**2.** What is the effect of shorter days?
**3.** What does this cause?
**4.** What other change results from a decrease in the amount of light?
**5.** What is the final result?

**PRACTICE 5**

*Chain Organization for
Cause and Effect Order*

Fill in the boxes to complete the flowchart, which illustrates the cause and effect chain described in the model essay "SAD."

---

[1] **ensuing:** following immediately
[2] **natural clock:** normal cycle of sleep and wakefulness
[3] **lethargy:** inactivity; tiredness
[4] **simulates:** gives the effect of; imitates
[5] **remedy:** cure

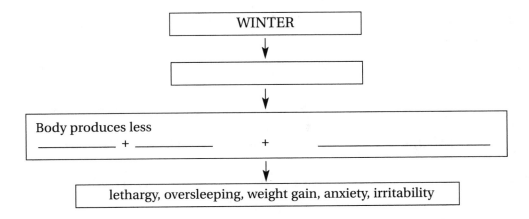

## Cause and Effect Structure Words

Just as there are transition signals that show time order and logical division, there are words and phrases that show cause and effect relationships. They are called cause and effect structure words. You are probably familiar with many of them.

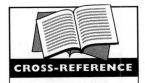

**CROSS-REFERENCE**

Reason clauses, result clauses, and purpose clauses help show cause and effect relationships. See pages 199–202.

| CAUSE STRUCTURE WORDS | EFFECT STRUCTURE WORDS |
|---|---|
| the first cause . . .<br>the next reason . . .<br>because of . . . | the first effect . . .<br>as a result, . . .<br>therefore, . . . |

It is important to distinguish between causes and effects. Remember that a cause is the *reason* for something; it happens earlier. An effect is the *result* of something; it happens later.

CAUSE    People clear land for agriculture by cutting down trees.

↓

EFFECT    The topsoil[6] washes away.

Remember also that in a chain of events, an effect becomes the cause of another effect, and that effect becomes the cause of still another effect, and so on. The example above can be expanded into the cause and effect chain that follows.

---

[6] **topsoil:** top layer of earth that is most nutrient-rich for agriculture

| | | |
|---|---|---|
| CAUSE | ↓ | People move into new areas and clear land for agriculture by cutting down trees. |
| EFFECT | ↓ | The tree roots no longer hold the soil in place. |
| CAUSE | ↓ | The tree roots don't hold the soil in place. |
| EFFECT | ↓ | The topsoil washes away during heavy rains. |
| CAUSE | ↓ | The topsoil washes away during heavy rains. |
| EFFECT | ↓ | There is no good soil to grow crops in. |
| CAUSE | ↓ | There is no good soil to grow crops in. |
| EFFECT | | People move to new areas and clear land by cutting down trees. |

Many of the most common cause and effect structure words are listed in the following chart. Learn to use different ones so that you don't always use *because* in your sentences.

## CAUSE STRUCTURE WORDS

| SENTENCE CONNECTORS | CLAUSE CONNECTORS | | OTHERS |
|---|---|---|---|
| | COORDINATORS | SUBORDINATORS | |
| | 1. for | 2. because<br>since<br>as | 3. to result from<br>to be the result of<br>4. due to<br>because of<br>5. the effect of<br>the consequence of<br>6. as a result of<br>as a consequence of |

**Note:** The sentence numbers correspond to the chart numbers.

### Examples

1. In the 1980s and 1990s, the U.S. government passed new immigration laws, **for** many people were concerned about illegal immigration.
2. **Because/Since/As** most illegal immigrants enter the United States seeking employment, a 1986 law tried to counteract[1] this by fining[2] employers who hire illegal immigrants.

---

[1] **counteract:** cancel the effects of
[2] **fining:** charging a financial penalty

3. Ten years later, a law limiting government assistance to immigrants **resulted from/was the result of** some people's concern about the cost of immigrants to taxpayers.
4. The United States has always welcomed people who leave their homeland **because of/due to** war or political persecution.[3]
5. Not only illegal but also legal immigrants felt the **effects of/consequences of** the 1996 law.
6. **As a result of/As a consequence of** the 1996 law, legal immigrants who had not become U.S. citizens were no longer eligible for certain benefits.

## EFFECT STRUCTURE WORDS

| SENTENCE CONNECTORS | CLAUSE CONNECTORS | | OTHERS |
|---|---|---|---|
| | COORDINATORS | SUBORDINATORS | |
| 1. as a result<br>as a consequence<br>therefore<br>thus<br>consequently<br>hence | 2. so | | 3. to result in<br>to cause<br>4. to have an effect on<br>to affect<br>5. the cause of<br>the reason for |

### Examples

1. The 1996 law eliminated many benefits for legal immigrants who had not become citizens; **as a result/as a consequence/therefore/thus/consequently/hence**, most of them applied for citizenship.
2. Welfare assistance for immigrants was restricted, **so** even legal immigrants who were poor and needy could not receive aid.
3. The new law **resulted in/caused** an immediate increase in the number of applications for citizenship.
4. The new law also **had an effect on/affected** students and businesspeople with visas who overstayed their visa time limit.
5. Overstaying a visa became **a cause of/a reason for** being barred[4] from the United States for three or more years.

**PRACTICE 6**

*Recognizing Cause Structure Words*

STEP 1    Underline the part of the sentence that states a cause.
STEP 2    Circle the word or words that introduce the cause.
STEP 3    Be able to discuss the use of each structure word or phrase that you have circled. What kind of grammatical structure follows each one? Notice especially the difference between the use of *because* and *because of.*

---

[3] **persecution:** bad treatment because of race, religion, or politics
[4] **barred:** prohibited from entering

**Example**

The computer is a learning tool (since) it helps children to master math and language skills.

1. Due to the ability of computers to keep records of sales and inventory, many big department stores rely on them.
2. A medical computer system is an aid to physicians because of its ability to interpret data from a patient's history and provide a diagnosis.[1] (How would you rewrite this sentence using *because* instead of *because of*?)
3. War, famine, and ethnic violence have caused a flood of refugees in the past fifty years.
4. Hollywood movies are known for their special effects because American audiences seem to demand them.
5. Since European audiences seem to prefer movies that explore psychological or philosophical issues, European movies are generally quieter and more thought-provoking.
6. Smog results from chemical air pollutants being trapped under a layer of warm air.
7. The patient's death was the result of the doctor's negligence.[2]
8. Little is known about life on the ocean floor, for scientists have only recently developed the technology to explore it.
9. One effect of prolonged weightlessness is the loss of muscle tone,[3] which can be a problem for astronauts who spend long periods of time in space.

---

**PRACTICE 7**

*Recognizing Effect Structure Words*

**STEP 1**  Underline the part of the sentence that states an effect.
**STEP 2**  Circle the word or words that introduce the effect.
**STEP 3**  Be able to discuss the use of each structure word or phrase. What kind of grammatical structure follows each one? How is the sentence punctuated?

1. The performance of electric cars is inferior to the performance of cars with conventional internal combustion engines; consequently, some improvements must be made in them if they are to become popular.
2. However, electric cars are reliable, economical, and nonpolluting; therefore, the government is spending millions of dollars to improve their technology.
3. Electric cars use relatively inexpensive electricity for power; thus, they cost less to operate than cars that use gasoline.
4. The cost of gasoline is rising; as a result, some automobile manufacturers have begun to produce electric models.
5. His refusal to attend classes resulted in his dismissal from the school.
6. The cause of the patient's death was the doctor's negligence.
7. It has been documented that heavy cigarette smoking affects the heart as well as the lungs.
8. Cold water is denser than warm water and will, therefore, sink.
9. Fresh water is less dense than salt water, so it tends to float on the surface of a body of salt water.

---

[1] **diagnosis:** identification of a disease or illness
[2] **negligence:** carelessness
[3] **muscle tone:** healthy elastic quality

Practice using structure words from the charts on pages 136 and 137 to write sentences.

**PRACTICE 8**

*Cause and Effect
Structure Words*

**STEP 1**  Decide which sentence in each item is a cause and which is an effect. Write C for cause or E for effect next to each sentence.

**STEP 2**  Combine the sentences in each item into a new sentence that shows a cause and effect relationship. Use a different structure word or phrase in each new sentence, and circle the word.

**Example**

_E_ The death rate among women from lung cancer is increasing.

_C_ Women are smoking more.

⟨Because⟩ women are smoking more, their death rate from
lung cancer is increasing.

**or**

The increase in the death rate of women from lung cancer
is ⟨the result of⟩ their smoking more.

1. _____ Cancer is increasing in industrialized nations.
   _____ Air pollution and the use of chemicals in food are increasing in these countries.
   _____
   _____

2. _____ The saltiest water is found at the bottom of the ocean.
   _____ Salt water, being denser than fresh water, sinks.
   _____
   _____

3. _____ Heat energy is carried by electrons.
   _____ Metals have many free-moving electrons.
   _____ Metals are good conductors of heat.
   _____
   _____

4. _____ Some businesses have flexible working hours.
   _____ Productivity has increased.
   _____ Absenteeism has declined.
   _____
   _____

5. _____ Radiation escaped into the atmosphere.
   _____ The Chernobyl nuclear power plant had no confinement shell.
   _____
   _____

6. _____ Operators at the Chernobyl plant disregarded safety rules.
   _____ The nuclear reactor underwent a meltdown.
   _____
   _____

7. _____ During a weather phenomenon known as El Niño, a mass of warm water
   flows eastward across the Pacific Ocean toward South America.
   _____ The temperature of the water off the coast of Peru rises as much as 10°F.
   _____
   _____

8. _____ Weather around the world changes.
   _____ During an El Niño, the jet stream[1] blows in a different pattern.
   _____
   _____

9. _____ Heavy rains fall in some areas of the world.
   _____ Devastating floods and mudslides happen.
   _____
   _____

10. _____ Thousands of people suffer starvation.
    _____ Drought happens in other parts of the world.
    _____
    _____

**WRITING PRACTICE**

Choose one of the suggested topics that follow, and write an essay that discusses it in terms of cause and effect. Use either block or chain organization or a combination of both. If you use block organization, be sure to insert a transition paragraph between the two blocks in the body of the essay.

Follow these steps to success:

1. Write your thesis statement at the top of your paper.
2. Brainstorm by using one of the prewriting techniques that you prefer.
   Hint: Divide your paper into two columns. List the causes in the first column and the effects in the second column.
3. Then brainstorm for ideas and details to support each cause and effect.
4. Write an outline from your brainstorming activity.
5. Write your first rough draft from your outline. Be sure to use a variety of cause and effect structure words, and begin each paragraph with a transition expression.
6. Revise your rough draft as you have learned. Ask a classmate to check your final essay against the Peer Editing Checklist on page 12..

## Topic Suggestions

Rising divorce rate
One type of pollution (air, water, soil)
Inflation
Stress
Any social, economic, or political
   problem in another country or the
   United States

Gender discrimination
Increasing life expectancy in a country
World refugees
Any scientific cause and effect
   phenomenon such as global warming,
   El Niño, etc.

---

[1] **jet stream:** high-speed, high-altitude air current.

# *Comparison and Contrast Order*

A very common and useful method of essay organization is comparison and contrast. You practiced writing paragraphs using comparison and contrast in Chapter 5, pages 65–67. The techniques for writing comparison/contrast paragraphs and essays are essentially the same; the main difference is in the size of the topic. Because the topic of an essay is much larger, you will need to learn some advanced patterns of organization.

As you read the following model essay, study its organization. Then answer the writing technique questions that follow.

**MODEL**

*Comparison and Contrast Essay*

### Japan and the USA—Different but Alike

The culture of a place is an integral[2] part of its society whether that place is a remote Indian village in Brazil or a highly industrialized city in Western Europe. The culture of Japan fascinates Americans because, at first glance, it seems so different. Everything that characterizes the United States—newness, racial heterogeneity,[3]
5  vast[4] territory, informality, and an ethic of individualism[5]—is absent in Japan. There, one finds an ancient and homogeneous[6] society, an ethic that emphasizes the importance of groups, and a tradition of formal behavior governing every aspect of daily living, from drinking tea to saying hello. On the surface at least, American and Japanese societies seem totally opposite.

10  One obvious difference is the people. Japan is a homogenous society of one nationality and a few underrepresented minority groups, such as the ethnic Chinese and Koreans. All areas of government and society are controlled by the Japanese majority. In contrast, although the United States is a country with originally European roots, its liberal immigration policies have resulted in its becoming a
15  heterogeneous society of many ethnicities—Europeans, Africans, Asians, and Latinos. All are represented in all areas of American society, including business, education, and politics.

Other areas of difference from Japan involve issues of group interaction and sense of space. Whereas Americans pride themselves on individualism and
20  informality, Japanese value groups and formality. Americans admire and reward a person who rises above the crowd; in contrast, a Japanese proverb says, "The nail that sticks up gets hammered down." In addition, while Americans' sense of size and scale developed out of the vastness of the North American continent, Japanese genius lies in the diminutive and miniature.[7] For example, America builds airplanes,
25  while Japan produces transistors.

In spite of these differences, these two apparently opposite cultures share several important experiences.

Both, for example, have transplanted cultures. Each nation has a "mother"

---

[2] **integral:** necessary for completeness
[3] **heterogeneity:** variety
[4] **vast:** very large
[5] **ethic of individualism:** belief in the value of the individual person over the group

[6] **homogeneous:** characterized by sameness; consistency
[7] **diminutive and miniature:** very small

society—China for Japan and Great Britain for the United States—that has influenced
30   the daughter in countless ways: in language, religion, art, literature, social customs, and
ways of thinking. Japan, of course, has had more time than the United States to work
out its unique interpretation of the older Chinese culture, but both countries reflect
their cultural ancestry.

Both societies, moreover, have developed the art of business and commerce, of
35   buying and selling, of advertising and mass producing, to the highest levels. Few sights
are more reassuring to Americans than the tens of thousands of bustling[1] stores
seen in Japan, especially the beautiful, well-stocked department stores. To American
eyes, they seem just like Macy's or Neiman Marcus at home. In addition, both Japan
and America are consumer societies. The people of both countries love to shop and
40   are enthusiastic consumers of convenience products and fast foods. Vending
machines selling everything from fresh flowers to hot coffee are as popular in Japan
as they are in America, and fast-food noodle shops are as common in Japan as
McDonald's restaurants are in America.

A final similarity is that both Japanese and Americans have always emphasized
45   the importance of work, and both are paying penalties for their commitment to it:
increasing stress and weakening family bonds. Americans, especially those in
business and in the professions, regularly put in twelve or more hours a day at their
jobs, just as many Japanese executives do. Also, while the normal Japanese
workweek is six days, many Americans who want to get ahead[2] voluntarily work on
50   Saturday and/or Sunday in addition to their normal five-day workweek.

Japan and America: different, yet alike. Although the two societies differ in many
areas such as racial heterogeneity versus racial homogeneity, individualism versus
group cooperation, and informal versus formal forms of behavior, they share more
than one common experience. Furthermore, their differences probably contribute as
55   much as their similarities toward the mutual interest the two countries have in each
other. It will be interesting to see where this reciprocal fascination leads in the future.

## Writing Technique Questions

**1.** In which paragraph(s) are the similarities discussed? In which paragraph(s) are
the differences discussed? Is the organization of this essay similar to cause and
effect block or chain style organization, discussed earlier in this chapter?

**2.** What is the function of the fourth paragraph?

*Comparison
Structure
Vocabulary*

The first key to writing successful comparison and contrast essays is the appropriate
use of comparison and contrast structure words. These are words that introduce
points of comparison and points of contrast.

The following table lists some of the words and phrases used to discuss
similarities.

---

[1] **bustling:** busy
[2] **get ahead:** win promotions and higher salaries

## COMPARISON STRUCTURE WORDS

| SENTENCE CONNECTORS | CLAUSE CONNECTORS | | OTHERS |
|---|---|---|---|
| | SUBORDINATORS | COORDINATORS/ CORRELATIVE CONJUNCTIONS | |
| 1. similarly<br>likewise<br>also<br>too | 2. as<br>just as | 3. and<br>both . . . and<br>not only . . .<br>but also<br>neither . . .<br>nor | 4. like (+ noun)<br>just like (+ noun)<br>similar to (+ noun)<br>5. (be) similar (to)<br>(be) the same as<br>6. (be) the same<br>7. (be) alike<br>(be) similar (to)<br>8. to compare (to/with) |

**Examples**

1. Human workers can detect malfunctions in machinery; **likewise/similarly**, a robot can be programmed to detect equipment malfunctions.
   Human workers can detect malfunctions in machinery; a robot can **also**.
   Human workers can detect malfunctions in machinery; a robot can, **too**.
2. Robots can detect malfunctions in machinery, **as/just as** human workers can. (**Note:** Use a comma when *as* and *just as* show comparison even when the dependent clause follows the independent clause.)
3. Robots **and** human workers/**Both** robots **and** human workers/**Not only** robots **but also** human workers can detect malfunctions in machinery.
   **Neither** robots **nor** human workers are infallible.[3]
4. Robots, **like/just like/similar to** human workers, can detect malfunctions in machinery.
5. Robots **are similar to/are the same as** human workers because they can both detect malfunctions in machinery.
6. In their ability to detect malfunctions in machinery, robots and human workers **are the same**.
7. Robots and human workers **are alike/are similar** because they can both detect malfunctions in machinery.
8. Robots can **be compared to/be compared with** human workers in their ability to detect malfunctions in machinery.

**PRACTICE 9**

*Using Comparison Structure Words*

**A.** Add comparison structure words to connect the following comparisons. The items contain both sentences and short phrases. You should write one complete new sentence for each item and use different comparison structure words in each new sentence. The information in this practice is from the field of political science. The items compare the systems of government of Great Britain and the United States.

---

[3] **infallible:** perfect; without errors

**Example**

The United States has a democratic form of government. Great Britain has a democratic form of government.

The United States has a democratic form of government,
just as Great Britain does.

1. The United States operates under a two-party system. Great Britain operates under a two-party system.

   _____

   _____

2. The British Parliament has two separate houses, the House of Commons and the House of Lords. The United States Congress has two separate houses, the Senate and the House of Representatives.

   _____

   _____

3. The U.S. House of Representatives = the British House of Commons. The U.S. Senate = the British House of Lords.

   _____

   _____

4. The members of the U.S. House of Representatives are elected by district. The members of the British House of Commons are elected by district.

   _____

   _____

5. The method of choosing cabinet members in the United States. The method of choosing cabinet members in Great Britain. (Use the structure phrase *the same*.)

   _____

   _____

6. In Great Britain, the cabinet is appointed by the prime minister. The U.S. president appoints the cabinet.

   _____

   _____

7. The British monarch has the right to veto[1] any law passed by Parliament. The U.S. president has the right to veto any law passed by Congress.

   _____

   _____

B. Now write five sentences of your own, comparing two things with which you are familiar. Use a different comparison signal in each sentence. Possible topics: bicycles and motorcycles; two cities; two siblings,[2] two friends; two cars; two sports; two sports stars; two teachers; two classes; two restaurants.

*Contrast Structure Vocabulary*

Contrast structure words fall into two main groups according to their meaning. The first group shows contrast in the sense of concession or unexpected result. The second group shows contrast in the sense of direct opposition. The clauses connected by the words in the second group are reversible. This means, for example, that *while* and *whereas* may be placed at the beginning of either clause with no change in meaning:

---

[1] **veto:** cancel                          [2] **siblings:** brothers and sisters

*I am short, whereas my brother is tall* and *Whereas I am short, my brother is tall* are both possible and are equal in meaning.

It is not always possible to do this with words from the first group. For example, the subordinator *even though* must be placed at the beginning of the clause *it began to rain* in the following sentence: *We continued our hike even though it began to rain.* It would not make sense to write *Even though we continued our hike, it began to rain.*

Notice that *but* and *however* belong to both groups.

## CONTRAST STRUCTURE WORDS—CONCESSION (UNEXPECTED RESULT)

| SENTENCE CONNECTORS | CLAUSE CONNECTORS | | OTHERS |
|---|---|---|---|
| | SUBORDINATORS | COORDINATORS | |
| 1. however<br>    nevertheless<br>    nonetheless<br>    still | 2. although<br>    even though<br>    though | 3. but<br>    yet | 4. despite (+ noun)<br>    in spite of (+ noun) |

**Examples**

1. It began to rain; **however/nevertheless/nonetheless/still,** we continued our hike.
2. We continued our hike **although/even though /though** it began to rain.
3. It began to rain, **but/yet** we continued our hike.
4. **Despite/In spite of** the rain, we continued our hike.

## CONTRAST STRUCTURE WORDS—DIRECT OPPOSITION

| SENTENCE CONNECTORS | CLAUSE CONNECTORS | | OTHERS |
|---|---|---|---|
| | SUBORDINATORS | COORDINATORS | |
| 1. however<br>    in contrast<br>    in (by) comparison<br>    on the other hand<br>2. on the contrary | 3. while<br>    whereas | 4. but | 5. differ from<br>6. compared (to/with)<br>7. (be) different (from)<br>    (be) dissimilar to<br>    (be) unlike |

**Examples**

1. The term *rock music* commonly refers to music styles after 1959 that were influenced primarily by white musicians; **however/in contrast/in comparison/on the other hand**, rhythm-and-blues music styles were influenced primarily by black musicians.
2. Innovation in rock music comes not just from the United States; **on the contrary**, the Beatles and the Rolling Stones were from Great Britain, and the music style known as reggae came from the Caribbean island of Jamaica. (**Note:** *On the contrary* contrasts an untruth and a truth.)
3. The term *rock music* commonly refers to music styles after 1959 that were influenced primarily by white musicians, **while/whereas** rhythm-and-blues music styles were influenced primarily by black musicians. (**Note:** Use a comma with *while* and *whereas* even when the dependent clause follows the independent clause.)
4. The term *rock music* commonly refers to music styles after 1959 that were influenced primarily by white musicians, **but** rhythm-and-blues music styles were influenced primarily by black musicians.
5. Early rock music **differs from** later styles in that later styles make use of electronics to produce new sounds.
6. **Compared to/Compared with** earlier rock styles, later styles have a harder sound.
7. The punk, rap, grunge, and techno styles of the '90s are very **different from/dissimilar to/unlike** the rock music played by Elvis Presley in the '50s, but they have the same roots.

**CROSS-REFERENCE**

Look at both Concession Clauses and Contrast Clauses on pages 202–203 for additional examples of contrast subordinators.

**PRACTICE 10**

*Using Contrast Structure Words*

A. Add contrast structure words to connect the following items. The items contain both sentences and short phrases. You should write one complete new sentence for each item, and use a different contrast signal in each new sentence.

**Example**

The government of the United States/the government of Great Britain/dissimilar in several aspects

*The governments of the United States and Great Britain are dissimilar in several aspects.*

1. The chief executive in Great Britain is called the prime minister. The chief executive in the United States is called the president.

2. In the United States, the president fulfills the functions of both political leader and head of state. These two functions are separate in Great Britain.

3. In other words, Great Britain has both a monarch and a prime minister. The United States has only a president.

**4.** The president of the United States may be of a different political party than the majority of Congress. The British prime minister is the head of the political party that has the most seats in Parliament.

_____

_____

**5.** The United States has a written constitution. Great Britain has no written constitution.

_____

_____

**6.** In the United States, elections are held on a regular schedule, no matter how popular or unpopular the government is. In Great Britain, elections are held whenever the prime minister loses a vote of confidence.[1]

_____

_____

**7.** The members of the U.S. Senate are elected. The members of the British House of Lords are appointed or inherit their positions.

_____

_____

**8.** As you can see, the two systems of government differ in several major aspects. They are both democracies.

_____

_____

**B.** Now write five sentences of your own, contrasting two things with which you are familiar. Use a different contrast signal in each sentence. Possible topics: computers/humans; English/your first language; taking public transportation/driving your own car; city life/country life; schools in two countries; the cost of living in two countries; family life in two countries.

## *Organization for Comparison and Contrast Order*

Just as there are two ways to organize a cause and effect essay, there are at least two ways to organize a comparison and contrast essay. You may use block organization or point-by-point organization. One type of organization is illustrated in each of the following models. Study each model very carefully. Notice how the thesis statement tells the reader what type of organization will be used.

In block organization, you discuss all of the similarities in one block (which can be one or more paragraphs), and all of the differences in another block (which can be one or more paragraphs). The essay on Japan and the United States on pages 141–142 is an example of block organization.

In point-by-point organization, you make a sentence-by-sentence comparison of the features in any order that seems appropriate for the topic. You might even use order of importance (most important feature first or last.)

Suppose you needed to compare two jobs. You might compare them on these points: salary, fringe benefits,[2] opportunities for advancement, and workplace atmosphere. If you use block organization, your outline might look like this:

---

[1] **vote of confidence:** vote of approval
[2] **fringe benefits:** employment benefits other than salary (vacation time, health insurance, etc.)

**MODEL**

*Block Organization*

| | |
|---|---|
| **Thesis Statement** | One way to decide between two job offers is to evaluate what the similarities and differences are before making a decision. |

**I.** The salary and fringe benefits of Job X and Job Y are almost the same.
   **A.** Salary (Job X and Job Y)
   **B.** Fringe benefits (Job X and Job Y)

**II.** Although the salary and fringe benefits are equal, there are big differences in the areas of workplace atmosphere and opportunity for advancement.
   **A.** Workplace atmosphere
      1. Job X
      2. Job Y
   **B.** Opportunity for advancement
      1. Job X
      2. Job Y

**Conclusion**

Of course, you could discuss the differences first and the similarities last. It is more usual, however, to discuss similarities first.

If you used point-by-point organization to compare the same two jobs, your outline might look like this:

**MODEL**

*Point-by-Point Organization*

| | |
|---|---|
| **Thesis Statement** | One way to decide between two job offers is to make a point-by-point comparison of their features. |

**I.** The salaries of Job X and Job Y are approximately equal.
   **A.** Job X's salary
   **B.** Job Y's salary

**II.** Job X offers the same fringe benefits as Job Y.
   **A.** Job X's fringe benefits
   **B.** Job Y's fringe benefits

**III.** In contrast to Job Y, Job X offers good opportunities for advancement.
   **A.** Job X's opportunities for advancement
   **B.** Job Y's opportunities for advancement

**IV.** Unlike the high-pressure and competitive atmosphere at Company X, the atmosphere at Company Y seems congenial[1] and supportive.
   **A.** Atmosphere at Company X
   **B.** Atmosphere at Company Y

**Conclusion**

---

[1] **congenial:** friendly

With both types of organization, as you discuss each feature of Job Y, refer back to the same feature of Job X and use comparison and contrast structure vocabulary to show whether they are the same or different. In other words, it is not sufficient simply to describe each job or each feature; you must constantly refer back and forth to make the similarities and differences clear.

> Like Job X, Job Y . . .
>
> In contrast to Job X, Job Y . . .
>
> Job X and Job Y both have . . .

**WRITING PRACTICE**

Choose one of the suggested topics and write an essay using comparison/contrast organization. Use either point-by-point or block organization. Follow these steps to success:

1. Brainstorm by freewriting, clustering, or listing all of the ideas that come into your mind. (*Hint:* Divide your paper into columns. List the similarities in the first column and the differences in the second.)
2. Decide whether to use point-by-point or block organization.
3. Brainstorm for specific supporting details.
4. Make an outline. Refer to the outlines on page 148 to guide you.
5. Write your first rough draft from your outline. Be sure to use comparison and contrast structure words.
6. Revise your rough draft as you have learned. Ask a classmate to edit your work using the Peer Editing Checklist on page 128.

### Topic Suggestions

Two cultures, or one aspect of two cultures such as family life, schools, child-raising practices, courtship and marriage customs, etc.

Living at home and living away from home

Two family members, two friends

Two classes, two teachers, two restaurants, two jobs you have had

High school and college or university

Public schools and private schools

## Review

Four common patterns of essay organization in English are

- Chronological order
- Logical division of ideas
- Cause and effect order
- Comparison and contrast order

With each pattern, use special transition signals and structure words to help your reader understand your ideas and follow your discussion. Of course there are other patterns of organization in academic writing such as definition and argumentation. Also, of course that you may need to use a combination of patterns at times, especially for long essays or term papers.

# PART III

# Sentence Structure

# CHAPTER 10 Types of Sentences

Thai manuscript

## Clauses

Clauses are the building blocks of sentences. A **clause** is a group of words that contains (at least) a subject and a verb.

These are clauses:

> ecology is a science
> because pollution causes cancer

These are not clauses:

> to protect the environment
> after working all day

There are two kinds of clauses: independent and dependent.

152

**Independent Clauses**

An **independent clause** contains a subject and a verb and expresses a complete thought. It can stand alone as a sentence by itself. An independent clause is formed with

| subject + verb (+ complement) |
| --- |
| **Students normally spend four years in college.**<br><br>**I will declare my major[1] now,** but **I may change it later.**<br><br>**Many international students experience culture shock** when they come to the United States. |

**Dependent Clauses**

A **dependent clause** begins with a subordinator such as *when, while, if, that,* or *who.* A dependent clause does not express a complete thought and cannot stand alone as a sentence by itself. A dependent clause is formed with

| subordinator + subject + verb (+ complement) |
| --- |
| **. . . although students normally spend four years in college . . .**<br><br>**. . . if I declare my major now . . .**<br><br>**. . . when they come to the United States . . .**<br><br>**. . . who was accepted at Harvard University . . .**<br><br>**. . . that the experiment was a success . . .** |

A partial list of subordinators follows in the chart of clause connectors. Study the chart, and then refer to it when you do Practice 1.

**Clause Connectors**

Three groups of words are used to connect clauses in order to form different kinds of sentences. They are subordinators (subordinating conjunctions), coordinators (coordinating conjunctions), and conjunctive adverbs.

---

[1] **declare my major:** officially register a major field of study with the university

## CLAUSE CONNECTORS

| SUBORDINATORS (SUBORDINATING CONJUNCTIONS) | | | | |
|---|---|---|---|---|
| after | before | that | when | which |
| although | even though | though | whenever | while |
| as | how | unless | where | who |
| as if | if | until | wherever | whom |
| as soon as | since | what | whether | whose |
| because | so that | | | |

### COORDINATORS (COORDINATING CONJUNCTIONS)

You can remember the seven coordinators by the phrase FAN BOYS:

for    and    nor    but    or    yet    so

### CONJUNCTIVE ADVERBS

| | | | | |
|---|---|---|---|---|
| accordingly | furthermore | in contrast | meanwhile | on the other hand |
| besides | hence | indeed | moreover | otherwise |
| consequently | however | instead | nevertheless | therefore |
| for example | in addition | likewise | nonetheless | thus |

**PRACTICE 1**

*Independent and Dependent Clauses*

Write INDEP next to the independent clauses and put a period (.) after them. Write DEP next to the dependent clauses.

_____ **1.** Jet lag affects most long-distance travelers

_____ **2.** Which is simply the urge to sleep at inappropriate times

_____ **3.** During long journeys through several time zones, the body's inner clock is disrupted

_____ **4.** For some reason, travel from west to east causes greater jet lag than travel from east to west

_____ **5.** Also, changes in work schedules can cause jet lag

_____ **6.** When hospital nurses change from a day shift to a night shift, for example

_____ **7.** Although there is no sure way to prevent jet lag

_____ **8.** There are some ways to minimize it

_____ **9.** Because jet lag is caused at least partially by loss of sleep, not just a change in the time of sleep

_____ **10.** A traveler should plan to arrive at his or her destination as late as possible

_____ **11.** Upon arriving, he or she should immediately go to bed

_____ **12.** Then the traveler should start to live in the new time frame immediately

# Kinds of Sentences

A sentence is a group of words that you use to communicate your ideas. Every sentence is formed from one or more clauses and expresses a complete thought.

There are basically four kinds of sentences in English: simple, compound, complex, and compound-complex. The kind of sentence is determined by the kind of clauses used to form it.

## Simple Sentences

A **simple sentence** is one independent clause.

> I enjoy playing tennis with my friends every weekend.
> I enjoy playing tennis and look forward to it every weekend.
> My friends and I play tennis and go bowling every weekend.

Notice that the second sentence has two verbs, *enjoy* and *look forward to*. This is called a compound verb. Because there is only one clause, this is a simple sentence. The third sentence has a compound subject as well as a compound verb, but it is still a simple sentence because it has only one clause.

**PRACTICE 2**

*Simple Sentences*

1. Write two simple sentences with one subject and one verb.
2. Write two simple sentences with one subject and two verbs.
3. Write two simple sentences with two subjects and two verbs.

## Compound Sentences

A **compound sentence** is two or more independent clauses joined together. There are three ways to join the clauses:

| | |
|---|---|
| 1. With a coordinator | I enjoy tennis, **but** I hate golf. |
| 2. With a conjunctive adverb | I enjoy tennis; **however,** I hate golf. |
| 3. With a semicolon | I enjoy tennis; I hate golf. |

Let's study each type of compound sentence in more detail.

### 1. Compound Sentences with Coordinators

A compound sentence can be formed as follows:

> Independent clause, + coordinator + independent clause

Notice that there is a comma after the first independent clause. The following sentences illustrate the meanings of the seven "FAN BOYS" coordinators.

| for | Women live longer than men, **for** they take better care of their health. (The second clause gives the reason for the first clause.) |
| --- | --- |
| and | Women follow more healthful diets, **and** they go to doctors more often. (The two clauses express equal, similar ideas.) |
| nor | Women don't smoke as much as men do, **nor** do they drink as much alcohol. (*Nor* means "and not." It joins two negative independent clauses. Notice that question word order is used after *nor*.) |
| but | Men may exercise harder, **but** they may not exercise as regularly as women do. (The two clauses express equal, contrasting ideas.) |
| or | Both men and women should limit the amount of fat in their diets, **or** they risk getting heart disease. (The two clauses express alternative possibilities.) |
| yet | Women used to be known as the "weaker sex," **yet** in some ways, they are stronger than men. (The second clause is a surprising or unexpected contrast to the first clause.) |
| so | Men are less cautious than women, **so** more men die in accidents. (The second clause is the result of the first clause.) |

**PRACTICE 3**

*Compound Sentences with Coordinators*

**A.** Add another independent clause to the following independent clauses to form compound sentences. Be sure to write a complete clause containing a subject and a verb. Circle the coordinator and add punctuation.

**Example**

The college campus is located in the center of the city, (so) it is very easy to do my shopping.

1. Students can attend day classes and _____

2. Students can live in dormitories or _____

3. I have finished my math homework but _____

4. I have studied English for six years yet _____

5. My adviser suggested a word processing class for _____

6. Some students do not like to write term papers nor _____

7. The instructor gave us eight weeks to write our term papers yet _____

8. Most students had not even chosen a topic nor _____
   _____

9. The instructor was very upset for _____
   _____

10. My roommate scored very high on the English placement test so _____
    _____

**B.** For each pair of sentences below, choose a coordinator that best fits the meaning, and join the two independent clauses to form a compound sentence. Use each FAN BOYS coordinator once. Write your new sentences on a separate sheet of paper, and punctuate them correctly.

### Example

Nuclear accidents can happen. Nuclear power plants must have strict safety controls.

Nuclear accidents can happen, so nuclear power plants must have strict safety controls.

1. The accident at the nuclear power plant at Three Mile Island in the United States created fears about the safety of this energy source. The disaster at Chernobyl in the former Soviet Union confirmed[1] them.
2. Solar heating systems are economical to operate. The cost of installation is very high.
3. Energy needs are not going to decrease. Energy sources are not going to increase. (Use *nor* and question word order in the second clause, deleting the word *not*.)
4. Burning fossil fuels causes serious damage to our planet. We need to develop other sources of energy.
5. Ecologists know that burning fossil fuels causes holes in the ozone layer. People continue to do it.
6. Poorer nations especially will continue this harmful practice. They don't have the money to develop "clean" energy sources.
7. All nations of the world must take action. Our children and grandchildren will suffer the consequences.

**C.** On a separate sheet of paper, write seven compound sentences of your own, using each coordinator once.

## 2. Compound Sentences with Conjunctive Adverbs

A compound sentence can also be formed as follows:

> Independent clause; + conjunctive adverb, + independent clause

Notice the punctuation: a semicolon follows the first independent clause, and a comma follows the conjunctive adverb. Also, just like the FAN BOYS coordinators, conjunctive adverbs express relationships between the clauses. The following chart shows the coordinators and conjunctive adverbs that express similar meanings.

_____

[1] **confirmed:** proved that they were correct

| COORDINATORS | CONJUNCTIVE ADVERBS | SENTENCE |
|---|---|---|
| **and** | besides<br>furthermore<br>moreover<br>also | Community colleges offer preparation for many occupations; **moreover,** they prepare students to transfer to a four-year college or university. |
| **but**<br>**yet** | however<br>nevertheless<br>nonetheless | Many community colleges do not have dormitories; **however,** they provide housing referral services. |
| **or** | otherwise | Students must take final exams; **otherwise,** they will receive a grade of Incomplete. |
| **so** | accordingly<br>consequently<br>hence<br>therefore<br>thus | Native and nonnative English speakers have different needs; **therefore,** most schools provide separate English classes for each group. |

**PRACTICE 4**

*Compound Sentences with Conjunctive Adverbs*

**A.** Add another independent clause to each independent clause that follows to form compound sentences. Be sure to add a complete clause containing a subject and a verb. Circle the conjunctive adverb and add punctuation. Notice that some of these sentences are from Practice 3A on pages 156–157.

**Example**

The college campus is located in the center of the city; (therefore,) it is very easy to do my shopping.

**1.** Students can attend day classes moreover _____

_____

**2.** Students can live in dormitories otherwise _____

_____

**3.** I have finished my math homework however _____

_____

**4.** I have studied English for six years nevertheless _____

_____

**5.** The instructor gave us eight weeks to write our term papers nonetheless

_____

_____

**6.** My roommate scored very high on the English placement test consequently

_____

_____

**B.** On a separate sheet of paper, combine the pairs of sentences in items 2, 4, 5, and 7 from Practice 3B on page 157, using conjunctive adverbs instead of coordinators. Punctuate your new sentences correctly.

**Example**

Nuclear accidents can happen. Nuclear power plants should have strict safety controls.

Nuclear accidents can happen; therefore, nuclear power plants should have strict safety controls.

**C.** On a separate sheet of paper, write four compound sentences, using each of these conjunctive adverbs once: *furthermore, however, therefore,* and *otherwise.*

### 3. Compound Sentences with Semicolons

A compound sentence can also be formed with a semicolon alone:

| Independent clause; independent clause |
| --- |
| My older brother studies law; my younger brother studies medicine.<br><br>Poland was the first Eastern European country to turn away from communism; others soon followed. |

This kind of compound sentence is possible only when the two independent clauses are closely related in meaning. If they aren't closely related, they should be written as two simple sentences, each ending with a period.

**PRACTICE 5**

*Compound Sentences with Semicolons*

**A.** Place a semicolon between the two independent clauses in the following compound sentences.

1. The American way of life apparently does not foster[1] marital happiness half of all American marriages end in divorce.
2. Motherhood causes some women to quit their jobs others continue working despite having young children to care for.
3. Three hundred guests attended his wedding two attended his funeral.

**B.** Write three compound sentences of your own, using a semicolon to join the independent clauses.

**PRACTICE 6**

*Combining Simple Sentences*

Use what you have learned about forming compound sentences to improve the following mini-essay, which contains many short, simple sentences. Combine sentences wherever possible. Try to use each of the three methods at least once. There is not just one correct way to combine the sentences; there are many possible ways.

---

[1] **foster:** encourage

**Robots**

[1]A robot is a mechanical device that can perform boring, dangerous, and difficult tasks. [2]First of all, robots can perform repetitive tasks without becoming tired or bored. [3]They are used in automobile factories to weld[*] and paint. [4]Robots can also function in hostile environments. [5]They are useful for exploring the ocean bottom as well as deep outer space. [6]Finally, robots can perform tasks requiring pinpoint accuracy. [7]In the operating room, robotic equipment can assist the surgeon. [8]For instance, a robot can kill a brain tumor. [9]It can operate on a fetus[†] with great precision.

[10]The field of artificial intelligence is giving robots a limited ability to think and to make decisions. [11]However, robots cannot think conceptually. [12]Robots cannot function independently. [13]Humans have to program them. [14]They are useless. (Use *otherwise* to combine sentences 13 and 14.) [15]Therefore, humans should not worry that robots will take over the world—at least not yet.

## *Writing Technique Questions*

**1.** What is the main idea of each paragraph? What sentences state the main ideas?
**2.** What method of organization is used to develop the first paragraph?

**Complex Sentences**

A **complex sentence** contains one independent clause and one (or more) dependent clause(s). In a complex sentence, one idea is generally more important than the other one. The more important idea is placed in the independent clause, and the less important idea is placed in the dependent clause.

There are three kinds of dependent clauses: adverb, adjective, and noun. The following chart presents an overview of them. You will study all of these kinds of clauses in greater detail in Chapters 11, 12, and 13.

## DEPENDENT CLAUSES

| **ADVERB CLAUSES** |
| --- |
| A dependent adverb clause begins with an adverbial subordinator such as *when, while, because, although, if, so that,* etc.<br><br>**1.** **Although women in the United States could own property,** they could not vote until 1920.<br>**2.** In the United States, women could not vote until 1920 **although they could own property.**<br><br>Notice that there are two possible positions for an adverb clause: before or after the independent clause. If it comes before the independent clause, it is followed by a comma (sentence 1). If it comes after the independent clause, no comma is used (sentence 2). |

---

[*] **weld:** join metal by applying heat
[†] **fetus:** unborn baby

## ADJECTIVE CLAUSES

A dependent adjective (relative) clause begins with a relative pronoun such as *who, whom, which, whose,* or *that,* or with a relative adverb such as *where* or *when.* An adjective clause functions as an adjective; that is, it modifies a noun or pronoun. The position and punctuation of dependent adjective clauses is discussed in Chapter 13.

**3.** Men **who are not married** are called bachelors.
**4.** Last year we vacationed on the Red Sea, **which features excellent scuba diving.**

## NOUN CLAUSES

A dependent noun clause functions as a noun and begins with a *wh-*question word, *that, whether,* or sometimes *if.* A dependent noun clause can be either a subject (sentence 5) or an object (sentence 6). No commas are necessary.

**5.** **That there is a hole in the ozone layer of the earth's atmosphere** is well known.
**6.** Scientists believe **that excess chlorofluorocarbons in the atmosphere are responsible for creating it.**

**PRACTICE 7**

*Complex Sentences*

A. **STEP 1**   Underline the independent clause of each sentence with a solid line.
   **STEP 2**   Underline the dependent clause with a broken line.
   **STEP 3**   Write SUB above the subordinator. Refer to the chart on page 154 for a list of subordinators.

**Example**

SUB
Because the cost of education is rising, many students must work part-time.

1. When students from other countries come to the United States, they often suffer from culture shock.
2. Because the cost of education has risen, many students are having financial problems.
3. Please tell me where the student union is.
4. Engineers, who have an aptitude for drafting and mechanics, must also be artistic and imaginative.
5. While the contractor follows the blueprint, the engineer checks the construction in progress.
6. Since the blueprint presents the details of the engineer's plans, it must be interpreted accurately by the contractor.
7. Students should declare a major by their junior year unless they have not made up their minds.
8. Even though students declare a major now, they can change it later.
9. Last year, the government reported that drug use is increasing.
10. Doctors are concerned about drug use by young people, who think that smoking marijuana is risk-free.

**B.  STEP 1**    Add a logical independent clause to each of the following dependent clauses.

**STEP 2**    Punctuate each sentence correctly.

1.  _____ until I pay my tuition.

2.  _____

unless I take twelve units.

3.  _____ that computer engineering is a popular major.

4.  _____ who is chair of the Communications Department.

5.  Because I had to look for a part-time job _____

6.  _____ if I want to get to school on time.

7.  _____

_____ whether I should take advanced calculus.

8.  _____ whom I met at the social club meeting last month.

9.  _____ when I left my country.

10. _____ that my college adviser recommends.

## Compound-Complex Sentences

A **compound-complex sentence** is a combination of two or more independent clauses and one (or more) dependent clauses. Many combinations are possible, and their punctuation requires careful attention.

**1.**  I wanted to travel after I graduated from college; however, I had to go to work immediately.

**2.**  After I graduated from college, I wanted to travel, but I had to go to work immediately.

**3.**  I wanted to travel after I graduated from college, but I had to go to work immediately because I had to support my family.

**4.**  I couldn't decide where I should work or what I should do, so I did nothing.

- Punctuate the compound part of a compound-complex sentence like a compound sentence; that is, use a semicolon/comma combination (sentence 1), or put a comma before a coordinator joining two clauses (sentences 2, 3, and 4).

- Punctuate the complex part like a complex sentence. With adverb clauses, put a comma after a dependent adverb clause (sentence 2) but not before them (sentence 3). With noun clauses, use no commas (sentence 4).

**PRACTICE 8**

*Compound-Complex Sentences*

Punctuate these compound-complex sentences.

**STEP 1**    Underline the independent clauses with a solid line and the dependent clauses with a broken line.

**STEP 2**    Add commas and/or semicolons as necessary.

1.  If housework and childcare are included women work more hours per week than men every place in the world except North America and Australia but they also earn less than men everywhere.

**2.** In Africa, women work harder than men because they work 67 hours per week but men work only 53.

**3.** Although Latin American women work 60 hours Latin men work only 54 and in Asia women work 62 hours to men's 48.

**4.** Men in Western Europe work the least they put in only 43 hours per week although women average 48.

**5.** The report stated that even when men's working hours were reduced they used the extra time for leisure activities rather than for housework or childcare.

# Compound Sentences (Coordination) versus Complex Sentences (Subordination)

Good writing requires a mixture of all four kinds of sentences: simple, compound, complex, and compound-complex. A composition with only short, simple sentences is boring and ineffective, as is writing that uses too many compound sentences. Writing with complex sentences and participial phrases,[1] structures that use subordination, is generally considered more mature, interesting, and effective in style.

Compare the two models that follow. The first model is an example of overcoordination, or writing with too many compound sentences. In the second model, some of the coordination has been replaced by subordination—complex sentences in sentences 5, 6, 7, 9, 11, and 12 and participial phrases in sentences 5 and 10. Notice, however, that coordination has been preserved where the ideas expressed are equal (sentences 1, 4, and 8).

**MODEL**

*Overcoordination*

## The People's Princess

[1]Diana, Princess of Wales, was born in Norfolk, England, in 1961, and she died in Paris, France, in 1997. [2]People around the world were fascinated by the transformation of this shy kindergarten teacher into an independent, self-assured young woman. [3]Her sudden death in a car crash while being chased by photographers prompted worldwide discussion and grief.

[4]Diana Spencer was born to a wealthy, upper-class English family, and she was educated in private schools in England and Switzerland. [5]She loved children, so she became a kindergarten teacher. [6]She led a quiet life in London, but then she met Charles, Prince of Wales, and her life changed dramatically. [7]She and Charles married in 1981, and her life as the wife of the future king of England began. [8]She gave birth to two sons and became active in charity work. [9]Diana's life should have been a happy one, but it was not to be. [10]She and Charles began having marital problems, and they separated in 1992, and they agreed to divorce in 1996.

[11]Diana worked very hard at her job as princess, and she supported many causes, especially those related to children and AIDS victims. [12]She lived for only a short time, but she touched people all over the world because of her beauty, her compassion for others, and her style.

---

[1] Participial phrases are presented in Chapter 14.

**The People's Princess**

[1]Diana, Princess of Wales, was born in Norfolk, England, in 1961 and died in Paris, France, in 1997. [2]People around the world were fascinated by the transformation of this shy kindergarten teacher into an independent, self-assured young woman. [3]Her sudden death in a car crash while being chased by photographers prompted worldwide discussion and grief.

[4]Diana Spencer was born to a wealthy, upper-class English family and educated in private schools in England and Switzerland. [5]Because she loved children, she became a kindergarten teacher, leading a quiet life in London. [6]However, when she met Charles, Prince of Wales, her life changed dramatically. [7]After she and Charles married in 1981, her life as the wife of the future king of England began. [8]She gave birth to two sons and became active in charity work. [9]Although Diana's life should have been a happy one, it was not to be. [10]She and Charles began having marital problems, separating in 1992 and agreeing to divorce in 1996.

[11]Diana, who worked very hard at her job as princess, supported many causes, especially those related to children and AIDS victims. [12]Even though she lived for only a short time, she touched people all over the world because of her beauty, her compassion for others, and her style.

**PRACTICE 9**

*Subordination*

Change the following compound sentences to complex sentences by subordinating one of the clauses. Use the subordinator given. **Note:** Be sure to add the subordinator to the correct clause so that the resulting sentence is logical.

**Example**

It was raining, so I took an umbrella to work. (because)

Not logical:    It was raining because I took an umbrella to work.

Logical:    I took an umbrella to work because it was raining.

1. In the former Soviet Union, men and women had access to equal education and job opportunities, for that reflected the Soviet philosophy. (since)

2. The 1937 Soviet constitution declared that women and men had equal rights and responsibilities, and women joined the workforce. (after)

3. Also, millions of Russian men were away in the military during World War II, so Russian women filled their places at work. (because)

4. Soviet women worked full time at their jobs, but they also had the primary responsibility for taking care of the family. (although)

5. They finished their work, and they had to shop, cook the evening meal, and perhaps wash, iron, or mend the family's clothes. (as soon as)

**PRACTICE 10**

*Combining Sentences in Different Ways*

Use what you have learned about the four kinds of sentences to improve this paragraph, which contains too many short, simple sentences. Use different methods of combining the sentences. You may want to refer to the chart on page 154 for a list of coordinators and subordinators.

### Nonverbal Communication

¹Nonverbal communication, or body language, is used everywhere in the world. ²It is a very powerful means of communication. ³It communicates much more than spoken words. ⁴One example of nonverbal communication is what occurs between parents and child. ⁵Parents smile at their child. ⁶They communicate love, acceptance, and reassurance. ⁷The child feels comfortable and safe. ⁸The smile signifies approval. ⁹The child is happy and well-adjusted. ¹⁰Another example of such communication is the image a person projects* in public. ¹¹A woman is walking alone on an unfamiliar and possibly dangerous street. ¹²She wants to appear confident. ¹³She should walk briskly.† ¹⁴She may be tired. ¹⁵She should walk with her shoulders straight and her head held high. ¹⁶Her eyes should be focused straight ahead. ¹⁷Someone is looking at her. ¹⁸She should return the glance without hesitation. ¹⁹In contrast, a nervous woman will appear afraid. ²⁰She walks slowly with her shoulders drooping‡ and her eyes looking downward. ²¹Indeed, body language can express more than spoken language. ²²It is a very strong method of communication. ²³People use their body signals carelessly. ²⁴They can sometimes be misinterpreted.

## *Review*

These are the important points in this chapter so far:

**1. Clauses** are the main building blocks of sentences. There are two kinds of clauses: independent and dependent.

| | |
|---|---|
| An **independent clause** <br> • expresses a complete thought. <br> • can be a sentence by itself. | English grammar is easy. |
| A **dependent clause** <br> • begins with a subordinator. <br> • cannot be a sentence by itself. <br> • is one of three types: **adverb, adjective,** or **noun.** | Adverb:. . . because grammar is easy . . . <br> Adjective:        . . . which is in Spanish . . . <br> Noun:  . . . that grammar is easy . . . |

---

\* **project:** show
† **briskly:** fast
‡ **drooping:** hanging down

**2.** There are **four kinds of sentences** in English: simple, compound, complex, and compound-complex. Each kind is punctuated differently.

| | |
|---|---|
| A **simple sentence** has one independent clause. | English grammar is easy. |
| A **compound sentence** has two independent clauses joined by<br><br>• a coordinator.<br>• a conjunctive adverb.<br>• a semicolon. | Grammar is easy, so I learned it quickly.<br>Grammar is easy; therefore, I learned it quickly.<br>Grammar is easy; I learned it quickly. |
| A **complex sentence** has one independent and one (or more) dependent clauses. The punctuation depends on the kind of dependent clause(s). | With an adverb clause:<br>Because grammar is easy, I learned it quickly.<br>I learned grammar quickly because it is easy.<br><br>With an adjective clause:<br>One of my favorite films is *Like Water for Chocolate*, which is in Spanish.<br><br>With a noun clause:<br>She doesn't agree that grammar is easy. |
| A **compound-complex sentence** has two independent clauses and one (or more) dependent clauses. | Because grammar is easy, I learned it quickly, but it took me several years to master writing. |

**3.** Although good writers use all four kinds of sentences, the use of subordination (complex and compound-complex sentences) is considered a more mature, interesting, and effective writing style.

# *Parallelism*

**Parallelism** is an important element in English writing, especially when you are listing and comparing and contrasting items or ideas. Parallelism means that each item in a list or comparison follows the same grammatical pattern. If you are writing a list and the first item in your list is a noun, write all of the following items as nouns also. If the first item is an infinitive verb phrase, make all of the others infinitive verb phrases; if it is a dependent clause, make all of the others dependent clauses. If you are making a comparison or contrast, make sure that the items you are comparing or contrasting are the same.

Notice how the rule of parallelism is followed in the second sentence in each of the following sets.

| | |
|---|---|
| *Not parallel* | My English conversation class is made up of Chinese, Spaniards, and some are from Bosnia. |
| *Parallel* | My English conversation class is made up of Chinese, Spaniards, and Bosnians. |

| | |
|---|---|
| *Not parallel* | The students who do well attend class, they do their homework, and practice speaking in English. |
| *Parallel* | The students who do well attend class, do their homework, and practice speaking in English. |

| | |
|---|---|
| *Not parallel* | The teacher wanted to know which country we came from and our future goals. |
| *Parallel* | The teacher wanted to know which country we came from and what our future goals were. |

| | |
|---|---|
| *Not parallel* | The language skills of the students in the evening classes are the same as the day classes. |
| *Parallel* | The language skills of the students in the evening classes are the same as the language skills of the students in the day classes. |

You may also substitute a pronoun for the second "the language skills":

> The language skills of the students in the evening classes are the same as those of the students in the day classes.

All of the words in the first item do not always have to be repeated in the second. You may repeat all or some of the words, depending upon what you wish to emphasize.

> Before you write a paper or (before) (you) take a test, you must organize your thoughts.

"Before" and/or "you" may be deleted from the second item without breaking the rule of parallelism.

> Before you write a paper or take a test, you must organize your thoughts.

## Coordinators— And, Or, But

Words, phrases, and clauses that are joined by *and, or,* and *but* are written in parallel form. Notice the parallel structures joined by coordinators in the following sentences:

> The Federal Air Pollution Control Administration regulates automobile exhausts, **and** the Federal Aviation Administration makes similar regulations for aircraft.

> The states regulate the noise created by motor vehicles **but** not by commercial aircraft.

> Pesticides cannot be sold if they have an adverse[1] effect on humans, on animal life, **or** on the environment.

---

[1] **adverse:** unfavorable

## Correlative Conjunctions

Use parallel forms with the correlative conjunctions *both . . . and, either . . . or, neither . . . nor,* and *not only . . . but also.*

Correlative conjunctions are placed directly *before* the elements they join in the sentence. Notice the parallel structure in these clauses joined by correlative conjunctions:

> A new law provides the means for **both** regulating pesticides **and** ordering their removal if they are dangerous.

> Air pollutants may come **either** from the ocean as natural contaminants given off by sea life **or** from the internal combustion engines of automobiles.

> If **neither** industry **nor** the public works toward reducing pollution problems, future generations will suffer.

> Many people are **neither** concerned about pollutants **nor** worried about their future impact.

> At the present time, air pollution is controlled through laws passed **not only** to reduce the pollutants at their sources **but also** to set up acceptable standards of air quality.

**PRACTICE 11**

*Parallelism*

**A.** Two or more items in each of the following sentences are written in parallel grammatical form. Underline the items or ideas that are parallel, and circle the word or words that connect the parallel structures.

**Example**

An ideal environment for studying includes good lighting, a spacious desk, (and) a comfortable chair.

1. You know you are truly bilingual when you can calculate in your second language and when you begin to dream in it.
2. People often spend as much time worrying about the future as planning for it.
3. You can learn a second language in the classroom, at home, or in a country where the language is spoken.
4. My new personal computer is both fast and reliable.
5. My old typewriter is neither fast nor reliable.
6. Ann is growing older but unfortunately not wiser.
7. Young people buy computers not only to do schoolwork but also to play games.
8. If industrial nations continue to burn fossil fuels and if developing nations continue to burn their rain forests, the level of $CO_2$ in the atmosphere will continue to increase.
9. Before the judge announced the sentence,[1] he asked the murderer if he wanted to speak either to the victim's family or to the jury.
10. The criminal neither admitted guilt nor asked for forgiveness before he was executed.

---

[1] **sentence:** punishment

**B.** Rewrite the following sentences in parallel form. Underline the part of the sentence that is not parallel and correct it.

**Example**

The disadvantages of using a credit card are overspending and <u>you pay</u> high interest rates.

<u>The disadvantages of using a credit card are overspending and paying</u>

<u>high interest rates.</u>

1. Credit cards are accepted by department stores, airlines, and they can be used in some gas stations.

_____

_____

2. You do not need to risk carrying cash or to risk to pass up² a sale.

_____

_____

3. With credit cards, you can either pay your bill with one check, or you can stretch out your payments.

_____

_____

4. You can charge both at restaurants and when you stay at hotels.

_____

_____

5. Many people carry not only credit cards but they also carry cash.

_____

6. Many people want neither to pay off their balance monthly nor do they like paying interest.

_____

_____

7. Not making any payment or to send in only minimum payments every month is poor money management.

_____

_____

**COMPUTER TIP**

Computer programs that check your style are available. However, these programs alert you only to certain stylistic problems. They are not able to detect problems in grammar.

**C.** Write seven original sentences in parallel form, using the coordinating conjunctions *and, or,* and *but* and the correlative conjunctions *both . . . and, either . . . or, neither . . . nor,* and *not only . . . but also* one time each.

## *Sentence Problems*

In this section, you will learn to recognize and correct some common errors in sentence structure: sentence fragments as well as choppy, run-on, and stringy sentences.

*Sentence Fragments*

**Sentence fragments** are incomplete sentences or parts of sentences. Remember that a complete sentence must contain at least one main or independent clause.

_____

² **pass up:** miss an opportunity

Study the following four examples of sentence fragments and the suggested methods for correcting them.

**1.** Because some students work part-time while taking a full load of courses.

    Problem:    This is a dependent clause.
    To correct:   Attach it to an independent clause.

                Because some students work part-time while taking a full load of courses, they have very little free time.

**2.** For example, the increase in the cost of renting an apartment.

    Problem:    There is no verb.
    To correct:   Rewrite the sentence so that it has a verb.

                For example, the cost of renting an apartment increased.

**3.** Feeling lonely and failing most of his classes.

    Problem:    This is a participial phrase.
    To correct:   (a) Add a subject and change the participles to verbs, or
                   (b) attach the phrase to an independent clause.

                (a) He felt lonely and was failing most of his classes.
                (b) Feeling lonely and failing most of his classes, the student wisely decided to make an appointment with his counselor.

**4.** Many young people who leave home at an early age.

    Problem:    This is a noun phrase + a relative clause. The independent clause is unfinished.
    To correct:   (a) Change the relative clause into an independent clause, or
                   (b) complete the unfinished independent clause.

                (a) Many young people leave home at an early age.
                (b) Many young people who leave home at an early age do not manage their money well.

Always check your own writing for sentence fragments. Pay particular attention to your sentences beginning with subordinating conjunctions (*although, since, because, if, before,* etc.). These are DANGER WORDS! Make sure that every subordinate clause beginning with these words is attached to an independent clause.

**PRACTICE 12**

*Rewriting Sentence Fragments*

**A.** Read the following sentences. Mark them FRAG if they are sentence fragments, or COMP if they are complete sentences. On a separate piece of paper, rewrite each fragment to make a complete sentence.

_____ **1.** The desire of all humankind to live in peace and freedom, for example.
_____ **2.** Second, the fact that men are physically stronger than women.
_____ **3.** The best movie that I saw last year.
_____ **4.** <u>Titanic</u> was the most financially successful movie ever made.
_____ **5.** For example, many students have part-time jobs.
_____ **6.** Although people want to believe that all men are created equal.
_____ **7.** Finding a suitable marriage partner is a challenging task.
_____ **8.** Many of my friends who didn't have the opportunity to go to college.
_____ **9.** Working during the morning and attending classes during the afternoon.

_____ **10.** Because I don't feel that grades in college have any value.

_____ **11.** The nuclear accident that occurred in Russia in 1986, the worst nuclear accident in history.

_____ **12.** The first hint of the tragedy came two days after the accident occurred.

_____ **13.** When radiation monitors[1] in Sweden indicated an increase in radiation levels over Scandinavia.

_____ **14.** Radiation escaping into the atmosphere, drifting west over other countries, and causing crops and dairy products to become contaminated.

_____ **15.** Opponents of nuclear power plants pointing to the Chernobyl disaster and the near-disaster at a U.S. plant in Pennsylvania.

**B.** Read the following short essay. Put brackets [ ] around any sentence fragments that you find and mark them FRAG. Then correct all fragments on a separate piece of paper.

### Women Drivers

Male chauvinism[2] extends even into the area of automobile driving, it seems. Believing that they are far better drivers than women. Men consider women drivers incompetent, inattentive, and even dangerous behind the wheel.

However, statistics prove that women are, in fact, safer drivers than
5  men. For example, insurance rates. Insurance rates for women are 20 percent lower than they are for men. Another proof is that more accidents are caused by male drivers between the ages of 18 and 25 than by any other group. Also, the greater percentage of accidents involving deaths caused by men. Although women are criticized for being too cautious. They are really just
10  being safe drivers.

The reasons for women drivers' safer driving habits can perhaps be found in the differing attitudes of the sexes toward automobiles. On the one hand, women drivers who regard the automobile as a convenience. Like a washing machine. On the other hand, men regard the automobile as an extension of
15  their egos.[3] Using it as a weapon when they feel particularly aggressive. Or using it as a status symbol.

All in all, women are safer drivers. Because of their attitude. Men can learn to become safe drivers. If they adopt the attitude that an automobile is merely a convenience.

*Choppy Sentences*

**Choppy sentences** are sentences that are too short. Although short sentences can be effective, overuse of them is considered poor style in academic writing.

Choppy sentences are easy to correct. Just combine two or three short sentences to make one compound or complex sentence. Your decision to make a compound or a complex sentence should be based on whether the ideas in the short sentences are equal or whether one idea is dependent on the other.

---

[1] **monitors:** machines to check radiation levels
[2] **male chauvinism:** men's belief in male superiority
[3] **egos:** self-importance

**1.** If the sentences express equal ideas, use coordination to combine them.

*Choppy sentences*    Wind is an enduring source of power. Water is also an unlimited energy source. Dams produce hydraulic power. They have existed for a long time. Windmills are relatively new.

*Corrected*    Both wind and water are enduring sources of power. Dams have produced hydraulic power for a long time, but windmills are relatively new.

**2.** If the sentences express unequal ideas, that is, if one sentence expresses a less important idea than the other, use subordination to combine them.

*Choppy sentences*    We must find new sources of energy. Natural sources of energy are dwindling.[1] Solar energy is a promising new source of energy. Solar energy is energy from the sun.

*Corrected*    We must find new sources of energy because natural sources of energy are dwindling. Solar energy, which is energy from the sun, is a promising new source.

Examine your own writing carefully. Do you use too many short sentences? If you do, practice combining them.

**PRACTICE 13**

*Rewriting Choppy Sentences*

Improve the following choppy sentences by combining them to make either compound, complex, or compound-complex sentences.

**1.** Gasoline became expensive. Automobile manufacturers began to produce smaller cars. Smaller cars use less gasoline.

_____

_____

**2.** The computer has undoubtedly benefited humanity. The computer has also created problems for humanity.

_____

_____

**3.** Government and private agencies have spent billions of dollars advertising the dangers of smoking. The number of smokers is still increasing.

_____

_____

**4.** Some students go to a vocational school to learn a trade. Some students go to college to get a degree.

_____

_____

**5.** The grading system at our college should be abolished.[2] The students don't like getting grades. The instructors don't enjoy giving grades.

_____

_____

## Run-On Sentences and Comma Splices

A **run-on sentence** is a sentence in which two or more independent clauses are written one after another with no punctuation. A similar error happens when two independent clauses are incorrectly joined by a comma without a coordinating conjunction. This kind of error is called a **comma splice.**

Run-on:    My family went to Australia then they emigrated to Canada.

Comma splice:    My family went to Australia, then they emigrated to Canada.

_____

[1] **dwindling:** decreasing
[2] **abolished:** gotten rid of; abandoned

The ways to correct these two sentence errors are the same.

1. Add a period:       My family went to Australia. Then they emigrated to Canada.

2. Add a semicolon:    My family went to Australia; then they emigrated to Canada.

3. Add a coordinator:  My family went to Australia, and then they emigrated to Canada.

4. Add a subordinator: My family went to Australia before they emigrated to Canada.
                       After my family went to Australia, they emigrated to Canada.

**PRACTICE 14**

*Run-On/Comma Splice
Sentences*

**A.** Correct the following run-on/comma splice sentences using the method indicated.

1. A newly arrived international student faces many problems, for example, he has to cope with a new culture.
   a. (Add a period.) _____
   _____
   b. (Add a semicolon.) _____
   _____

2. New York City is very cosmopolitan, there are people from many cultures and ethnic groups living there.
   a. (Add a period.) _____
   _____
   b. (Add a semicolon.) _____
   _____
   c. (Add a subordinator.) _____
   _____
   d. (Add a coordinator.) _____
   _____

3. Learning a new language is like learning to swim it takes a lot of practice.
   (Add a coordinator.) _____
   _____

4. Ask for assistance at the reference desk in the library, there is always a librarian on duty.
   (Add a semicolon.) _____
   _____

5. Skiing is a dangerous sport you can easily break your leg or your neck.
   (Add a subordinator.) _____
   _____

**B.** Some of the following sentences are run-ons or comma splices, and some are correct. Check each sentence. If it is incorrect, write RO or CS in the space at the left. If it is correct, leave the space blank. Then, on a separate piece of paper, correct the incorrect sentences.

**Example**

   _RO_        Two letters arrived on Monday a third one came on Wednesday.

               *Two letters arrived on Monday; a third one came on*
               *Wednesday.*

**COMPUTER TIP**

Your school library probably has other computerized reference materials such as dictionaries and bibliographies. Ask your school librarian to show them to you.

———  **1.** An encyclopedia is a valuable source of information, it contains summaries of every area of knowledge.

———  **2.** Because of the rapid expansion of human knowledge, it is difficult to keep encyclopedias current.

———  **3.** A printed encyclopedia becomes obsolete[1] almost as soon as it is published, also it is quite expensive to purchase.

———  **4.** Encyclopedias on CD-ROMs are inexpensive, convenient to use, and easily updated.

———  **5.** Articles in encyclopedias are written by experts in each subject, who are often university professors.

———  **6.** An editor of an encyclopedia doesn't write articles he only collects and edits articles written by other experts.

———  **7.** To find a book on a certain subject, you used to look in a card catalog, to find a magazine article on a subject, you used to look in a periodical index.

———  **8.** Now, most libraries have thrown away their card catalogs, they have computerized catalogs that are much more efficient to use and update.

———  **9.** Many periodical indexes, which only list titles of magazine articles and indicate where to find them, have been replaced by computer indexes, some of which display synopses[2] and even entire articles instantly.

——— **10.** If you can't find any information on a subject, you can always ask a librarian to help you, they are paid to assist students.

**C.** Locate the run-on/comma splice sentences in the following paragraphs. Mark them by writing RO or CS above them. Then, on a separate piece of paper, rewrite both paragraphs, correcting the mistakes that you found.

### Grade Inflation

Teachers at Stone Mountain State College give higher grades than teachers at twelve of the nineteen other colleges in the state college system, according to a recent report from the State Institutional Research Committee. This report showed that more than one-third of the undergraduate grades awarded
5 in the spring semester, 1997, were A's, only 1.1 percent were F's. The percentage of A's awarded to graduate students was even higher, almost two-thirds were A's.

While students may be happy to receive high grades, there is evidence that this trend is having negative consequences. Investigation of the admissions cri-
10 teria[3] of some graduate and professional schools indicates that the admissions offices of these schools are discounting high grades on the transcripts of SMSC students, this means that an A from SMSC is not equal to an A from other universities. Grade inflation may, therefore, hurt a student from Stone Mountain State College who intends to apply to a graduate or professional
15 school, he or she may not be accepted despite a high grade point average.

---

[1] **obsolete:** out of date; old
[2] **synopses:** summaries
[3] **criteria:** standards by which a judgment is made

## *Stringy Sentences*

A **stringy sentence** is a sentence with too many independent clauses, usually connected with *and, but, so,* and *because*. It often results from writing the way you speak, going on and on like a string without an end.

There is no rule limiting the number of independent clauses allowed in one sentence, but two is a good maximum. To correct a stringy sentence, divide it and/or recombine the clauses, remembering to subordinate when appropriate.

Stringy sentence | Many students attend classes all morning, and then they work all afternoon, and they also have to study at night, so they are usually exhausted by the weekend.

Corrected | Many students attend classes all morning and work all afternoon. Since they also have to study at night, they are usually exhausted by the weekend.

Because many students attend classes all morning, work all afternoon, and study at night, they are usually exhausted by the weekend.

**PRACTICE 15**

*Stringy Sentences*

Improve these stringy sentences.

1. He enrolled in an advanced calculus class, but he found it too difficult, so he dropped it.

2. The tidal wave ruined the crops, and it destroyed several villages, and it caused many deaths, so it was a real disaster.

3. The analysts worked many hours on the computer program, but they couldn't find the cause of the problem, so they finally gave up, and they went home.

4. Junk food is bad for your health, and it also contains no vitamins, and it damages your stomach, so people shouldn't eat it.

5. The lack of rainfall has caused a severe water shortage, so people have to conserve water every day, and they also have to think of new ways to reuse water, but the situation is improving.

# *Review*

These are the important points in the second half of this chapter:

**1. Parallelism**

Lists of items joined by coordinating conjunctions and correlative conjunctions must be parallel in structure. The same is true of contrasts and comparisons of items. If the first item is a noun, make all others nouns; if it is a phrase, make all of the others phrases; if it is a clause, make all of the others clauses.

| NOT PARALLEL | PARALLEL |
|---|---|
| I enjoy snow skiing in the winter and waterski summers. | I enjoy snow skiing in the winter and waterskiing in the summer. |
| My grandmother not only speaks four languages but also she understands six | My grandmother not only speaks four languages but also understands six. |

**2. Sentence Problems**

The four main kinds of problem sentences that students may write are fragments, run-ons, comma splices, and choppy and stringy sentences.

| | |
|---|---|
| **Fragments** are incomplete sentences. | |
| Fragment: The subject that I enjoyed the most in high school. | Corrected: The subject that I enjoyed the most in high school was physics. |
| **Run-ons** and **comma splices** are incorrectly joined independent clauses. | |
| Run-on: Getting married is easy staying married is another matter.<br><br>Comma splice: Getting married is easy, staying married is another matter. | Corrected: Getting married is easy, but staying married is another matter.<br><br>or: Although getting married is easy, staying married is another matter. |
| **Choppy sentences** are sentences that are too short. | |
| Choppy: My family left our homeland. Then we lived in a refugee camp. We livedthere for several months. Then we got our documents. We traveled to. Canada. We live there now. | Corrected: After my family left our homeland, we lived in a refugee camp for several months. As soon as we got our documents, we traveled to Canada, where we live now. |

---

**Stringy sentences** are sentences with too many independent clauses.

| Stringy: My family left our homeland, and we lived in a refugee camp for several months, but finally we got our documents, so we traveled to Canada, and we live there now. | Corrected: After my family left our homeland, we lived in a refugee camp for several months. As soon as we got our documents, we traveled to Canada, where we live now. |
|---|---|

---

**EDITING PRACTICE**

Edit the following paragraph for errors in parallel structure and other sentence problems. Identify the problem sentences and correct them. (**Note:** Not every sentence has a problem.)

### America: Melting Pot or Salad Bowl?

[1]The United States counts its population every ten years, and each census* reveals that the racial and ethnic mix is changing dramatically, so by the year 2050, the "average" American will not be descended from† Europeans, but the majority of U.S. residents will trace their ancestry‡ to Africa, Asia, the Hispanic world, the Pacific Islands, or the Middle East. [2]Once the United States was a microcosm§ of European nationalities, today the United States is a microcosm of the world. [3]The United States is no longer considered a "melting pot" society by many of its residents. [4]Instead, many people prefer the term "salad bowl." [5]They use this term to describe American society. [6]American society will soon be predominantly nonwhite. [7]"Melting pot" implies that the different ethnic groups blend together into one homogeneous mixture, "salad bowl" implies that nationalities, like the ingredients in a mixed green salad, retain their cultural identities. [8]Earlier generations of immigrants believed they had to learn English quickly not only to survive but also for success. [9]Now, many immigrant groups do not feel the same need. [10]Because there are many places in America where you can work, shop, get medical care, marry, divorce, and die without knowing English. [11]For example, Chinatown in San Francisco and New York. [12]Also, Los Angeles has many Vietnamese immigrants and immigrants from Mexico. [13]In addition, many immigrant groups want their children to know their own culture. [14]Many Hispanics, for instance, want their children to learn both English and study the Spanish language in school. [15]They are fighting for the right to bilingual education in many communities. [16]In many communities they are in the majority.

---

* **census:** population count
† **be descended from:** be the children, grandchildren, etc., of

‡ **ancestry:** a person's origins
§ **microcosm:** small community representing a large one

# CHAPTER

 **Noun Clauses**

Japanese writing from the Edo period (1615–1868)

## *Introduction*

**A noun clause** is a dependent clause that functions as a noun. It can be a subject, object, or subject complement. However, in this chapter you will study the noun clause only as it is used as an object.

Because a noun clause is dependent, it must be connected to an independent clause to form a complex sentence. A noun clause used as an object is preceded by an

178

independent clause called an introductory clause. The noun clause is the object of the introductory clause verb, which is often a verb of speaking *(say, tell, report)* or mental activity *(know, believe, wonder)*.

| INTRODUCTORY CLAUSE | | NOUN CLAUSE |
|---|---|---|
| SUBJECT | VERB | OBJECT |
| I | know | **that people have different opinions about capital punishment.** |

# *Types of Noun Clauses*

There are three types of noun clauses:

- *That*-clauses are made from statements and are introduced by the subordinator *that*.

  | | | |
  |---|---|---|
  | The bulletin states | **that** | **science courses require a laboratory period.** |
  | It also points out | **that** | **lab attendance is mandatory.**[1] |

- *Wh*-word clauses are formed from *wh*-questions and are introduced by *wh*-words such as *who, whoever, what, whatever, where, wherever, when, which, how, how much, how many,* etc.

  | | | |
  |---|---|---|
  | I don't know | **where** | **the student cafeteria is.** |
  | The professor explained | **how** | **shock waves are formed.** |
  | Do you know | **which answer** | **is correct?** |

- *If/whether*-clauses are formed from yes/no questions and are introduced by the subordinator *whether* or *if*. The phrase *or not* may be added.

  | | | |
  |---|---|---|
  | I don't know | **whether (or not)** | **I should take computer science (or not).** |
  | An engineer determines | **if** | **the measurements are correct (or not).** |

  The punctuation of sentences with noun clauses is easy.

- No comma is used to separate the introductory clause from the noun clause.
- The introductory clause, which may be a statement or a question, determines the end-of-sentence punctuation.

    If the introductory clause is a question, use a question mark at the end of the sentence.

    If the introductory clause is a statement, use a period.

    **Do you know** when he called?
    **I don't know** when he called.

---

[1] **mandatory:** required

## Sequence of Tenses

The verb in the introductory clause controls the tense of the verb in the noun clause. If the introductory clause verb is simple present, present perfect, or future, the verb in the noun clause is in whatever tense expresses the meaning that the introductory clause intends.

The prime ministers **agree** that global warming[1] **is** a serious world problem.

They **hope** that all nations **will be** responsible for solving this serious problem.

Scientists **believe** that atmospheric warming **has** already **begun**.

Measurements **have indicated** that the average temperature of the earth **has risen** in the past one hundred years.

Further research **will prove** that carbon dioxide **is** largely responsible.

However, when the verb in the introductory clause is in the past tense, the verb in the dependent clause is usually in a past form[2]:

The prime ministers **agreed** that global warming **was** a serious world problem.

They **hoped** that all nations **would be** responsible for solving this problem.

Scientists **believed** that atmospheric warming **had** already **begun**.

Measurements **indicated** that the average temperature of the earth **had risen** in the past one hundred years.

Further research **proved** that carbon dioxide **was** largely responsible.

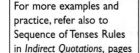

**CROSS-REFERENCE**

For more examples and practice, refer also to Sequence of Tenses Rules in *Indirect Quotations*, pages 87–88.

# That-Clauses

*That*-clauses are made from statements and are introduced by the subordinator *that*. The word *that* is often omitted if the meaning is clear without it. A *that*-clause is composed of

---

*that* + subject + verb + complement

---

. . . that the language center of the brain differs in each person.

. . . that different aspects of language, such as nouns and verbs, are processed in different areas of the brain.

---

Here are examples of complex sentences containing an independent introductory clause and a dependent *that*-clause.

---

[1] **global warming:** rising temperature of the earth
[2] *Exception:* The verb in the dependent clause is in the present tense when it reports a general truth: We knew that food cooks more slowly at high elevations.

| INTRODUCTORY CLAUSE | | *THAT*-CLAUSE |
|---|---|---|
| I think | **that** | **the study of the brain is fascinating.** |
| The professor explained | **that** | **the brain is the master control for both mind and body.** |

The following verbs are used in introductory clauses followed by *that*-clauses. They are grouped according to whether or not they may take an indirect object.

## INTRODUCTORY CLAUSE VERBS

| GROUP I | GROUP II | GROUP III | GROUP IV |
|---|---|---|---|
| No indirect object | Indirect object optional; *to* required with indirect object | Indirect object required | Indirect object optional |
| agree<br>answer<br>assert<br>conclude<br>know<br>notice<br>realize<br>state<br>think | admit<br>explain<br>mention<br>point out<br>prove<br>reply | assure<br>convince<br>inform<br>notify<br>remind<br>tell | promise<br>show<br>teach<br>warn<br>write |

The verbs in Group I do not take an indirect object.

> We **know** that women have higher verbal IQs than men.

The verbs in Group II may or may not take an indirect object. However, if an indirect object is used, *to* must precede it.

> The defense attorney **proved (to the jury)** that his client was not guilty.

The verbs in Group III *must* be followed by an indirect object.

> The doctor **assured the worried parents** that their child would recover.

The verbs in Group IV may or may not be followed by an indirect object.

> He **promised (them)** that they could see their child immediately after the operation.

**Note:** In academic writing, especially in scientific writing, introductory clause verbs are often written in passive voice with the neutral subject *it*.

> **It was agreed/stated** that . . .     **It has been asserted/proven** that . . .

**A.** Complete the introductory clauses in the following sentences by adding a verb from the table and the subordinator *that*. Use a different verb in each sentence, and use passive voice verbs in sentences 4, 5, and 6.

**Examples**

Researchers <u>know that</u> men's and women's brains are different.

It <u>has been proven that</u> men's and women's brains are different.

1. Experts _____ women learn languages more easily than men do.
2. They _____ a certain area of the brain controls language.
3. A recent study _____ women have more brain cells in the language area than men do.
4. In the report, it _____ women are not more intelligent than men just because they have more cells in the brain's language area.
5. It _____ men and women have different abilities involving spatial[1] tasks; for example, men can read maps more easily, but women can remember the location of objects better.
6. It _____ men are, in general, better at math and reasoning than women.

**B.** Write six original sentences containing *that*-clauses. Use a different introductory clause verb in each sentence, and remember the sequence of tenses rules.

### Subjunctive Noun Clauses

After certain verbs and adjectives in an introductory clause, the verb in a *that*-clause is in the simple or base form, called the subjunctive. These verbs and adjectives indicate urgency, advisability, necessity, and desirability. The verbs and adjectives requiring the subjunctive form in the *that*-clause include:

| VERBS | | | ADJECTIVES | |
|---|---|---|---|---|
| advise | direct | recommend | advisable | important |
| ask | insist | suggest | essential | urgent |
| command | move | urge | necessary | vital |
| demand | propose | | | |

The company president **urged** that the marketing department **be** more aggressive.

She **insisted** that the company **not lose** any more customers to its competitors.

It is **necessary** that each salesperson **work** longer hours.

The subjunctive also occurs when the introductory clause verb is in passive voice:

It **was recommended** that the department **not hire** new staff at this time.

---

[1] **spatial:** concerning space

**PRACTICE 2**

*Subjunctive Noun
Clauses*

**A.** Background information: *A three-year drought has caused a serious water shortage in the fictitious[2] country of Sunnyland. As a result, Sunnyland's government is proposing restrictions on water use.*

Write complex sentences containing subjunctive noun clauses.

**STEP 1**   Rewrite the question in each item as an introductory clause.
**STEP 2**   Rewrite the statement as a subjunctive noun clause.
**STEP 3**   Combine the two clauses to make a new sentence.

**Example**

What did the government order?
Citizens must decrease their water use; they should not waste water.

_The government ordered that citizens decrease their water use and
that they not waste water._

**1.** What did the government demand?
Each family must reduce its water use by 40 percent.

_____

_____

**2.** What is necessary?
All citizens must comply with[3] the new restrictions.

_____

_____

**3.** What did the government propose for city-dwellers?
Everyone must take five-minute showers.

_____

_____

**COMPUTER TIP**

A computer spell check will find many errors. However, it will not find spelling errors such as *there/their/they're*, nor will it find a missing *-s* on a plural noun. You still need to check for errors yourself.

**4.** What is advisable?
People should conserve water whenever possible.

_____

_____

**5.** What has been demanded of farmers?
Farmers should cut their water use by 25 percent.

_____

_____

**6.** What was suggested?
Every farmer should install a drip irrigation system.

_____

_____

**7.** What did the government urge?
People must not use water to wash cars, sidewalks, or streets.

_____

_____

———————

[2] **fictitious:** not real
[3] **comply with:** obey

**B.** Write six original sentences with subjunctive noun clauses, using a different verb or adjective in the introductory clause in each sentence.

# Wh-Word Clauses

A *wh*-word clause is a dependent noun clause in which the subordinator is a *wh*-word such as *who, what, where, when, why, how much, how long, which,* etc. A *wh*-word clause is composed of either

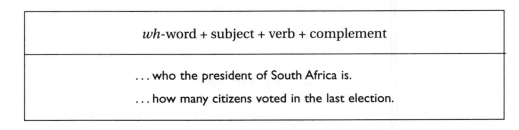

| *wh*-word + subject + verb + complement |
| --- |
| . . . who the president of South Africa is. |
| . . . how many citizens voted in the last election. |

or
(when the *wh*-word and the subject of the clause are the same word)

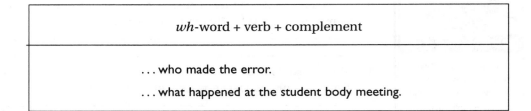

| *wh*-word + verb + complement |
| --- |
| . . . who made the error. |
| . . . what happened at the student body meeting. |

The word order in these clauses sometimes causes problems for learners of English as a second language. It may seem strange not to follow words such as *who* and *when* with a verb. However, just remember that the word order in a noun clause is like a statement, not like a question.

Study the word order in the *wh*-questions on the left side of the chart on page 184, and the *wh*-word clauses on the right. Notice that *wh*-word clauses always use normal SV statement word order. Also, since they are not questions, the helping verbs *do, does,* and *did* disappear.

| WH-QUESTIONS | WH-WORD CLAUSES |
|---|---|
| S   V<br>Who started the band? | S   V<br>... who started the band. |
| S   V<br>Which vocalists have sung with the group? | S   V<br>... which vocalists have sung with the group. |
| V   S<br>How often does the group perform during the year? | S   V<br>... how often the group performs during the year. |
| V   S<br>Who is the lead singer? | S   V<br>... who the lead singer is. |

To change a *wh*-question into a *wh*-word clause:

- Change the word order to SV statement word order if necessary.
- Delete *do, does,* or *did.*

Here are examples of complex sentences containing *wh*-word clauses:

| INTRODUCTORY CLAUSE | WH-WORD CLAUSE | | |
|---|---|---|---|
| | SUBORDINATOR-SUBJECT | | VERB (+ COMPLEMENT) |
| I don't know<br>Can you tell us | who<br>which vocalists | | started the band.<br>have sung with the group? |
| | SUBORDINATOR | SUBJECT | VERB (+ COMPLEMENT) |
| I can't remember<br><br>We asked | how often<br><br>who | the group<br><br>the lead singer | performs during the year.<br>was. |

**A.** Write new complex sentences containing *wh*-word clauses.

> **STEP 1**  Rewrite each question as a *wh*-word clause:
> - Change the word order to SV statement word order if necessary.
> - Delete *do, does,* or *did.*
>
> **STEP 2**  Combine your new *wh*-word clause with the introductory clause to form a new complex sentence, and observe the sequence of tenses rules.

**Example**

Who plays lead guitar in the band Behind Bars?

We don't know <u>who plays lead guitar in the band Behind Bars.</u>

1. Which company produces their CDs?
   We asked the music store manager ⎯⎯⎯⎯⎯⎯⎯⎯

2. Where will their next concert be held?
   They will announce tomorrow ⎯⎯⎯⎯⎯⎯⎯⎯

3. Where do they practice on the road[1]?
   The band's manager always arranges ⎯⎯⎯⎯⎯⎯

4. When did they last perform in Europe?
   I remember very clearly ⎯⎯⎯⎯⎯⎯⎯⎯

5. Who writes their songs?
   The group never says ⎯⎯⎯⎯⎯⎯⎯⎯

6. Which of their songs do you like the best?
   I can't really say ⎯⎯⎯⎯⎯⎯⎯⎯

7. How many members of the group have received formal music training?
   It is surprising ⎯⎯⎯⎯⎯⎯⎯⎯

8. What happened to their female vocalist?
   Their agent wouldn't reveal ⎯⎯⎯⎯⎯⎯⎯⎯

**B.** Write new sentences containing *wh*-word clauses.

> **STEP 1**  Rewrite each question as a *wh*-word clause.
> **STEP 2**  Combine your new *wh*-word clause with any introductory clause of your choice, and observe the sequence of tenses rules.

**Example**

Who was Pablo Picasso?

<u>Do you know who Pablo Picasso was?</u>

---

[1] **on the road:** traveling

**1.** Where was he born?

_____

**2.** Where did he live most of his life?

_____

**3.** How many of his paintings have been exhibited at the Louvre in Paris?

_____

**4.** What is the subject of his painting entitled <u>Guernica</u>?

_____

**5.** Where is the actual city of Guernica?

_____

**6.** Who was his favorite model?

_____

**7.** How old was Picasso at his death?

_____

**8.** How many masterpieces did he produce during his lifetime?

_____

**C.** Write six original complex sentences containing *wh*-word clauses.

# If/Whether-Clauses

*If/whether*-clauses are dependent noun clauses that are formed from yes/no questions and are introduced by the subordinator *whether* or *if*. An *if/whether*-clause is composed of

| *whether (if)* + subject + verb + complement |
| --- |
| . . . whether the president will win reelection. <br> . . . if the airplane landed safely. |

The following examples show how yes/no questions can become *if/whether*-clauses.

| YES/NO QUESTION | IF/WHETHER-CLAUSE |
| --- | --- |
| V    S <br> Does Dr. Chen practice acupuncture? | S    V <br> . . . if Dr. Chen practices acupuncture. |
| V    S <br> Is acupuncture an effective treatment for arthritis? | S    V <br> . . . whether acupuncture is an effective treatment for arthritis. |
| V S <br> Has it been used as an anesthetic during surgery? | S    V <br> . . . whether it has been used as an anesthetic during surgery or not. |

To change a yes/no question into an *if/whether*-clause:

- Change the word order to SV statement word order if necessary.
- Delete *do, does,* or *did.*
- Add the subordinator *if* or *whether. Whether* is more formal than *if.*
- (Optional) Add *or not* at the end of the clause or immediately after the subordinator *whether.* Add *or not* at the end of a clause beginning with *if.*

Here are examples of complex sentences containing *if/whether*-clauses.

| INTRODUCTORY CLAUSE | IF/WHETHER-CLAUSE | | |
| --- | --- | --- | --- |
| | SUBORDINATOR | SUBJECT | VERB (+ COMPLEMENT) |
| We want to know | if | Dr. Chen | practices acupuncture. |
| | if | Dr. Chen | practices acupuncture or not. |
| Doctors wonder | whether | acupuncture | is an effective treatment for arthritis. |
| | whether | acupuncture | is an effective treatment for arthritis or not. |
| | whether or not | acupuncture | is an effective treatment for arthritis. |

**PRACTICE 4**

*If/Whether-Clauses*

**A.** Write complex sentences containing *if/whether*-clauses.

**STEP 1**    Rewrite each question as an *if/whether*-clause.
- Change the word order to SV statement word order.
- Delete *do, does,* or *did.*
- Add the subordinator *whether* or *if.*
- If you wish, add *or not* in an appropriate location.

**STEP 2**    Add your new clause to the introductory clause to make a complex sentence, and observe the sequence of tenses rules.

You may write your new sentence in any of the five possible ways shown above.

1. Is acupuncture a risky medical procedure?
   Westerners would like to know ―――――――――――――――――――――――

2. Do acupuncture needles relieve pain after dental surgery?
   Please tell me ――――――――――――――――――――――

**3.** Has the safety of acupuncture, which is practiced widely in Asia and Europe, ever been tested?

A new report hadn't revealed ———————————————————————

———————————————————————————————————

**4.** Does acupuncture use the body's own energy to promote healing?

It has not been proven ————————————————————————

———————————————————————————————————

**5.** Can acupuncture strengthen your immune system?

It is not certain ——————————————————————————

———————————————————————————————————

**B.** Write complex sentences containing *if/whether*-clauses by adding an introductory clause and the subordinator *if* or *whether*. If you wish, add the phrase *or not* in an appropriate position. Add the appropriate end-of-sentence punctuation.

**Example**

_Do you know whether or not_ acupuncture relieves chronic pain?

**1.** ——————————————————— acupuncture treatments are expensive

**2.** ——————————————————— health insurance companies will pay for acupuncture treatments

**3.** ——————————————————— acupuncture is successful in helping people lose weight or stop smoking

**4.** ——————————————————— my doctor approves of acupuncture treatment

**5.** ——————————————————— acupuncture as an alternative medical practice will be an accepted form of treatment

**C.** Write five original sentences containing *if/whether* clauses. Use each possible pattern once.

# Review

**1.** A noun clause is a dependent clause that functions like a noun as a subject, a subject complement, or an object. A noun clause used as an object is the object of an introductory clause verb.

**2.** When writing a complex sentence with a noun clause, follow the sequence of tenses rules.

- If the introductory clause verb is in the present, present perfect, or future tense, the verb in the noun clause can be in any tense.

- If the introductory clause verb is in a past tense, the verb in the noun clause must be in a past tense. *Exception*: If the noun clause states a general truth, then use simple present tense.

**3.** Do not use a comma with noun clauses.

## TYPES OF NOUN CLAUSES

| | |
|---|---|
| **that-clauses:**<br>• formed from statements<br>• introduced by subordinator *that*<br>• *that* can be omitted | The Russian president and his wife told the press **(that) they were enjoying their visit.** |
| **subjunctive noun clauses:**<br>• verb in simple form<br>• occur after verbs and adjectives of urgency, advisability, necessity, and desirability | The president of the United States suggested **that Russia open its doors to American business.** |
| **wh-word clauses:**<br>• formed from *wh*-questions; *wh*-words are the subordinators: *who, where, which, how,* etc.<br>• use SV statement word order<br>• *do, does, did* disappear | Do you know **who the interpreter for the Russian leader was?**<br><br>The reporter asked **which companies planned to do business in Russia.** |
| **if/whether clauses:**<br>• formed from yes/no questions<br>• introduced by subordinator *if* or *whether. Whether* is more formal than *if.*<br>• *or not* may be added<br>• use SV statement word order<br>• *do, does, did* disappear | The question is **whether (or not) American and European companies understand the Russian business environment (or not).**<br><br>No one knows **if the experiment will succeed (or not).** |

You can improve your writing style by using noun clauses correctly. Doing the editing practice that follows will make you aware of potential errors in this sentence pattern and alert you to look for them in your own writing.

**EDITING PRACTICE**

Edit the following composition for errors in noun clauses. You should make 21 changes. Look for these kinds of errors:

| | |
|---|---|
| Incorrect word order: | We don't know who ~~is she~~. *(she is)* |
| Sequence of tense rule not followed: | The newspaper reported that world leaders ~~have~~ *(had)* failed to agree at the conference. |
| Subjunctive verb not used: | Environmentalists urged that carbon dioxide emissions ~~are~~ *(be)* decreased immediately. |
| Incorrect punctuation: | Everyone wonders when world peace will become a reality X Everyone hopes X that peace will come soon. |

### A College Lecture

¹Professor Sanchez gave a lecture on transistors last Tuesday. ²First, he explained what are transistors. ³He said, that they are very small electronic devices used in telephones, automobiles, radios, and so on. ⁴He further explained that transistors control the flow of electric current in electronic equipment. ⁵He wanted to know which popular technological invention cannot operate without transistors. ⁶Most students agreed, it is the personal computer. ⁷Professor Sanchez then asked if the students know how do transistors function in computers. ⁸He said that the transistors were etched* into tiny silicon microchips and that these transistors increase computers' speed and data storage capacity. ⁹Then he asked the class when had transistors been invented? ¹⁰Sergei guessed that they were invented in 1947. ¹¹The professor said that he is correct. ¹²Professor Sanchez then asked what was the importance of this invention? ¹³Many students answered that it is the beginning of the information age. ¹⁴At the end of the lecture, the professor assigned a paper on transistors. ¹⁵He requested that each student chooses a topic by next Monday. ¹⁶He suggested that the papers are typed.

---

* **etched:** cut into the surface

**WRITING PRACTICE**

*Letter of Inquiry*

Pretend you are going to graduate from the university a year from now, and you are interested in seeing what kinds of positions employers are offering to graduates in your field (business, engineering, teaching, etc.). You could look in your local newspaper to see what job opportunities are available. The following are examples of ads that you might find:

---

**College Grad**

Do you have a B.A. or B.S. degree in accounting or business? No experience necessary. Training program in national firm. Inquiries welcomed. Write: Billings, Goodwill, and Rush Accountants, Inc., 354 Waterfront Center, Suite 3790, New York, New York, 10017. Affirmative Action Employer.

---

**ENGINEERING GRADUATES**

Must possess degree in electrical/chemical/industrial engineering. Company is expanding. Job opportunities on U.S. West or East Coasts and in Middle East. Letters of inquiry are welcome. Write to: Frank Memry, MHC Engineering, Inc., 475 Evanston Drive, Santa Clara, CA 94301. Equal Opportunity Employer.

---

If you are planning to become an accountant or an engineer, you might answer one of these ads. If you have a different career preference, look in your local newspaper for an ad that fits your needs, and attach the ad to your assignment.

Write a letter of inquiry using noun clauses. Use *that*-clauses to state information that you already know ("Your ad stated that your company was seeking..."). Use *wh*-word clauses and *if/whether*-clauses to ask for information. You might want to inquire about the size of the company, travel requirements, salary, benefits, number of employees, advancement opportunities, support for further education, and so on.

Pay close attention to the following model business letter. Notice the punctuation in the addresses and the greeting and closing. Also note the capitalization of proper nouns, of the word *Dear*, and of the first word of the closing. Study the line spacing between different parts of the letter. When you write your own letter, follow this format exactly.

**MODEL**

*Business Letter*

*Your address*

777 Oak Avenue, Apt. 2C
Cleveland, OH 44106

*Date*

May 19, _____

*Employer's name and address*

Mr. Frank Memry
MHC Engineering, Inc.
475 Evanston Drive
Santa Clara, CA 94301

*Greeting*

Dear Mr. Memry:

*Body*

I am responding to an advertisement for engineering positions in today's *Metropolitan Tribune*. Although I will not graduate from the university for another year, I thought that this would be a good opportunity to inquire about what kinds of job opportunities are
5   available with your company for a new graduate in electrical engineering.
First of all, I would like to know how old your company is and where your branch offices are located both in the United States and internationally. I would also like to inquire about what the company's travel policy is for new employees. If travel is required, what is the
10   average time away from the office? Finally, please tell me whether or not your company encourages employees to study for advanced degrees.
I would appreciate this opportunity to learn about your company so that I can be prepared for the job market when I graduate.
Thank you very much for your kind attention to my inquiry.

*Closing*

Very truly yours,

*Your signature*

*Marvin Lemos*

*Your name*

Marvin Lemos

# CHAPTER 12

# Adverbial Clauses

Eighteenth-century English handwriting

## Introduction

An **adverbial clause** is a dependent clause introduced by an adverbial subordinator. It is used to modify the verb of the independent clause and tells when (time), where (place), why (reason), for what purpose, how, how long, or how far. It is also used to show contrast: concession (unexpected result) and direct opposition.

Adverbial clauses are composed of

| subordinator + subject + verb + complement |
| --- |
| Because scientists are interested in the planets . . . <br> . . . so that humans can learn more about the universe. |

**CROSS-REFERENCE**

Correct use of commas
and other marks helps
make your meaning clear.
To see how, look at
Appendix A: Punctuation,
pages 245–254.

Since the adverbial clause is a dependent clause, it cannot stand alone. It must be combined with an independent clause to form a complex sentence. An adverbial clause can come either before or after an independent clause. If it comes before an independent clause, a comma is placed after it.

**Because scientists are interested in the planets,** they send spacecraft to orbit them.

If the adverbial clause comes after the independent clause, no comma is necessary.

Scientists send spacecraft to orbit the planets **so that humans can learn more about the universe.**

## *Types of Adverbial Clauses*

There are several different kinds of adverbial clauses. The following chart lists the different kinds along with the subordinators that introduce them. In the pages that follow, you will study and practice each kind.

### ADVERBIAL SUBORDINATORS

|  | SUBORDINATOR | MEANING |
|---|---|---|
| **Time** | when<br>whenever<br>while<br>as soon as<br>after<br>since<br>as<br>before<br>until | a point in time/short duration<br>at any time<br>at the same time/longer duration<br>immediately at or instantly after the time that<br>following the time that<br>from that time/moment<br>while/when<br>earlier than the time when<br>up to the time of |
| **Place** | where<br>anywhere<br>wherever<br>everywhere | a definite place<br>anyplace<br>anyplace<br>everyplace |
| **Distance/frequency** | as + *adverb* + as | comparison |
| **Manner** | as<br>as if<br>as though | in the way or manner that/like |
| **Reason** | because<br>as<br>since | for the reason that |

*(Chart continues on the next page.)*

## ADVERBIAL SUBORDINATORS *(continued)*

| | SUBORDINATOR | MEANING |
|---|---|---|
| **Result** | so + *adjective* + that<br>so + *adverb* + that<br>such a(n) + *noun phrase* + that<br>so much/many/little/few + *noun phrase* + that | with the result that |
| **Purpose** | so that<br>in order that | for the purpose of |
| **Contrast (concession)** | although<br>even though<br>though | unexpected result |
| **Contrast (direct opposition)** | while<br>whereas | direct opposition |

# *Time Clauses*

An adverbial time clause tells when the action described by the independent clause verb took place. The action or situation in a time clause can occur at the same time or at a different time, as part of a sequence of events.

A time clause is introduced by the subordinators *when(ever), while, as soon as, after, since, as, before,* and *until.*

> **When people had to hunt for food,** they had continuous moderate exercise.
> People were eating a lot of protein **while they were living on farms.**
> **After people moved to urban areas,** they had less protein in their diet.
> Our eating habits changed **as soon as food processing methods improved.**

**PRACTICE I**

*Time Clauses*

**A.  STEP 1**   Add a time subordinator to the appropriate sentence in each pair to form an adverbial time clause. Use a different subordinator in each sentence.

**STEP 2**   Write a new sentence by combining the adverbial clause with the independent clause.

**STEP 3**   Circle the subordinator, and punctuate the sentence if necessary.

**Example**

Everyone should know what to do. An earthquake strikes.

Everyone should know what to do (when) an earthquake strikes.

1. If you are inside, move away from windows, and get under a desk or table, or stand in a doorway. You feel the floor begin to shake.

   _____

   _____

2. Try to stay calm. The earthquake is happening.

   _____

3. Don't move. The floor stops shaking.

   _____

4. You are sure the earthquake is over. You may begin to move around.

   _____

   _____

5. You have checked carefully for fallen power lines. You may go outside.

   _____

   _____

B. Write nine original sentences containing adverbial clauses of time. Use each time subordinator once.

# Place Clauses

An adverbial place clause tells where the action described by the main verb took place. A place clause is introduced by the subordinators *where* (a definite place), *wherever* (anyplace), *everywhere* (everyplace), and *anywhere* (anyplace).

> Most people prefer to shop **where they can be sure of quality.**
>
> Consumers usually prefer to do business **wherever credit cards are accepted.**
>
> **Everywhere** I shop, I use my credit cards.
>
> I usually stop for lunch **anywhere that is handy.**[1]

**PRACTICE 2**

*Place Clauses*

A.  **STEP 1**   Add a place subordinator to the appropriate sentence in each pair to form an adverbial clause. Use a different subordinator in each.
    **STEP 2**   Write a new sentence by combining the adverbial clause with the independent clause.
    **STEP 3**   Circle the subordinator, and punctuate the sentence if necessary.

**Example**

People prefer to shop. Credit cards are accepted.

People prefer to shop (where) credit cards are accepted.

1. Consumers have a tendency[2] to buy more. Credit cards are accepted for payment of merchandise.

   _____

   _____

2. You cannot use credit cards. You shop.

   _____

   _____

---

[1] **handy:** conveniently located
[2] **tendency:** possibly acting in a particular way

**3.** There are a few places of business. A credit card is not accepted.

_____

_____

**4.** They are accepted. Travelers can use credit cards in foreign countries.

_____

_____

**B.** Write four original sentences containing adverbial clauses of place. Use each place subordinator once.

# Manner, Distance, and Frequency Clauses

Adverbial clauses of manner, distance, and frequency are introduced by

_as_ + adverb + _as_
_as_
_as if/as though_[1]

Adverbial clauses of manner answer the question "How?"
Adverbial clauses of distance answer the question "How far?"
Adverbial clauses of frequency answer the question "How often?"

The demonstrators left **as the police had ordered**. (manner)

The students completed the experiment **as quickly as they could**. (manner)

Pat jogs on the beach **as far as she can.** (distance)

She jogs on the beach **as often as she can.** (frequency)

Kathleen spoke **as if (as though) she were an authority on the subject.** (manner)

**PRACTICE 3**

_Manner, Distance, and Frequency Clauses_

**A.** **STEP 1** Add a manner, distance, or frequency subordinator in each blank to form an adverbial clause. In some sentences, an adverb is suggested.

**STEP 2** Write a new sentence by combining the adverbial clause with the independent clause.

**Example**

The American people should try to conserve energy. _as often as_ they can (frequency)

_The American people should try to conserve energy as often as they can._

**1.** The public must conserve energy.

_____ the president has requested    (manner)

_____

_____

**2.** Many Americans want to move.

_____ they can from polluted cities    (distance)

_____

_____

_____

[1] When _as if/as though_ introduce a clause that expresses an untrue statement, the verb is similar to the verb in a conditional _if_-clause. (Use _were_, not _was_, with both singular and plural nouns.)

**3.** We should not consume our natural resources.

——————————————— we have in the past   (manner—*wastefully*)

————————————————————————————————————

————————————————————————————————————

**4.** Citizens should make a strong effort to conserve all natural resources.

——————————————— the government has advised   (manner)

————————————————————————————————————

————————————————————————————————————

**5.** The EPA[2] must remind people.

——————————————— they can about the dangers of pollution   (frequency)

————————————————————————————————————

————————————————————————————————————

**6.** No nation in the world can afford to act.

——————————————— pollution were not its problem   (manner—use *as if* or *as though*)

————————————————————————————————————

————————————————————————————————————

**B.** Write four original sentences containing adverbial clauses of manner, distance, and frequency. Use each of these subordinators once: *as, as often as, as far as, as though.*

## Reason Clauses

An adverbial reason clause answers the question "Why?" A reason clause is introduced by the subordinators *because, since,* and *as.*

> Europeans are in some ways better environmentalists than North Americans **because they are more used to conserving energy.**

> **Since many Europeans live, work, and shop in the same locale,** they are quite accustomed to riding bicycles, trains, and streetcars to get around.

> **As the price of gasoline has always been quite high in Europe,** if a European owns an automobile, it is likely to be a high-mileage model that uses diesel fuel.

 **PRACTICE 4**

*Reason Clauses*

**A.   STEP 1**   Add a reason subordinator to the appropriate sentence in each pair to form an adverbial clause.

**STEP 2**   Write a new sentence by combining the adverbial clause with the independent clause.

**STEP 3**   Circle the subordinator, and punctuate the sentence if necessary.

**Example**

Electricity is expensive. Europeans buy energy-saving household appliances such as washing machines that use less water.

⟨Since⟩ electricity is expensive, Europeans buy energy-saving household appliances such as washing machines that use less water.

---

[2] **EPA:** Environmental Protection Agency, a U.S. government agency

1. Europeans experienced hardship and deprivation[1] during and after World War II. They are used to conserving.

   _____

   _____

2. European nations are trying to reduce the level of carbon dioxide in the atmosphere. Carbon dioxide in the atmosphere causes global warming.

   _____

   _____

3. Coal pollutes the air and gives off a lot of carbon dioxide. Most European nations have switched to natural gas or nuclear power to produce electricity.

   _____

   _____

4. In the United States, in contrast, 56 percent of the nation's electricity is generated by burning coal. Coal is cheap and plentiful.

   _____

   _____

5. The parliamentary system in Europe is different. A European head of government has more power than an American president to force industry to make environment-friendly changes.

   _____

   _____

B. Write three sentences of your own containing adverbial clauses of reason. Use each reason subordinator once.

# Result Clauses

An adverbial result clause expresses the result of what is stated in the independent clause. A result clause is introduced by

> *so* + adjective/adverb + *that*
> *such a(n)* + noun phrase + *that*
> *so much/many* + noun phrase + *that*
> *so little/few* + noun phrase + *that*

New textbooks are **so** expensive **that many students buy used ones.**

The cost of education is rising **so** rapidly **that students are looking for ways to cut costs.**

The library is **such** a big place **that I couldn't find the book I needed.**

There is always **so much** noise in the dormitory **that I can't study there.**

There were **so many** students waiting in line to register for classes **that I decided to come back later.**

**PRACTICE 5**

*Result Clauses*

A. **STEP 1**  Add a result subordinator to the first sentence in the following pairs to form an adverbial clause.

   **STEP 2**  Write a new sentence by combining the adverbial clause with the second sentence.

   **STEP 3**  Circle the subordinator.

---

[1] **deprivation:** lack of necessities for living

**Example**

Anthropological museums have realistic displays. A visitor can gain insight into the life-styles of ancient people.

<u>Anthropological museums have (such) realistic displays (that) a visitor</u>
<u>can gain insight into the life-styles of ancient people.</u>

1. The Ancient Peru exhibit was popular. It was held over for two weeks.
   _____
   _____

2. The artifacts[2] were of historic value. Anthropologists from several universities came to study them.
   _____
   _____

3. The exhibits were precious. A museum guard was posted in every room.
   _____
   _____

4. Computer graphics allowed the exhibit's curators[3] to present the lives of ancient Peruvians realistically. You felt that you were actually there.
   _____
   _____

5. There were many exhibits. We couldn't see all of them.
   _____
   _____

B. Write four sentences of your own containing adverbial clauses of result. Use each of the four variants of result subordinators once.

# Purpose Clauses

An adverbial purpose clause states the purpose of the action in the independent clause. The purpose clause is introduced by the subordinators *so that* or *in order that*. The modals *may/might, can/could, will/would,* or *have to* usually occur in a purpose clause. *In order that* is formal.

> Farmers use chemical pesticides **so that they can grow bigger harvests.**
>
> Farmers also spray their fields **in order that consumers might enjoy unblemished[4] fruits and vegetables.**

**Note:** When the subjects of the two clauses are the same, purpose is often expressed by an infinitive phrase (*to grow bigger harvests*), or by an infinitive phrase with *in order to (in order to grow bigger harvests)*, instead of by an adverbial clause. The structure is possible in the first example above but not in the second.

---

[2] **artifacts:** objects such as tools, weapons, pottery, clothing, etc.
[3] **curators:** museum employees who plan, design, and build displays
[4] **unblemished:** free of imperfections

PRACTICE 6

*Purpose Clauses*

**A.** **STEP 1**  Add a purpose subordinator—either *so that* or *in order that*—to the appropriate sentence in order to form an adverbial clause.

**STEP 2**  Write a new sentence by combining the adverbial clause with the independent clause.

**STEP 3**  Circle the subordinator.

**Example**

Chemists are constantly creating new products in the laboratory. People can have substitutes for scarce or unavailable products.

Chemists are constantly creating new products in the laboratory (so that) people can have substitutes for scarce or unavailable products.

**1.**  Chemicals are used in many food products. They will stay fresh longer.

_____

_____

**2.**  They can increase food crops. Most farmers use chemical fertilizers and pesticides.

_____

_____

**3.**  They can produce organic[1] crops. Some farmers use only natural pest control methods.

_____

_____

**4.**  People pay more for organic farm produce. They can avoid food with chemicals.

_____

_____

**5.**  They might avoid potential health risks. They prefer eating organic food.

_____

_____

**B.**  Write two original sentences containing adverbial clauses of purpose. Use each purpose subordinator once.

# Concession (Unexpected Result) Clauses

Adverbial clauses of concession are used to express ideas or actions that are not expected. The information in the independent clause indicates a concession or an unexpected result of something described in the dependent clause. Adverbial clauses of concession are introduced by the subordinators *although, even though,* and *though.*

> **Although I studied all night,** I failed the test.
>
> I failed the test **although I studied all night.**

Notice the difference in meaning between *because* and *even though.*

> **Because the weather was cold,** I didn't go swimming. (expected result)
>
> **Even though the weather was cold,** I went swimming. (unexpected result)

_____

[1] **organic:** grown without chemicals

**PRACTICE 7**

*Concession (Unexpected Result) Clauses*

A. **STEP 1**  Add a concession subordinator to the appropriate sentence, which is always the first action.

**STEP 2**  Rewrite the sentence by combining the adverbial clause with the independent clause, which is the unexpected resulting action.

**STEP 3**  Circle the subordinator, and punctuate the sentence as necessary.

**Example**

She is a famous movie star. She is unhappy.

(Even though) she is a famous movie star, she is unhappy.

1. Beethoven wrote some of the Western world's greatest music. He became totally deaf in mid-life.

2. Global warming is a real problem. Governments have been slow to take action.

3. Korea is becoming an economic superpower. Korea is a small country with few natural resources.

4. Abraham Lincoln became one of the great presidents of the United States. He came from humble[2] origins.

5. Scientists know why earthquakes happen. Scientists are still not able to predict them.

6. Fax machines appeared only recently. They are now the preferred means of transmitting business documents.

B. Write three original sentences containing adverbial clauses of concession (unexpected result). Use each of the subordinators once.

## Contrast (Direct Opposition) Clauses

In this type of adverbial clause, the information in the first clause is the direct opposite of the information in the second clause of the sentence. Use the subordinators *while* or *whereas* to introduce either clause. Place a comma between the two clauses. (This is an exception to the rule.)

San Francisco is very cool during the summer, **whereas San Juan is extremely hot.**

**While San Juan is extremely hot during the summer,** San Francisco is very cool.

---

[2] **humble:** low status

**PRACTICE 8**

*Contrast (Direct Opposition) Adverbial Clauses*

**A.** **STEP 1**   Add a contrast subordinator to either sentence in each pair to form an adverbial clause.

**STEP 2**   Write a new sentence by combining the adverbial clause and the independent clause.

**STEP 3**   Circle the subordinator, and add a comma.

**1.** The West Coast suffered a severe drought. The East Coast had heavy rainfall.

_____

_____

**2.** The Northwest rainfall averages hundreds of inches annually. The Southwest averages less than twelve inches per year.

_____

_____

**3.** The air is polluted in industrial areas. The air is clean in many rural areas.

_____

_____

**4.** Smokers claim the right to smoke in public places. Nonsmokers claim the right to clean air.

_____

_____

**5.** College graduates with degrees in technology are in demand. Graduates with degrees in music are not.

_____

_____

**6.** The most recent spacecraft landed in the desert. Earlier spaceships splashed down in the ocean.

_____

_____

**B.** Write two sentences of your own using adverbial clauses of contrast—direct opposition. Use each subordinator once.

# Review

**1.** An adverbial clause is a dependent clause that answers such questions as Where? When? Why? How? For what purpose?

**2.** Place an adverbial clause either before or after an independent clause. If the adverbial clause comes before an independent clause, it is followed by a comma. If it comes after an independent clause, do not use a comma (except with *whereas/while*).

**3.** There are different types of adverbial clauses, each with its own subordinators.

## ADVERBIAL SUBORDINATORS

| Time | when, whenever, while, as soon as, after, since, as, before, until | **Whenever I had to speak in front of people,** I was paralyzed by fear. |
|---|---|---|
| Place | where, wherever, everywhere, anywhere | I saw unfriendly, critical faces **everywhere I looked.** |
| Manner Distance Frequency | as as + *adverb* + as, as if/as though | I tried **as hard as I could** to calm myself. I tried to act **as if I were not afraid.** |
| Reason | because, since, as | **Since I need to make speeches for career advancement,** I enrolled in a speech class. |
| Purpose | so that, in order that | I took a speech class **so that I could overcome my fear of public speaking.** |
| Result | so + *adjective/adverb* + that such a(n) + *noun* + that so much/little + *noun* + that so many/few + *noun* + that | At first, making a speech made me **so nervous that I got a stomachache before every class.** During the semester, I made **so many speeches that I lost some of my fear.** |
| Concession (unexpected result) | although, even though, though | **Even though I am a politician,** I still don't enjoy speaking in public. |
| Contrast (direct opposition) | while, whereas | As a child, I never tried out for school plays, **whereas my best friend usually got a starring role.** |

You can use adverbial clauses to improve your writing style. As you learned in Chapter 10, good writing in English requires the use of subordinated structures. Adverbial clauses are a common kind of subordinate clause.

**WRITING PRACTICE**

**A.** Complete the following sentences by adding the kinds of adverbial clauses indicated in the parentheses. Circle the subordinators, and add commas if necessary.

**Example**

I reviewed my class notes (before) I took the final exam _____ (time)

1. I bought all of my textbooks _____
_____ . (time)

2. Tom rode on the subway _____
_____ . (distance)

3. _____
_____ the company hired me. (reason)

4. I study in the library _____
_____ . (purpose)

5. _____
_____ I will study for a master's degree. (time)

6. I registered for my classes early _____
_____ . (purpose)

7. A serious student spends time studying _____
_____ . (reason)

8. Tom wanted to become a doctor _____
_____ . (concession)

9. _____
_____ many young couples prefer living together. (concession)

10. Pollution becomes a problem _____
_____ . (place)

11. City living is stressful _____
_____ . (contrast/direct opposition)

12. A single person leads a carefree life _____
_____ . (contrast/direct opposition)

**B.** Fill in the blanks with the correct adverbial subordinators, and punctuate the sentences correctly.

**A Harrowing Experience**

Several years ago _____ (time) I was driving toward Miami from Tampa a tire on my old Toyota blew out. _____ (time phrase) I realized my problem I brought my car to a stop on the side of the highway. _____ (time) I was checking the damaged tire a
5  man stopped his car. _____ (concession) he could not help me I was glad he was there. _____ (time) he left he told me that he would notify the highway patrol. _____ (time) he left I felt nervous again _____ (reason) it was dark, foggy, and windy. _____ (at any time) I saw a car approaching I thought it was
10  someone coming to help me. _____ (time) an hour had passed I saw the flashing lights of a tow truck and my heart sang songs of joy.

_____ (time) the driver would tow my car to Miami I had to
pay him _____ (reason) I didn't carry insurance. Now
_____ (anyplace) I decide to go I doublecheck my car
15  _____ (time) I leave. _____ (concession) I
carry insurance I still don't want to have such a frightening experience again.

**EDITING PRACTICE**

_Adverbial Clauses_

Edit the following essay for errors in adverbial clauses. There are thirteen errors. Look for these kinds of mistakes:

| | |
|---|---|
| An incorrect sentence connector (subordinator or coordinator) is used: | I made an appointment with my history professor,_so_ I could ask his advice about graduate schools. Corrected: I made an appointment with my history professor so that I could ask his advice about graduate school. |
| There are too many sentence connectors: | <u>Even though</u> I am studying five hours a night, <u>but</u> I am still getting low grades. Corrected: Even though I am studying five hours a night, I am still getting low grades. or I am studying five hours a night, but I am still getting low grades. |
| A subordinator is used with the wrong clause: | <u>Because</u> we arrived late, we had a flat tire. Corrected: We arrived late because we had a flat tire. |
| Commas should be added or deleted: | He doesn't eat meat, because he is a vegetarian. Corrected: He doesn't eat meat because he is a vegetarian. |

## Addicted to the Net*

[1] A lot of people enjoy surfing the Net.† [2] They look for interesting Websites and chat with people all over the world. [3] However, some people spend such many hours on-line that they are Internet addicts. [4] Although an average person spends about eight to twelve hours per week, but an addict spends eight to twelve hours per day on-line. [5] Because addicts spend so much time interacting with the computer so it can affect their lives negatively. [6] They

---

* **Net:** shortened from Internet
† **surfing the Net:** exploring the Internet

become social recluses,[*] because they stop going out and talking to people face-to-face. [7]They avoid real-life social situations, preferring instead to be in a dimly lit room with only the glowing screen to light up their lives.

[8]Internet addiction negatively affects not only the addicts themselves, but also the people around them. [9]For example, John's marriage to Marta broke up until he insisted on spending so many hours on the Net. [10]As soon as he arrived home from work he was at his computer. [11]While he finished dinner, he would disappear into his computer room again. [12]He paid so little attention to her, that she finally divorced him.

[13]As college students are especially technologically skilled they can easily become nonstop Net-surfers. [14]Many colleges provide computers at several locations around campus since students can use them at any time day or night. [15]As a result, students can spend too much time surfing the Net instead of "surfing" their textbooks. [16]Last semester, nine freshmen at Berkshire College flunked out[†] although they became Internet addicts.

[17]In short, even though the Internet is an excellent source of information and entertainment, but we must not let it take over our lives.

---

[*] **recluses:** people who withdraw from the world and live in isolation
[†] **flunked out:** left school because of failing grades

# CHAPTER 13

# Relative Clauses

1890s typewriter

## *Introduction*

**A relative clause** is a dependent clause that functions as an adjective; that is, it modifies a noun or pronoun. For this reason, relative clauses are also called **adjective clauses.**

The first American thanksgiving feast**, which took place in 1621,** lasted three days.

Everyone **who studied for the exam** passed it easily.

In the first sentence, the dependent clause *which took place in 1621* is a relative clause that modifies the noun phrase *the first American thanksgiving feast.* This noun phrase is the **antecedent** of the relative clause.

What is the relative clause in the second sentence? What is the antecedent? Is the antecedent a noun or a pronoun?

**Relative Pronouns and Adverbs**

A relative clause begins with a **relative pronoun** or **relative adverb.**

| Pronouns | who, whom, whose, that which, that, whose | refer to humans refer to nonhumans and things |
|---|---|---|
| Adverbs | when, where | refer to a time or a place |

A chart summarizing their use is in the review section at the end of this chapter on page 226.

**Position of Relative Clauses**

Place a relative clause after its antecedent and as close to it as possible to avoid confusion.

Confusing:    He left the gift in his friend's car **that he had just bought.**
    (It is not clear whether the relative clause modifies *car* or *gift*.)

Corrected:    He left the gift **that he had just bought** in his friend's car.
    (The relative clause clearly modifies *gift*.)

Occasionally, a prepositional phrase comes between the antecedent and the relative clause.

Manuel was visited by **a friend** (from San Juan) **who was touring the country.**

Try writing **a sentence** (of your own) **that contains a relative clause.**

**Verb Agreement in Relative Clauses**

The verb in a relative clause should agree in number with its antecedent.
    Compare:

A person **who works part-time** usually receives no benefits.
(The verb *works* is singular to agree with the singular antecedent *person*.)

People **who work part-time** usually receive no benefits.
(The verb *work* is plural to agree with the plural antecedent *people*.)

**Punctuation of Relative Clauses**

Relative clauses are either restrictive (necessary) or nonrestrictive (unnecessary). A restrictive clause is necessary because it identifies its antecedent for the reader. Do not use commas with restrictive clauses.

The professor **who teaches my biology class** won a Nobel Prize two years ago.

(Which professor won a Nobel Prize two years ago? The clause *who teaches my biology class* is necessary to identify the professor.)

He won the prize for research **that might lead to a cure for AIDS**.

(For which research did he win the prize? We need the clause *that might lead to a cure for AIDS* to tell us.)

A nonrestrictive clause is not necessary to identify its antecedent; it merely gives the reader some extra information. Because it can be omitted without loss of meaning, separate it from the rest of the sentence with commas.

Professor Jones**, who teaches my biology class,** won a Nobel Prize two years ago.

(The person who won a Nobel Prize is identified by his name, so the clause *who teaches my biology class* is extra, unnecessary information about Professor Jones. If it were omitted, we would still know which person won the Nobel Prize.)

He won the prize for his research into the structure of T-cells**, which might lead to a cure for AIDS.**

(We already know which research he won the prize for: his research into the structure of T-cells. The information *which might lead to a cure for AIDS* is not necessary to identify the research; it merely gives us extra information about it.)

**PRACTICE 1**

*Restrictive and
Nonrestrictive Clauses*

**STEP 1**   Underline the relative clause or clauses in each sentence. (Some sentences have two.)

**STEP 2**   In the parentheses, write R for a restrictive and NR for a nonrestrictive clause.

**STEP 3**   Add commas to the nonrestrictive clauses.

**Example**

(R)   Families <u>whose incomes are below a certain level</u> pay no income tax.

(NR)   My family, <u>whose income is more than $50,000,</u> pays about 25 percent income tax.

(   ) **1.** The sun which in forty minutes can produce enough solar energy to meet humankind's needs for a year is one of Earth's potential sources of power.

(   ) **2.** According to an article that appeared in <u>Time</u> magazine we are at the beginning of a medical computer revolution.

(   ) **3.** A medical computer is a machine that analyzes the results of laboratory tests and electrocardiograms.

(   ) **4.** Laser beams which are useful in both medicine and industry were first predicted in science fiction stories seventy-five years ago.

(   ) **5.** Physicians who feed patient symptoms into the computer receive a list of diseases that fit the symptoms of their patients.

(   ) **6.** The country that has the highest per capita[1] income is not the United States which is in third place.

(   ) **7.** Kuwait which is a small country in the Middle East is in first place.

(   ) **8.** It was a thrilling experience to meet the author of the book that we had been reading all semester.

(   ) **9.** The public is highly critical of the tobacco industry whose profits have been increasing in spite of the health risks of smoking.

---

[1] **per capita:** per person (literally, "per head" in Latin)

( ) **10.** Carbohydrates which are composed of carbon, hydrogen, and oxygen are organic compounds.

( ) **11.** People who use body language[1] to express themselves are interesting to watch.

( ) **12.** My brother-in-law who is from Italy moves his hands a lot when he is talking.

( ) **13.** The man whom my sister married is Italian; he uses his hands as much as he uses his mouth to communicate.

( ) **14.** X-ray machines are gradually being replaced by machines that can provide clearer, more detailed images of the human body, its tissues, and its organs.

( ) **15.** X-ray machines are gradually being replaced by CAT scanners and MRI devices which can provide clearer, more detailed images of the human body, its tissues, and its organs.

( ) **16.** The company promised to reimburse[2] everyone who had bought a defective[3] product.

( ) **17.** Students whose grade point averages fall below 2.0 will be placed on probation.

( ) **18.** She plans to marry her childhood sweetheart whom she has known since they were five years old.

( ) **19.** The Republican party whose goal is to win the election accused the Democrats of using fund-raising practices that are unethical and possibly illegal.

( ) **20.** My English teacher enjoys novels that combine history and fiction; <u>Pillars of Stone</u> which tells about the construction of the great Gothic cathedrals in Europe during the Middle Ages is one of her favorites.

There are different types of relative clauses. In each different kind, the relative pronoun has a different function. It may be a subject or an object in its own clause, or it may replace a possessive word.

# Relative Pronouns as Subjects

A relative pronoun may be the subject of its own clause. Subject pattern relative clauses are formed as follows:

| | |
|---|---|
| *who* | |
| *which* | + verb + complement |
| *that* | |

Football, **which is the most popular American sport,** began at Harvard University.

Study the following examples to see how sentences a and b in each set are combined to form new sentence c, which contains a subject pattern relative clause. The subject in sentence b, which changes to a relative pronoun, is crossed through. Notice how *that* is used in restrictive clauses only.

---

[1] **body language:** communication by body movements
[2] **reimburse:** pay money back to
[3] **defective:** flawed; not in working condition

## RELATIVE PRONOUNS FOR HUMANS

| Restrictive<br>*who, that* | **1. a.** People save time and energy.<br>**b.** ~~They~~ use microwave ovens.<br>**c.** People **who use microwave ovens** save time and energy.<br>People **that use microwave ovens** save time and energy. (informal) |
|---|---|
| Nonrestrictive<br>*who* | **2. a.** Microwave cooking is not popular with most professional chefs.<br>**b.** ~~Professional chefs~~ say that fast cooking doesn't allow flavors to blend.<br>**c.** Microwave cooking is not popular with most professional chefs**, who say that fast cooking doesn't allow flavors to blend.** |

## RELATIVE PRONOUNS FOR NONHUMANS/THINGS

| Restrictive<br>*that* | **3. a.** Ovens are capable of cooking food quickly.<br>**b.** ~~They~~ use microwave energy.<br>**c.** Ovens **that use microwave energy** are capable of cooking foods quickly. |
|---|---|
| Nonrestrictive<br>*which* | **4. a.** An electron tube in the oven produces microwaves.<br>**b.** ~~Microwaves~~ cook by agitating[4] the water molecules in food.<br>**c.** An electron tube in the oven produces microwaves**, which cook by agitating the water molecules in food.** |

**PRACTICE 2**

*Relative Pronouns as Subjects*

**A.** Combine the two sentences in each pair to make a new complex sentence containing a relative clause in the subject pattern. Follow these steps:

**STEP 1** Change the subject of the second sentence to a relative pronoun. Use *who, which,* or *that* as appropriate.

**STEP 2** Combine the two sentences, placing the relative clause as close to its antecedent as possible.

**STEP 3** Add commas if the relative clause is nonrestrictive.

**1.** John Fish explained the complex structure of DNA. He is a research chemist.

_____

**2.** While he lectured, he showed us a slide. The slide diagrammed the double helix structure of DNA.

_____

_____

[4] **agitating:** moving very quickly

3. Words in English are often difficult for foreigners to pronounce. They begin with the consonants th.

_____

_____

4. Foreigners also have difficulty with English spelling. English spelling is not always consistent with its pronunciation.

_____

_____

5. Anyone must have a logical mind. He or she wants to be a computer programmer.

_____

_____

6. Fans quickly lose interest in a sports team. The team loses game after game.

_____

_____

B. Write six sentences of your own that contain relative clauses in the subject pattern. Use the following prompts, and then write two sentences of your own. Write both restrictive and nonrestrictive clauses.

1. My father, who _____

_____

2. _____

_____ anyone who _____

3. _____ is a sport that _____

_____

4. Mount Everest, which _____

_____

5. _____

_____

6. _____

_____

# Relative Pronouns as Objects

A relative pronoun may be an object in its own clause. Object pattern relative clauses are formed as follows:

| | |
|---|---|
| *whom*<br><br>*which*<br><br>*that*<br><br>*ø*[1] | + subject + verb + complement |
| The address **that he gave me** was incorrect. | |

---

[1] The symbol ø indicates that relative pronouns can be left out.

In the following examples, notice how sentences a and b are combined to make sentence c, which contains an object pattern relative clause. The object in sentence b, which changes to a relative pronoun, is crossed through. Notice how *that* is used in restrictive clauses only and may be left out entirely in object pattern clauses.

<table>
<tr><td colspan="2" style="text-align:center">**RELATIVE PRONOUNS FOR HUMANS**</td></tr>
<tr>
<td>**Restrictive**<br>*whom, that, ø*</td>
<td>**1. a.** The professor is chair of the English Department.<br>**b.** You should see ~~the professor~~.<br>**c.** The professor **whom you should see** is chair of the English Department.<br>The professor **that you should see** is chair of the English Department. (informal)<br>The professor **you should see** is chair of the English Department.</td>
</tr>
<tr>
<td>**Nonrestrictive**<br>*whom*</td>
<td>**2. a.** Dr. White is an ecologist.<br>**b.** You met ~~Dr. White~~ in my office.<br>**c.** Dr. White, **whom you met in my office,** is an ecologist.</td>
</tr>
<tr><td colspan="2" style="text-align:center">**RELATIVE PRONOUNS FOR NONHUMANS/THINGS**</td></tr>
<tr>
<td>**Restrictive**<br>*that, ø*</td>
<td>**3. a.** The book was written in German.<br>**b.** The professor translated ~~the book~~.<br>**c.** The book **that the professor translated** was written in German.<br>The book **the professor translated** was written in German.</td>
</tr>
<tr>
<td>**Nonrestrictive**<br>*which*</td>
<td>**4. a.** Environmental science is one of the most popular courses in the college.<br>**b.** Dr. White teaches ~~environmental science~~.<br>**c.** Environmental science, **which Dr. White teaches,** is one of the most popular courses in the college.</td>
</tr>
</table>

**PRACTICE 3**

*Relative Pronouns as Objects*

**A.** Combine the two sentences in each pair to make a new sentence containing a relative clause in the object pattern. Follow these steps:

**STEP 1**   Change the object in the second sentence to a relative pronoun. Use *whom, which, that,* or no pronoun as appropriate. Move the relative pronoun to the beginning of its clause.

**STEP 2**   Combine the two sentences, placing the new relative clause as close to its antecedent as possible.

**STEP 3**   Add commas if the relative clause is nonrestrictive.

   1. Albert Einstein was a high school dropout. The world recognizes him as a genius.
      _____
      _____

   2. As a young boy, Einstein had trouble in elementary and high school. He attended these schools in Germany.
      _____
      _____

   3. He did poorly in subjects. He disliked them.
      _____
      _____

   4. The only subjects were mathematics and physics. He loved them.
      _____
      _____

   5. He developed theories. We use theories to help us understand the nature of the universe.
      _____
      _____

   6. Einstein is best known for his General Theory of Relativity. He began to develop this theory while living in Switzerland.
      _____
      _____

   **B.** Write six sentences of your own that contain relative clauses in the object pattern. Use the prompts given, and then write two sentences of your own. Write both restrictive and nonrestrictive clauses.

   1. My mother, whom _____

   2. _____ the homework that _____

   3. _____ someone whom _____

   4. The islands of the Caribbean, which _____

   5. _____

   6. _____

# Possessive Relative Clauses

In these clauses, which show possession, the relative pronoun *whose* replaces a possessive word such as *Mary's, his, our, their, the company's,* or *its.* Possessive relative clauses can follow the subject or the object pattern, and they may be restrictive or nonrestrictive.

***Subject Pattern***    Subject pattern possessive clauses are formed as follows:

| |
|---|
| *whose* + noun    + verb + complement |
| Princess Diana, **whose life ended suddenly in a Paris car crash,** was the most photographed woman in the world. |

In the following examples, notice how sentences a and b are combined to make sentence c, which contains a possessive relative clause in the subject pattern. The possessive word in sentence b, which changes to *whose*, is crossed through.

| POSSESSIVE RELATIVE PRONOUNS FOR HUMANS AND NONHUMANS/THINGS[1] | |
|---|---|
| **Restrictive** *whose* | **1. a.** Opportunities for college graduates are on the upswing.[2] <br><br> **b.** ~~College graduates~~' degrees are in computer engineering. <br><br> **c.** Opportunities for college graduates **whose degrees are in computer engineering** are on the upswing. |
| **Nonrestrictive** *whose* | **2. a.** Santa Claus is the symbol of Christmas gift-giving. <br><br> **b.** ~~His~~ portly[3] figure appears everywhere during the Christmas season. <br><br> **c.** Santa Claus, **whose portly figure appears everywhere during the Christmas season,** is the symbol of Christmas gift-giving. |

**PRACTICE 4**

*Possessive Relative Clauses—Subject Pattern*

Combine the two sentences in each pair to make a new sentence containing a possessive relative clause in the subject pattern. Follow these steps:

**STEP 1**    Find a possessive expression in the second sentence and change it to *whose*.

**STEP 2**    Combine the two sentences, placing the new relative clause as close to its antecedent as possible.

**STEP 3**    Add commas if the relative clause is nonrestrictive.

1. Securities Corporation's president is a man. His expertise[4] on financial matters is well known.

_____

_____

---

[1] Some teachers feel that *whose* may only be used to refer to humans. For nonhumans, they recommend using *of which*. Compare: I returned the book **whose** cover was torn. I returned the book, the cover **of which** was torn. Other teachers feel that *whose* is acceptable in all but the most formal writing.

[2] **on the upswing:** increasing

[3] **portly:** comfortably fat

[4] **expertise:** skill; knowledge

**2.** First National Bank tries to attract female customers. The bank's president is a woman.

_____

_____

**3.** Companies conduct market research to discover trends among consumers. Consumers' tastes change rapidly.

_____

_____

**4.** A manufacturer can offer lower prices. Its costs are lower because of mass production.

_____

_____

## *Object Pattern*

Object pattern possessive clauses are formed as follows:

| *whose* + noun        + subject + verb + complement |
| --- |
| Maya Angelou, **whose poetry we have been reading in our English class,** is one of America's most famous female poets. |

In the following examples, notice how sentences a and b are combined to make sentence c, which contains a possessive relative clause in the object pattern. The possessive word in sentence b, which changes to *whose*, is crossed through.

| POSSESSIVE RELATIVE PRONOUNS FOR HUMANS AND NONHUMANS/THINGS | |
| --- | --- |
| **Restrictive** *whose* | **1.** **a.** The citizens could do nothing. <br> **b.** The government had confiscated[1] ~~their~~ property. <br> **c.** The citizens **whose property the government had confiscated** could do nothing. |
| **Nonrestrictive** *whose* | **2.** **a.** *Consumer Reports* magazine publishes comparative evaluations of all kinds of products. <br> **b.** Shoppers trust ~~the magazine's~~ research. <br> **c.** *Consumer Reports,* **whose research shoppers trust,** publishes comparative evaluations of all kinds of products. |

**PRACTICE 5**

*Possessive Relative Clauses—Object Pattern*

Combine the two sentences in each pair to make a new sentence containing a possessive relative clause in the object pattern. Follow these steps:

**STEP 1**  Find a possessive expression in the second sentence and change it to *whose*. Move the *whose* + noun phrase to the beginning of the clause.

**STEP 2**  Combine the two sentences, placing the new relative clause as close to its antecedent as possible.

**STEP 3**  Add commas if the relative clause is nonrestrictive.

---

[1] **confiscated:** taken by government authority

1. Princess Diana was mourned by rich and poor people alike. The whole world watched her funeral on television.

   _____

   _____

2. William Shakespeare lived and wrote 400 years ago. High school students struggle to understand his English.

   _____

   _____

3. Nike is a sporting goods company. Most people recognize the company's "swoosh" symbol.

   _____

   _____

4. The actress has starred in several successful films. I can't remember her name.

   _____

   _____

**PRACTICE 6**

*Possessive Relative Clauses—Subject or Object Pattern*

Write four sentences containing possessive relative clauses in either the subject or the object pattern. Use the following prompts if you wish, or write sentences that are entirely your own.

1. (a child whose parents) _____

   _____

2. (Michael Jordan, whose picture) _____

   _____

3. (my cousin, whose car) _____

   _____

4. (teachers whose classes) _____

   _____

# *Relative Pronouns as Objects of Prepositions*

A relative pronoun may be the object of a preposition in its own clause. These relative clauses are formed in two ways, the formal way and the informal way. The clauses may be either restrictive or nonrestrictive.

| **Formal** | preposition + *whom* / *which* + subject + verb + complement |
|---|---|
| | The person **to whom I mailed the letter** never received it. |
| **Informal** | *whom* *which* *that* ø + subject + verb + complement + preposition |
| | The person **whom I mailed the letter to** never received it. |

In the formal pattern, the preposition comes before the relative pronoun. In the informal pattern, the preposition comes at the end of the clause.

In the following examples, notice how sentences a and b are combined to make a new sentence containing a relative clause. The object of the preposition in sentence b, which changes to a relative pronoun, is crossed through. Sentence c is formal, and the sentences in d are informal. Notice how *that* is used only in informal pattern restrictive clauses; it may also be omitted.

| RELATIVE PRONOUNS FOR HUMANS | |
|---|---|
| **Restrictive**<br>*whom, that, ø* | **1. a.** The candidate lost the election.<br>  **b.** I voted for ~~the candidate~~.<br>  **c.** The candidate **for whom I voted** lost the election.<br>  **d.** The candidate **whom I voted for** lost the election.<br>    The candidate **that I voted for** lost the election.<br>    The candidate **I voted for** lost the election |
| **Nonrestrictive**<br>*whom* | **2. a.** Mayor Pyle lost the election.<br>  **b.** I voted for ~~Mayor Pyle~~.<br>  **c.** Mayor Pyle, **for whom I voted,** lost the election.<br>  **d.** Mayor Pyle, **whom I voted for,** lost the election. |
| RELATIVE PRONOUNS FOR NONHUMANS/THINGS | |
| **Restrictive**<br>*which, that, ø* | **3. a.** No one had read the book.<br>  **b.** He quoted from ~~the book~~.<br>  **c.** No one had read from the book **from which he quoted.**<br>  **d.** No one had read the book **which he quoted from.**<br>    No one had read the book **that he quoted from.**<br>    No one had read the book **he quoted from.** |
| **Nonrestrictive**<br>*which* | **4. a.** The position of office manager has been filled.<br>  **b.** He applied for ~~the position of office manager~~.<br>  **c.** The position of office manager, **for which he applied,** has been filled. |

**PRACTICE 7**

*Relative Pronouns as Objects of Prepositions*

**A.** Change the second sentence in each pair to a relative clause, and combine it with the first sentence. The prepositional phrase that you should change is underlined. Write each new sentence twice: once in the formal pattern and once in an informal pattern.

1. Finding reasonably priced housing in big cities is a problem. Many young people are concerned <u>about the problem</u>.

   Formal pattern: ⸺⸺⸺⸺⸺⸺⸺⸺⸺⸺⸺

   Informal pattern: ⸺⸺⸺⸺⸺⸺⸺⸺⸺⸺

2. Affordable apartments are scarce. Young people would like to live <u>in them</u>.

   Formal pattern: ⸺⸺⸺⸺⸺⸺⸺⸺⸺⸺⸺

   Informal pattern: ⸺⸺⸺⸺⸺⸺⸺⸺⸺⸺

3. Of course, many young people share apartments, but they have to choose roommates carefully. They will share living space and expenses <u>with these roommates</u>.

   Formal pattern: ⸺⸺⸺⸺⸺⸺⸺⸺⸺⸺⸺

   Informal pattern: ⸺⸺⸺⸺⸺⸺⸺⸺⸺⸺

4. Living with people can be stressful, but it can also be fun. You are not related <u>to the people</u>.

   Formal pattern: ⸺⸺⸺⸺⸺⸺⸺⸺⸺⸺⸺

   Informal pattern: ⸺⸺⸺⸺⸺⸺⸺⸺⸺⸺

5. In many countries, young people continue to live with their parents in the same house. They grew up <u>in that house</u>.

   Formal pattern: ⸺⸺⸺⸺⸺⸺⸺⸺⸺⸺⸺

   Informal pattern: ⸺⸺⸺⸺⸺⸺⸺⸺⸺⸺

6. In the United States, young people don't want to live with their parents. They typically declare their independence <u>from their parents</u> at age eighteen.

   Formal pattern: ⸺⸺⸺⸺⸺⸺⸺⸺⸺⸺⸺

   Informal pattern: ⸺⸺⸺⸺⸺⸺⸺⸺⸺⸺

B. Now write two sentences of your own. Write each sentence twice: once in the formal pattern and once in the informal pattern.

1. Formal pattern: ⸺⸺⸺⸺⸺⸺⸺⸺⸺⸺⸺

   Informal pattern: ⸺⸺⸺⸺⸺⸺⸺⸺⸺⸺

2. Formal pattern: ⸺⸺⸺⸺⸺⸺⸺⸺⸺⸺⸺

   Informal pattern: ⸺⸺⸺⸺⸺⸺⸺⸺⸺⸺

# *Relative Pronouns in Phrases of Quantity and Quality*

A relative pronoun can also occur in phrases of quantity:

> some of which, one of whom, all of whom, each of which, etc.

and in phrases of quality:

> the best of which, the most important of whom, the more economical of which, the loveliest of which, the oldest of whom, the least expensive of which, etc.

Relative clauses containing these phrases can follow the subject or object pattern, and they are always nonrestrictive.

| | |
|---|---|
| *many of which* | + (subject) + verb + complement |
| *the oldest of whom* | + (subject) + verb + complement |

> While scuba diving in the Caribbean, I saw tropical fish, **many of which I photographed with my new underwater camera.**
>
> He has three daughters, **the oldest of whom is studying abroad.**

In the following examples, notice how sentence a and b are combined to form a new sentence c, which contains a relative clause. The object in sentence b (always following the preposition *of*) is crossed through and replaced by a relative pronoun (always *whom* or *which*).

| RELATIVE PRONOUNS FOR HUMANS | |
|---|---|
| **Nonrestrictive** *whom* | **1. a.** The citizens of Puerto Rico are well educated. <br> **b.** Ninety percent of ~~them~~ are literate.[1] <br> **c.** The citizens of Puerto Rico, **ninety percent of whom are literate,** are well educated. |

| RELATIVE PRONOUNS FOR NONHUMANS/THINGS | |
|---|---|
| **Nonrestrictive** *which* | **2. a.** There are many delicious tropical fruits in Puerto Rico. <br> **b.** I have never tasted most of ~~them~~ before. <br> **c.** There are many delicious tropical fruits in Puerto Rico, **most of which I have never tasted before.** |

---

[1] **literate:** able to read and write

**PRACTICE 8**

*Relative Clauses with Phrases of Quantity and Quality*

**A.** Change the second sentence in each pair to a relative clause, and combine it with the first sentence. Follow the examples in the chart.

**1.** There is a chain of islands in the Caribbean Sea. The most charming of the islands is Puerto Rico, "The Land of Enchantment."

_____

_____

**2.** Puerto Rico attracts thousands of visitors. Most of them come for the sunny weather, the beautiful beaches, and the Spanish atmosphere.

_____

_____

**3.** Puerto Rico has many historic sites. The most famous of them are in the Old San Juan area of the capital city.

_____

_____

**4.** Puerto Rico's economy is growing. The most important sector² of the economy is clothing manufacturing.

_____

_____

**5.** Puerto Ricans have strong ties to the United States. All of them are U.S. citizens.

_____

_____

**6.** Puerto Rico has three political parties. One of them favors Puerto Rico's becoming a state.

_____

_____

**B.** Now write two sentences of your own. Write one sentence with *of whom* and one sentence with *of which*.

**1.** _____

_____

**2.** _____

_____

# Adverbial Relative Clauses

Relative clauses may also be introduced by the **relative adverbs** *when* and *where*. **Adverbial relative clauses** refer to a time or a place, and they replace entire prepositional phrases like *on Sunday* and *in the city*. Adverbial relative clauses may be restrictive or nonrestrictive. They are composed of

| | |
|---|---|
| *when* *where* | + subject + verb + complement |

| |
|---|
| The lives of thousands of Germans changed during the night of August 13, 1961, **when East German soldiers began building the Berlin Wall.** |

² **sector:** part; division

| RELATIVE ADVERBS FOR TIME AND PLACE | | | |
|---|---|---|---|
| *when* | refers to a time | restrictive | The lives of thousands of Germans suddenly changed on the night **when East German soldiers began building the Berlin Wall.** |
| | | nonrestrictive | On November 9, 1989, **when the wall was torn down,** their lives changed again. |
| *where* | refers to a place | restrictive | The city **where citizens had lived, worked, and shopped relatively freely** was suddenly divided. |
| | | nonrestrictive | Berlin, **where citizens had lived, worked, and shopped relatively freely,** was suddenly divided. |

In the following examples, notice how sentences a and b are combined to form a new sentence c, which contains an adverbial relative clause. The prepositional phrase in sentence b, which is entirely replaced by the relative adverb, is crossed through.

| TIME | |
|---|---|
| **Restrictive and nonrestrictive *when*** | **1. a.** Ramadan is the month.<br>    **b.** Devout[1] Muslims fast[2] ~~during the month~~.<br>    **c.** Ramadan is the month **when devout Muslims fast.** |

| PLACE | |
|---|---|
| **Restrictive and nonrestrictive *where*** | **2. a.** The Saudi Arabian city of Mecca is the holiest city in Islam.<br>    **b.** Mohammed was born ~~in Mecca~~.<br>    **c.** The Saudi Arabian city of Mecca, **where Mohammed was born,** is the holiest city in Islam. |

**PRACTICE 9**

*Adverbial Relative Clauses*

**A.** Combine the two sentences in each pair, changing the second sentence into an adverbial relative clause. Add commas if necessary.

**1.** Germany had been divided into two countries since 1945. It was defeated in World War II in 1945.

_____

_____

**2.** 1989 was the year. The Berlin Wall was torn down in that year.

_____

_____

---
[1] **devout:** religious
[2] **fast:** voluntarily do not eat food

**3.** In 1990, Germany became one country again. East and West Germany were reunited in 1990.

_____

_____

**4.** East Germany became part of the Federal Republic of Germany. People had lived under communist rule in East Germany.

_____

_____

**5.** There was rejoicing in areas. Germans looked forward to reunification with their fellow citizens in some areas.

_____

_____

**6.** There was anxiety in places. People feared losing their jobs in some places.

_____

_____

**B.** Write four sentences of your own containing adverbial relative clauses, two sentences using _when_ and two sentences using _where_. Try to write both restrictive and nonrestrictive clauses. You may use the prompts given or write sentences that are entirely your own.

**1.** My grandmother enjoys telling about the time when _____

_____

**2.** _____

_____

**3.** _____ my hometown, where _____

_____

**4.** _____

_____

# Review

**1.** A relative clause is a dependent clause that functions as an adjective; that is, it modifies a noun or pronoun in the independent clause. For this reason, relative clauses are also called adjective clauses. The modified noun or pronoun is called the antecedent.
**2.** A relative clause begins with a relative pronoun or a relative adverb.
**3.** Place a relative clause after its antecedent and as close to it as possible to avoid confusion of meaning.
**4.** The verb in a relative clause should agree in number with its antecedent.
**5.** Relative clauses are either restrictive (necessary) or nonrestrictive (unnecessary). Add commas before and after nonrestrictive clauses.

| RELATIVE PRONOUNS | | | | |
|---|---|---|---|---|
| **who** | refers to humans | subject in its own clause | restrictive or nonrestrictive | The professor **who teaches my biology class** won a Nobel Prize two years ago. Professor Jones, **who teaches my biology class,** won a Nobel Prize two years ago. |
| **whom** | refers to humans | object in its own clause | restrictive or nonrestrictive | She loaned her car to someone **whom she didn't know.** Professor Jones, **whom I have for biology,** won a Nobel Prize two years ago. |
| **whose** | refers to humans, nonhumans, and things; shows possession | subject or object in its own clause | restrictive or nonrestrictive | I studied algebra from a professor **whose name I have forgotten.** Apple Computer, **whose Macintosh computer changed computing,** was started by two men working in a garage. |
| **which** | refers to nonhumans and things | subject or object in its own clause | nonrestrictive only | She teaches biology, **which is my favorite subject.** Her husband teaches algebra, **which I enjoy the least.** |
| **that** | refers to nonhumans and things; informally, refers to humans | subject or object in its own clause; if *that* is an object, it may be omitted | restrictive only | The class **that meets in the next room** is very noisy. The subject **that I enjoy the least** is algebra. The subject **I enjoy the least** is algebra. The salesman **that sold me my car** was fired. (informal) |
| RELATIVE ADVERBS | | | | |
| **when** | refers to a time | | restrictive or nonrestrictive | I work full time on days **when I don't have classes.** I didn't work last week, **when I had my final exams.** |
| **where** | refers to a place | | restrictive or nonrestrictive | She has never returned to the city **where she was born.** First City Bank, **where I have a checking account,** was robbed last week. |

You can use relative clauses to improve your writing style. As you know, writing that contains subordinate structures is more sophisticated than writing that contains mostly simple simple and compound sentences. Relative clauses are one of the ways to subordinate. (However, take care not to use too many relative clauses. A paragraph or essay that is filled with too many *who*'s and *which*'s is not good either.)

**EDITING PRACTICE**

*Relative Clauses*

**A.** Edit the following essay for errors in relative clauses. You should make 17 changes. Look for these kinds of errors:

| | |
|---|---|
| Incorrect relative pronoun was chosen: | I telephoned the student ~~which~~ *whose* wallet I found in the parking lot. |
| Verb and antecedent don't agree: | People who ~~lives~~ *live* in earthquake zones need earthquake insurance. |
| Nouns or pronouns are repeated: | My friend whom I loaned my car to ~~him~~ returned it with several dents. |
| Commas should be added or deleted: | Electronic pagers, which always seem to beep at inappropriate times, should be turned off during concerts, lectures, and naps. |

### El Niño

Recently, scientists have begun studying an ocean event who is the cause of

drastic changes in weather around the world. This event is an increase in the

temperature of the Pacific Ocean that appear around Christmas off the coast of

Peru. Hence, the Peruvian fishermen whom first noticed it named it El Niño

5   whose its name means "the Christ child" in Spanish. The causes of this rise in

ocean temperatures are unknown, but its effects are obvious and devastating.

One of El Niño's far-reaching effects is that it threatens Peru's vital

anchovy harvest, that could mean higher prices for food. The warm water of

El Niño keeps the nutrient-rich cold water which anchovies need down at the

10  bottom of the ocean. Anchovies are the primary source of fish meal which is

the main ingredient in livestock and chicken feed. In addition, guano[1] from

birds who feed off the anchovies is a major source of fertilizer for farmers.

---

[1] **guano:** droppings of seabirds and bats

As a result of decreasing supplies of anchovies and guano, the price of chicken feed, livestock feed, and fertilizer rises. This causes farmers, who they

15  must pay more for feed and fertilizer, to charge more for the food that they produces. The price of eggs, meat, and even bread has soared as a result of El Niños in past years.

El Niño has other global effects. It can cause heavy rains, floods, and mudslides along the coasts of North and South America and droughts[1] in

20  other parts of the world. In the 1982–83 El Niño, West Africa suffered a terrible drought which caused crop failures and food shortages. Lack of rain also created problems for Indonesia whose forests burned for months during the 1997–98 El Niño. Winds spread smoke from these fires as far north as Malaysia and Singapore, resulting in choking smog, that closed schools and

25  caused pedestrians to don[2] masks.

Indeed, El Niño is an unpredictable and uncontrollable phenomenon of nature, that we need to study it and understand it in order to prepare for and perhaps lessen its devastating effects in the future.

**B.**  Improve the following essay. Combine some of the sentences, using relative clauses.

### Two Childhood Friends

My two best friends from high school were complete opposites. Their names were Rafael and Cecilia. Rafael was an introverted, studious, dependable friend. Rafael lived in a small house down the street from us. His two sisters were younger than he. His mother was divorced. Cecilia, on the other

5  hand, was extroverted, not at all studious, and totally undependable. She lived next door to us.

The house next door was very noisy. Cecilia lived in the house with five siblings. Music blaring from at least two radios fought constantly with noise blasting from the TV. The TV was always turned on. The six Garcia children

10  often invited me over to play. Each of them had lots of friends. As a result, there was always a group of children at the Garcias. I went over to Cecilia's house sometimes. I was bored and lonely sometimes.

---

[1] **droughts:** periods of little rainfall
[2] **don:** put on

Rafael's house was in total contrast to Cecilia's. It was calm and peaceful in his house. I used to go there on evenings. I needed to study on those

15    evenings. Rafael and his friends spent most evenings doing homework together or surfing the Net. His friends were quiet types.

Mrs. Garcia, Cecilia's mother, never seemed to mind fixing snacks for fifteen or twenty kids. She loved to cook. Mrs. Menendez, Rafael's mother, was always too busy to fix us snacks, but she didn't mind if we made our own. She

20    owned a small bookstore. She worked there every day. She often did her bookkeeping at night. She came home at night.

Cecilia, Rafael, and I were good friends during all of our high school years. I still don't understand how people could be friends. The people are so different from each other.

## Writing Technique Questions

**1.** What kind of organization does each of the two essays in this practice use?
**2.** What is the thesis statement of each?
**3.** Circle the transition signals and structure words in each essay.

# CHAPTER

# 14 Participial Phrases

1990s computer screen

## *Participles*

A **participle** is a word that is formed from a verb and used as an adjective to modify nouns.

Notice how an active voice verb is changed to a present participle by adding the suffix *-ing* to the verb. An active voice verb (present, past, or future tense) becomes a present participle.

230

## CHANGING ACTIVE VERBS TO PARTICIPLES

| Verbs | Present Participles |
|---|---|
| The custom **fascinates** me.<br>The woman **jogged** in the park.<br>The hostages **will return** soon. | The **fascinating** custom interests me.<br>The **jogging** woman ran through the park.<br>The **returning** hostages were treated like heroes. |

Now notice how a passive voice verb (present or past tense) becomes a past participle.

## CHANGING PASSIVE VERBS TO PARTICIPLES

| Verbs | Past Participles |
|---|---|
| The movie **is rated "X."**<br>The steak **was burned.**<br>My heart **was broken.** | The **X-rated** movie was banned.[1]<br>The **burned** steak tasted terrible.<br>My **broken** heart will never heal. |

**Note:** The terms *present* and *past participle* are misleading because these forms have nothing to do with present tense or past tense. Rather, they are based on active or passive voice. The present participle comes from an active voice verb, and the past participle comes from a passive voice verb.

There are also perfect and continuous forms of participles, as shown in the following chart.

## SUMMARY OF PARTICIPLE FORMS[2]

| Forms | Active | Passive |
|---|---|---|
| The **general forms** do not indicate time; time is determined by the main clause verb. | verb + *ing*<br>opening | verb + *ed, en, t, d*<br>opened    bought<br>taken      sold |
| The **continuous form** emphasizes action going on *right now*; may also express future time. | | *being* + past participle<br>being opened |
| The **perfect forms** emphasize that the action happened before the time of the main clause verb. | *having* + past participle<br>having opened | *having been* + past participle<br>having been opened |

---

[1] **banned:** forbidden
[2] There is a sixth participle form, the perfect continuous active: Having been playing tennis all morning, my hand has become cramped. It is not included here because it is not commonly used.

# Participial Phrases

**Participial phrases** are groups of words that contain participles + other modifiers. They are used to modify nouns and pronouns as follows:

A car, **speeding the wrong way down the street,** struck a pedestrian.
**Speeding the wrong way down the street,** a car struck a pedestrian.
**While crossing the street,** a pedestrian was struck by a car.

Participial phrases can be formed by reducing relative clauses and adverbial clauses.

## Participial Phrases from Relative Clauses

Participial phrases are formed by reducing subject pattern relative clauses.

| ADJECTIVE CLAUSES | PARTICIPIAL PHRASES |
|---|---|
| The pedestrian, **who was bleeding from several wounds,** waited for someone to help him. | The pedestrian, **bleeding from several wounds,** waited for someone to help him. |
| An ambulance **that was summoned by a bystander** came quickly. | An ambulance **summoned by a bystander** came quickly. |

To form a participial phrase from a relative clause, delete the relative pronoun (*who, which,* or *that*) and change the verb to a participle. Put the word *not* at the beginning of a participial phrase to make it negative:

The car's driver, **not realizing what had happened,** continued on his way.

## Position and Punctuation of Participial Phrases

Participial phrases, like relative clauses, can be restrictive (necessary) or nonrestrictive (unnecessary). If the original clause was nonrestrictive, the phrase will be also. Nonrestrictive phrases are separated from the rest of the sentence by commas. Restrictive phrases use no commas.

The position of a participial phrase in a sentence depends on whether it is restrictive or nonrestrictive.

• A restrictive participial phrase follows the noun it modifies.

Restrictive:    There are twelve students **receiving awards this year.**

• A nonrestrictive phrase may precede or follow the noun it modifies.

Nonrestrictive:    Teresa, **hurrying to catch a bus,** stumbled and fell.
**Hurrying to catch a bus,** Teresa stumbled and fell.

> ***Caution!***   When you use an introductory participial phrase—one that appears at the beginning of a sentence—make certain that it modifies the noun immediately following it (which should be the subject of the sentence). If it does not, your sentence is incorrect.
>
> Incorrect:   Hoping for an "A," my exam grade disappointed me.
>
> (The participial phrase *Hoping for an A* cannot modify *my exam grade*. A grade cannot hope.)
>
> Correct:   Hoping for an "A," I was disappointed in my exam grade.

- Sometimes the participial phrase modifies an entire independent clause. In this case, it follows the clause and requires a comma.

  The team won the championship, **shocking the opponents.**

***General Form Participles— Active Voice***

The general form participle in the active voice ends in *-ing: crying, living, not knowing,* etc. It may come from present, past, or future tense verbs.

| VERB TENSE | SENTENCE WITH RELATIVE CLAUSE | SENTENCE WITH PARTICIPIAL PHRASE |
|---|---|---|
| Simple present | Many students **who study at this university** are from foreign countries. | Many students **studying at this university** are from foreign countries. |
| Present continuous | Students **who are taking calculus** must buy a graphing calculator. | Students **taking calculus** must buy a graphing calculator. |
| Simple past | The team members, **who looked happy after their victory,** were cheered by the fans. | The team members, **looking happy after their victory,** were cheered by the fans. |
| Past continuous | The crowd, **which was cheering wildly as the game ended,** wouldn't leave the stadium. | **Cheering wildly as the game ended,** the crowd wouldn't leave the stadium. |
| Future | Everyone **who will take the TOEFL next month** must preregister. | Everyone **taking the TOEFL next month** must preregister. |

**PRACTICE I**

*Participial Phrases—
Active Voice*

Rewrite each sentence, changing the relative clause into a participial phrase. Rewrite sentences 4 and 5 each in two ways: once with the participial phrase preceding and once with it following the noun it modifies. Punctuate nonrestrictive phrases.

1. Robotics is a complex field that combines electronics, computer science, and mechanical engineering.

   _____

   _____

2. The number of students who are studying robotics is growing.

   _____

   _____

3. Soon, robots that will work in assembly plants will be able to follow voice commands.

   _____

   _____

4. Robots, which have the ability to withstand extreme temperatures and radiation levels, can perform jobs that are too dangerous for humans.
   a. _____

   _____
   b. _____

   _____

5. Robots, which do not need to eat, sleep, or take restroom breaks, can work nonstop.
   a. _____

   _____
   b. _____

   _____

***General Form Participles— Passive Voice***

The general form participle in the passive voice is the "past participle" or third form of a verb: *opened, spoken, sold, cut.* This form is made from both present and past tense verbs.

| VERB TENSE | SENTENCE WITH RELATIVE CLAUSE | SENTENCE WITH PARTICIPIAL PHRASE |
|---|---|---|
| Simple present | Lab reports **that are not handed in by Friday** will not be accepted. | Lab reports **not handed in by Friday** will not be accepted. |
| Simple past | The prisoner, **who was surrounded by guards,** walked calmly to his execution. | The prisoner, **surrounded by guards,** walked calmly to his execution.<br><br>**Surrounded by guards,** the prisoner walked calmly to his execution. |

## Continuous Form Participles

Using the continuous form participle emphasizes that the action is happening now (or, less frequently, in the future). Make the continuous form with *being* + a past participle: *being shown, being held.*

| VERB TENSE | SENTENCE WITH RELATIVE CLAUSE | SENTENCE WITH PARTICIPIAL PHRASE |
|---|---|---|
| Present continuous | A law **that is currently being debated** concerns abortion rights. | A law **currently being debated** concerns abortion rights. |
| Past continuous | The signs **that were being posted around campus** support abortion rights. | The signs **being posted around campus** support abortion rights. |
| Future | A movie **that will be shown tomorrow** was made by an anti-abortion group. | A movie **being shown tomorrow** was made by an anti-abortion group. |

**PRACTICE 2**

*Participial Phrases— Passive Voice*

Rewrite each sentence, changing the relative clause to a participial phrase. Use continuous form participles to express actions that are happening *right now;* otherwise, use general form participles. Since the relative clauses in these sentences are all restrictive, no commas are necessary.

1. Computer programs that are known as expert systems will combine textbook knowledge and rules of experience to make decisions.

   _____

   _____

2. Computers that are programmed to diagnose[1] diseases accurately are important tools for doctors.

   _____

   _____

3. The uses of artificial intelligence that are now being suggested have created excitement around the world.

   _____

   _____

4. Robots that are currently being designed will do many dangerous jobs.

   _____

   _____

5. A robot that was built to work outside spaceships functioned perfectly during its first assignment.

   _____

   _____

---

[1] **diagnose:** identify

### *Perfect Form Participles*

Participles in perfect forms emphasize the completion of an action that takes place before the action of the main verb. There are both active forms (*having* + a past participle) and passive forms (*having been* + a past participle). Both present perfect or past perfect verbs can be changed into perfect form participles.

Active:   having discovered      Passive:   having been discovered

| Verb Tense | Sentence with Relative Clause | Sentence with Participial Phrase |
|---|---|---|
| Present perfect (active) | The secrets of the universe, **which have fascinated people for centuries,** are slowly being revealed. | The secrets of the universe, **having fascinated people for centuries,** are slowly being revealed. |
| Past perfect (passive) | The film, **which had been shown too often in movie theaters,** did not attract a large television audience. | The film, **having been shown too often in movie theaters,** did not attract a large television audience. |

---

**PRACTICE 3**

*Participial Phrases— The Perfect Forms*

Rewrite each sentence by changing the relative clause to a participial phrase. Since all of the clauses in these sentences are nonrestrictive, use commas. Write three of the sentences with the participial phrase positioned at the beginning of the sentence.

**1.** Women around the world, who have traditionally been without political power, are beginning to gain influence in politics and government.

_____

**2.** England, which has been ruled by queens several times in its history, elected a woman prime minister in 1979.

_____

**3.** On the other hand, voters in the United States, who have not experienced strong female leaders at the national level, may never elect a woman president.

_____

**4.** Both India and Pakistan, which have elected women prime ministers in the past, are more progressive in this area than the United States.

_____

**5.** Indira Ghandi, who had been raised in a political family, became one of India's most powerful leaders.

_____

_____

---

**PRACTICE 4**

*Participial Phrases— Mixed Forms*

Rewrite the following sentences, changing the relative clauses to participial phrases. Use the appropriate participle form (active or passive—general, continuous, or perfect), and use the same punctuation (commas or no commas) as in the original sentences. If it is possible, write each sentence twice: once with the participial phrase after the noun it modifies and once with the participial phrase at the beginning of the sentence.

**Example**

Alaska, which was purchased from Russia in 1867, became the 49th state of the United States in 1959.

    **a.** <u>Alaska, purchased from Russia in 1867, became the 49th state</u>
       <u>of the United States in 1959.</u>

    **b.** <u>Purchased from Russia in 1867, Alaska became the 49th state</u>
       <u>of the United States in 1959.</u>

**1.** The purchase of Alaska, which was negotiated by Secretary of State Seward, became a good investment.

    **a.** _____
    _____

    **b.** _____
    _____

**2.** The people of the United States, who did not understand the value of the purchase, called it "Seward's Folly."[1]

    **a.** _____
    _____

    **b.** _____
    _____

**3.** The state, which was once connected to Asia by a land bridge, is now separated from it by only a few miles of water.

    **a.** _____
    _____

    **b.** _____
    _____

**4.** The ancient inhabitants of Alaska, who had migrated across this land bridge from Asia, can be considered distant cousins of modern Asians.

    **a.** _____
    _____

    **b.** _____
    _____

**5.** The Eskimos, who have lived in Alaska for millions of years, have adapted well to their harsh environment.

    **a.** _____
    _____

    **b.** _____
    _____

**6.** The Eskimos have to live in cold and darkness most of the year, which causes them to develop a lively sense of humor and a hospitable[2] attitude.

    **a.** _____
    _____

    **b.** _____
    _____

---

[1] **folly:** silly act; foolishness
[2] **hospitable:** welcoming; friendly toward strangers

7. The Eskimos, who had been hunters and fishermen before the arrival of the Europeans, are experiencing a difficult time adapting to modern ways.

   a. _____

   _____

   b. _____

   _____

8. A problem that is being discussed by the Alaskan government concerns the rights of Alaska's natives.

   a. _____

   _____

   b. _____

   _____

9. Eskimos who want to preserve their traditional way of life do not care about the modern world.

   a. _____

   _____

   b. _____

   _____

10. On the other hand, Eskimos who want to improve their standard of living hope that they can combine both worlds—old and new.

   a. _____

   _____

   b. _____

   _____

You can use participial phrases to improve your writing style. When your essays contain too many relative clauses, change some of them to participial phrases. Occasionally using participial phrases at the beginning of sentences is considered especially mature style.

**EDITING PRACTICE**

*Participles and Participial Phrases*

A. Edit the following short autobiography[1] for errors in participles and participial phrases. You should make 5 changes. Look for these kinds of errors:

| An incorrect participle form was used: | Confused<br>C̶o̶n̶f̶u̶s̶i̶n̶g̶ by the question, I answered incorrectly. |
|---|---|
| A participial phrase at the beginning of a sentence doesn't modify the following noun: | Having worked around cars all my life, my auto mechanics class was quite easy. (Can an auto mechanics class work?)<br><br>Corrected: Having worked around cars all my life, I found my auto mechanics class to be quite easy. |

_____

[1] **autobiography:** a person's life story written by the person

### A Short Autobiography

Born on November 12, 1980, in a medium-sized town in the mountains of Peru, I learned responsibility at an early age. My family, consisted of my father, my mother, and seven younger brothers and sisters, is quite large. Being the oldest daughter, my responsibilities were many. I helped my mother

5  at home with the cooking and cleaning, and I was almost like a second mother to my younger siblings. By the time I was ten years old, I had learned how to soothe a crying baby, how to bandage an injuring knee or elbow, and especially how to get a boring schoolchild to finish his or her homework. Having been helped my brothers and sisters with their homework for so many years, I

10  have developed a love of teaching. I hope to get a college degree in elementary education and teach either math or science in my hometown in Peru.

**B.** Write five sentences about yourself, using a participial phrase in each.

**Example**

Having six older brothers, I have always been interested in sports.

1. _____
2. _____
3. _____
4. _____
5. _____

## *Participial Phrases from Adverbial Clauses*

Participial phrases can also be formed from adverbial clauses. Time and reason clauses introduced by the subordinators *after, while, when, before, since, because,* and *as* can be reduced to participial phrases if the subjects of both the adverbial and independent clauses are the same.

To change an adverbial clause to a participial phrase, follow these steps:

**STEP 1**   Make sure that the subject of the adverbial clause and the subject of the independent clause are the same.

While **technology** creates new jobs in some sectors of the economy, **it** takes away jobs in others.

**STEP 2**   Delete the subject of the adverbial clause. If necessary, move it to the subject position in the independent clause.

While **technology** creates new jobs in some sectors of the economy, ~~it~~ takes away jobs in others.

**STEP 3**   Change the adverbial clause verb to the appropriate participle.

While **creating** new jobs in some sectors of the economy, technology takes away jobs in others.

**STEP 4**   Delete or retain the subordinator according to the following rules:
   **a.**   Retain *before*, and retain *since* when it is a time subordinator.
   **b.**   Delete all three reason subordinators *because, since,* and *as.* Delete *as* when it is a time subordinator.
   **c.**   Retain *after, while,* and *when* if the participial phrase follows the independent clause. When the phrase is in another position, you may either retain or delete these subordinators.

A participial phrase from an adverbial clause may occupy several positions in a sentence. If a participial phrase from a reduced adverbial clause comes in front of or in the middle of the independent clause, punctuate it with commas. If it comes after the independent clause, do not use commas.

The following examples show you some of the possible variations of this structure. **Note:** There are many instances in which the "rules" given in the four steps above do not apply. The "rules" are only general guidelines and do not cover every situation.

*Reducing Adverbial Clauses to Participial Phrases*

| **Retain** | |
|---|---|
| *before* | Before a student chooses a college, he or she should consider several factors. |
| | **Before choosing a college,** a student should consider several factors. |
| | A student should consider several factors **before choosing a college.** |
| *since* (time) | Carlos hasn't been back home since he came to the United States three years ago. |
| | **Since coming to the United States three years ago,** Carlos hasn't been back home. |
| | Carlos hasn't been back home **since coming to the United States three years ago.** |

| **Delete** | |
|---|---|
| *because* *since* *as* (reason) | Because (Since/As) Carlos came from a very conservative family, he was shocked at the American system of coed[1] dormitories. |
| | **Coming from a very conservative family,** Carlos was shocked at the American system of coed dormitories.[2] |
| *as* (time) | As he gradually got used to American customs, he became less homesick. |
| | **Gradually getting used to American customs,** he became less homesick. |

---

[1] **coed:** shared by men and women
[2] Placing the participial phrase at the end of the sentence does not work well in this example: Carlos was shocked at the American system of coed dormitories coming from a very conservative family. It sounds as if the dormitories come from a conservative family.

| Retain or delete | |
|---|---|
| *after* | After he had passed the TOEFL exam, he became a freshman at his college.<br><br>**After passing the TOEFL exam,**[3] he became a freshman at his college.<br><br>**Having passed the TOEFL exam,** he became a freshman at his college.<br><br>He became a freshman at his college **after passing the TOEFL exam.**[3] |
| *while* | While he was preparing for the TOEFL, he lived with an American family.<br><br>**While preparing for the TOEFL,** he lived with an American American family.<br><br>**Preparing for the TOEFL,** he lived with an American family.<br><br>He lived with an American family **while preparing for the TOEFL.** |
| *when* | When he was asked about his life in the United States, he said that he was enjoying himself, but that he was a little homesick.<br><br>**When asked about his life in the United States,** he said that he was enjoying himself, but that he was a little homesick.[4]<br><br>**Asked about his life in the United States,** he said that he was enjoying himself, but that he was a little homesick. |

**PRACTICE 5**

*Reducing Adverbial Clauses to Participial Phrases*

**A.** Rewrite the following sentences, changing the adverbial clause in each to a participial phrase. If possible, write the sentence in more than one way.

**1.** Before I left home, I promised my parents that I would return.

_____

_____

**2.** Since I made that promise four years ago, I have thought about it often.

_____

_____

**3.** Since I am the eldest son, I am responsible for taking care of my parents.

_____

_____

**4.** As they grow older, they will need my assistance.

_____

_____

---

[3] The perfect form, *After having passed the TOEFL exam,* is not necessary because the word *after* already indicates the time relationship.

[4] Placing the participial phrase at the end of the sentence results in awkwardness: He said that he was enjoying himself, but that he was a little homesick when asked about his life in the United States. It sounds as if he is homesick only when he is asked about his life in the United States.

**5.** After I had received my B.A., I went to graduate school for two years.

_____

_____

**6.** While I was studying at the University of Chicago, I enjoyed living in a big city.

_____

_____

**7.** When I think about my future, I always remember my promise.

_____

_____

**B.** Write three sentences of your own, using a participial phrase in each one.

**1.** _____

_____

**2.** _____

_____

**3.** _____

_____

# Review

These are the important points you should have learned from this chapter.

**1.** Participles are adjectives formed from verbs. Some participles are from active voice verbs:

| | |
|---|---|
| The baby cried. | . . . the **crying** baby |
| The speaker bored the audience. | . . . the **boring** speaker |

Some participles are from passive voice verbs:

| | |
|---|---|
| The soldier was wounded. | . . . the **wounded** soldier |
| The audience was bored by the speaker. | . . . the **bored** audience |

The five commonly used participle forms and the times they indicate are shown in the following chart:

## PARTICIPLE FORMS

| Forms | Active | Passive |
|---|---|---|
| General—no time indicated | speaking | spoken |
| Continuous—current time (right now) and future | | being spoken |
| Perfect—time before that of the main verb | having spoken | having been spoken |

**2.** Participial phrases may be formed by reducing relative clauses.

> The audience, **which was listening intently to the music,** failed to notice the fire **that started to smolder[1] in the back of the auditorium.**

> The audience, **listening intently to the music,** failed to notice the fire **starting to smolder in the back of the auditorium.**

- A nonrestrictive participial phrase may precede or follow the noun it modifies and is set off by commas.

> The audience, **listening intently to the music,** . . .
> **Listening intently to the music,** the audience . . .

- A restrictive participial phrase must follow the noun it modifies and is not set off by commas.

> . . . the fire **starting to smolder in the back of the auditorium.**

- A nonrestrictive participial phrase may also modify an entire sentence, in which case it comes at the end of the sentence and is set off by a comma.

> The building collapsed, **killing three firefighters.**

**3.** Participial phrases may also be reduced from time and reason adverbial clauses.

**a.** Participial phrases reduced from time clauses may occupy various positions in a sentence, and the time subordinators are sometimes deleted and sometimes retained.

| Time clauses: | Participial phrases: |
|---|---|
| Since I arrived . . . | Since arriving . . . |
| After they had finished . . . | After finishing . . . |
| | Having finished . . . |

**b.** Participial phrases reduced from reason clauses may come before or after the independent clause in a sentence. Reason subordinators are always deleted.

| Reason clauses: | Participial phrases: |
|---|---|
| Because I wanted . . . | Wanting . . . |
| As he had been warned . . . | Having been warned . . . |

---

[1] **smolder:** burn without flame

Improve the following short essay by changing some of the adjective and adverbial clauses to participial phrases. There are ten places where such changes can be made.

**Global Warming**

One of the biggest problems that faces humankind in the next few decades is the problem of global warming. In the past 150 years, global temperatures have risen approximately 1°C (1.8°F). The year 1998 was the warmest year that was ever recorded. If temperatures continue to rise, the consequences
5   could be catastrophic. As the earth's temperature rises, polar ice will melt, which will cause the water level of the oceans to rise. Rising ocean levels, in turn, will cause flooding along the coasts. Global warming will also cause major changes in climate that will affect agriculture. For example, crops that were previously grown in Guatemala may not do so well because it will
10  become too hot.

Because they believe that the increase in carbon dioxide in the earth's atmosphere is the primary cause of global warming, scientists have urged immediate action to decrease $CO_2$ levels. They have asked the world's governments to write an agreement that will control the amount of carbon dioxide
15  that is released into the atmosphere. After each government signs such an agreement, each government will have to enforce it. Brazilians, for example, will have to stop burning their rain forests, and Americans will have to stop driving their gas-guzzling SUVs.[1]

Write a paragraph or two about yourself, and include at least three participial phrases in your composition. You may write facts about your family background, your education, and your career goals, or you may write more personal information—your characteristics, your likes and dislikes, your dreams and goals, etc. Use "A Short Autobiography" on page 239 as a model.

---

[1] **SUVs:** <u>s</u>port <u>u</u>tility <u>v</u>ehicles, a popular type of automobile that uses a lot of gas

# APPENDIX

# **A** Punctuation

Using correct punctuation is important because punctuation conveys meaning just as words do. Consider these two sentences:

> Eat children.
> Eat, children.

Both sentences are commands, but the first sentence would be correct only in a society of cannibals![1] Learn and practice the rules of punctuation until you are confident about using them correctly.

## *Commas*[2]

**Commas** are sometimes troublesome to learners of English because they are used differently in other languages. There are many comma rules in English, but you may remember them more easily if you realize that they can be organized into just four main groups: **introducers, coordinators, inserters,** and **tags.** Each group of commas relates to independent clauses in a particular way, except the coordinator group. Coordinator commas link not just independent clauses, but *any* coordinate (equal) elements in a sentence.

Study the examples for each comma group, and notice the kinds of elements that can be introducers, coordinators, inserters, and tags.

| INTRODUCER COMMAS | An introducer comma follows any element that comes in front of the first independent clause in a sentence. _____ , [ INDEPENDENT CLAUSE ]. |
|---|---|
| **Words** | **Therefore,** I plan to quit smoking. <br> **Nervously,** I threw away my cigarettes. |
| **Phrases** | **As a result,** I feel terrible right now. <br> **After sixteen years of smoking,** it is not easy to quit. <br> **Having smoked for sixteen years,** I find it difficult to quit. |
| **Dependent clauses** | **Because I have a chronic cough,** my doctor recommended that I quit immediately. |
| **Direct quotations** | **"Stop smoking today,"** she advised. |

---

[1] **cannibals:** people who eat human flesh
[2] Our thanks to Anne Katz of ARC Associates, Oakland, California, for permission to adapt her presentation of comma rules.

| **COORDINATOR COMMAS** | Together with a coordinating conjunction, a comma links coordinate (equal) elements in a sentence. |
|---|---|
| **Compound sentence with 2 independent clauses** | coord.<br>INDEPENDENT CLAUSE , conj. INDEPENDENT CLAUSE .<br><br>**She has a good job,**      yet      **she is always broke.**<br>**They were tired,**      so      **they went home early.** |
| **Series of 3 or more items:** | ☐ , ☐ , ☐ , and / or / but  ☐ . |
| **Words** | He doesn't enjoy **skiing, ice-skating,** or **sledding.**<br>Cecille speaks **English, Spanish, French,** and **Creole.**<br>(No comma with only 2 items: Chen speaks Mandarin and Taiwanese.) |
| **Phrases** | A nurse has to work **at night, on weekends,** and **on holidays.**<br>We **ran into the airport, checked our luggage, raced to the boarding gate, gave the attendant our boarding passes,** and **collapsed in our seats.** |

| **INSERTER COMMAS** | An inserter comma is used before and after any element that is inserted into the middle of an independent clause.<br>INDEPENDENT , _____ , CLAUSE . |
|---|---|
| **Words** | My uncle, **however,** refuses to quit smoking. |
| **Phrases** | My father, **on the other hand,** has never smoked.<br>There's no point in living, **according to my uncle,** if you don't do what you enjoy. |
| **Nonrestrictive phrases and clauses** | My aunt, **his wife,** died of lung cancer.<br>My cousins, **grieving over their mother's death,** resolved never to smoke.<br>My mother, **who just celebrated her fiftieth birthday,** enjoys an occasional cigarette. |
| **Reporting verbs in direct quotations** | "I've tried to quit dozens of times," **she says,** "but can't." |

| TAG COMMAS | A tag comma is used when adding certain elements to the end of a sentence. |
|---|---|
| | INDEPENDENT CLAUSE , _____. |
| **Words** | My uncle believes in drinking a daily glass of wine, **too.** |
| | He appears to be in good health, **however.** |
| **Phrases** | He swims for an hour every day, **for example.** |
| | He also plays tennis, **beating me most of the time** |
| **Tag questions** | It isn't logical, **is it?** |
| **Direct quotations** | He laughs as he says, **"I will outlive all of you."** |

**PRACTICE I**

*Using Commas*

**STEP 1**  Add commas wherever they are necessary. (Not all sentences need them, and some sentences need more than one.)

**STEP 2**  Name the function of each comma (introducer, coordinator, inserter, or tag).

**Function**

_____  **1.** The advertising industry which is one of the largest industries in the United States employs millions of people and spends billions of dollars.

_____  **2.** A company that wants to be successful must spend a great deal of money to advertise its products.

_____  **3.** Advertising is essential to the free enterprise system yet it can sometimes be very annoying.

_____  **4.** Every minute of the day and night people are exposed to ads on
_____  television on billboards in the newspapers and in magazines.

_____  **5.** You can't even avoid advertising in the privacy of your own car
_____  or your own home for advertisers have begun selling their products in those places too.

_____  **6.** In the last few years advertising agencies have started to hire young people to hand out circulars on street corners and in parking lots.

_____  **7.** You can often find these circulars stuck on your windshield thrust[1] through the open windows of your car stuffed in your mailbox or simply scattered on your front doorstep.

_____  **8.** Because Americans are exposed to so much advertising they have become immune[2] to it.

_____  **9.** As a result advertisers have to make louder commercials use
_____  brighter colors and hire sexier models to catch the public's attention.

_____

[1] **thrust:** pushed forcefully
[2] **immune:** cannot be affected

———————— **10.** Many people object to commercials that use sex as a sales strategy.

———————— **11.** Sexy commercials that sell everything from toothpaste to automobiles seem to imply that you will become sexier if you buy the product.

———————— **12.** Sex is used in many cigarette and liquor ads for example.

———————— **13.** The women in such ads are often dressed in revealing clothes and are surrounded by handsome men and the men in such ads are always extremely handsome and virile.

———————— **14.** As everyone knows smoking and drinking do not make you sexy or virile.

———————— **15.** On the contrary drinking makes you fat and smoking makes you sick.

———————— **16.** Recently smoking was banned in most public places in the United States.

———————— **17.** Many people opposed the law but it finally passed.

———————— **18.** Smoking is now prohibited in hospitals airports stores offices and even some restaurants.

———————— **19.** Many states however still allow smoking in bars.

———————— **20.** Anti-smoking groups want to ban smoking in those places too.

# Semicolons

Using **semicolons** is not difficult if you remember that a semicolon (;) is more like a period than a comma. It is a very strong punctuation mark. Semicolons are used in three places:

**1.** Between two sentences that are closely connected in idea
**2.** Before conjunctive adverbs and some transitional phrases
**3.** Between items in a series if the items themselves contain commas

## *Between Sentences*

Use a semicolon at the end of a sentence when the following sentence is closely connected in meaning. You could also use a period, but when the sentences are connected in meaning, it is better to use a semicolon.

| Independent clause ; independent clause. |
| --- |
| Alice is going to Harvard; she isn't going to M.I.T.<br>Computer use is increasing; computer crime is, too.<br>The meeting adjourned[1] at dawn; nothing had been accomplished. |

———————

[1] **adjourned:** ended

***Before Connectors***

Use a semicolon before conjunctive adverbs such as *however, therefore, nevertheless, moreover,* and *furthermore.* You may also use a semicolon before some transition phrases such as *for example, as a result, that is, in fact,* etc.

Independent clause  ;  conjunctive adverb or transition phrase  ,  independent clause.

Skiing is dangerous; nevertheless, millions of people ski.

I have never been to Europe; in fact, I have never been outside my country.

***Between Items in a Series***

Semicolons may be used to separate items in a series when some of the items already contain commas.

I cannot decide which car I like best: the Ferrari, with its quick acceleration and sporty look; the midsize Ford Taurus, with its comfortable seats and ease of handling; or the compact Geo, with its economical fuel consumption.

**PRACTICE 2**

*Using Semicolons and Commas*

**A.  STEP 1**  The following sentences need semicolons and commas; add the correct punctuation in the appropriate places.

**STEP 2**  In the space provided at left, indicate whether the semicolon is

**1.** Before two closely connected sentences
**2.** Before a conjunctive adverb or a transition phrase
**3.** Between items in a series if the items already contain commas

**Example**

_2_  Professor Smith is at a conference; however, Dr. Jones, who is the department chairman, will be glad to see you.

——  **1.** Grace works for a prestigious law firm she is their top criminal lawyer.
——  **2.** My favorite leisure-time activities are going to movies especially musicals reading novels[2] especially stories of love and adventure listening to music both rock and classical and participating in sports particularly tennis and volleyball.
——  **3.** The future of our wild animals is uncertain for example illegal shooting and chemical poisoning threaten the bald eagle.[3]
——  **4.** Homework is boring therefore I never do it.
——  **5.** The freeways are always crowded during the busy rush hours nevertheless people refuse to take public transportation.

[2] **novels:** fiction books
[3] **bald eagle:** a large bird of prey, symbol of the United States

——— **6.** The Smiths' marriage should succeed they share the same interests.

——— **7.** Hoping that he would pass the course he stayed up all night studying for the final exam unfortunately he overslept and missed the test.

——— **8.** In general I enjoy my English class the amount of homework our teacher assigns is definitely not enjoyable however.

——— **9.** If you are a college student, an average day is filled with challenges: you have to avoid running into Professor Jones whose class you missed because you overslept you have to race across the campus at high speed to reach your next class which is always at the other side of the campus and you have to secretly prepare your homework assignment during class hoping all the time that the teacher won't catch you.

**B.** Punctuate the following sentences by adding semicolons and commas. Use semicolons wherever possible.

**1.** My bus was late therefore I missed my first class.

**2.** The politician was discovered accepting bribes as a result his political career was ruined.

**3.** My father never cries in fact he never shows any emotion at all.

**4.** The restaurant was closed consequently we went home to eat.

**5.** Some people feel that grades are unnecessary on the other hand some people feel that grades motivate students.

**6.** Technology is changing our lives in insidious[1] ways for example the computer is replacing human contact.

**7.** The computer dehumanizes business nevertheless it has some real advantages.

**8.** Writing essays is easy it just takes a little practice.

**9.** Americans love pets every family seems to have at least one dog or cat.

**10.** The life expectancy of Americans is increasing for example the life expectancy of a man born today is 77.2 years which is an increase of 26.12 years since 1900.

**11.** Your proposal is a good one however I do not completely agree with your final suggestion.

**12.** Efficiency is a highly prized quality among Americans it has almost attained the status of a moral attribute.[2]

**C.** Write one original sentence for each of the three rules for using semicolons:

**1.** Between closely connected sentences
**2.** Before conjunctive adverbs and some transition phrases
**3.** Between items in a series

---

[1] **insidious:** secretly harmful
[2] **attribute:** characteristic; quality

# Colons

A **colon** (:) can be used in five ways:

## Lists

Use a colon to introduce a list.

Libraries have two kinds of periodicals: bound periodicals and current periodicals.

I need the following groceries: eggs, milk, and coffee.

The causes of the U.S. Civil War were as follows: the economic domination of the North, the slavery issue, and the issue of states' rights versus federal intervention.

**Note: Do not** use a colon to introduce a list after the verb *to be* unless you add *the following* or *as follows*.

To me, the most important things in life **are** health, happiness, good friends, and a lot of money.

To me, the most important things in life **are the following:** health, happiness, good friends, and a lot of money.

## Long Quotations

Use a colon to introduce a quotation longer than three lines. This type of quote is indented on both sides, and no quotation marks are used.

As Albert C. Baugh and Thomas Cable state in their book, *The History of the English Language:*

There is no such thing as uniformity in language. Not only does the speech of one community differ from that of another, but the speech of different individuals of a single community, even different members of the same family, is marked by individual peculiarities.[3]

## Subtitles

Use a colon between the main title and the subtitle of a book, article, or play.

A popular book on nonverbal communication is Samovar and Porter's *Intercultural Communication: A Reader.*

The name of an article from the *New York Times* is "Space Stations: Dream or Reality?"

## Time

Use a colon between the numbers for hours and minutes when indicating the time of day.

Helen left the class at 12:30.
Our plane arrived at 1:40, six hours late.

## Formal Salutations

Use a colon after the salutation of a formal letter.

Dear Professor Danielson:
Dear Sir or Madam:
Dear Ms. Smith:
To Whom It May Concern:

In informal letters, a comma is more appropriate.

Dear Mom,
Dear Mark,

---

[3] **peculiarities:** strange characteristics

**PRACTICE 3**

*Using Punctuation Marks*

**A.** Add commas, semicolons, and colons to the following.

**1.** The library offers many special services the Student Learning Center where students can receive individual tutoring special classes where you can improve your math composition and reading skills and computer skills in addition there are group study rooms.

**2.** Dear Dr. Patterson
Dear Alice
Dear Mr. Carter

**3.** To check a book out of the library you should follow this procedure write down the call number of the book find the book bring it to the circulation desk fill out the card and show your student I.D.

**4.** The principal sources of air pollution in our cities are factories airplanes and automobiles.

**5.** I have a dental appointment at 330 today. Please pick me up at 300.

**B.** Write a sentence in which you list two pieces of advice that you have received from your parents. Use a colon to direct attention to them.

_____

_____

**C.** Write the title and subtitle of the following book correctly. Remember to underline the full title.

(Title)    Paris            (Subtitle)    A Visitor's Guide to Restaurants

_____

_____

# Quotation Marks

**Quotation marks** ["..."] have three basic functions:

*Direct Quotations*

Use quotation marks to enclose a direct quotation that is shorter than three lines. A direct quotation states the *exact* words of a speaker.

Punctuation with quotation marks can be a little tricky. Here are some rules to follow:

**1.** Periods and commas go inside quotation marks.

"I thought he was responsible," he said, "but he isn't."

**2.** Colons and semicolons go outside quotation marks.

"Give me liberty or give me death": these are immortal[1] words.

**3.** Exclamation points (!) and question marks (?) go inside quotation marks if they are a part of the quotation; otherwise, they go outside.

"Is it eight o'clock?" she asked.
Did she say, "It's eight o'clock"?

---

[1] **immortal:** long–remembered

**4.** When a quoted sentence is divided into two parts, the second part begins with a small letter unless it is a new sentence.

"I thought he was responsible," he said, "but he isn't."

"I think he is responsible," he said. "Look at his fine work."

**5.** Use single quotation marks ('. . .') to enclose a quotation within a quotation.

As John F. Kennedy reminded us, "We should never forget the words of Martin Luther King, Jr., who said, 'I have a dream.'"

*Unusual Words*

Use quotation marks to enclose foreign words or words that are used in a special or uncommon way.

A lot of people talk about "machismo" these days, but few people really know what it means.

The "banquet" turned out to be no more than hot dogs and soft drinks.

*Titles*

Use quotation marks to enclose the titles of articles from periodical journals, magazines, and newspapers; chapters of books; short stories; poems; and songs.

In the article "The Future of Space," published in the July 19, 1974, issue of *Scientific American,* the authors explore the possibility of manned space stations.

The *New York Times* recently published an article entitled "Space Stations: Dream or Reality?" in which the potential of space cities in orbit was discussed.

**Note:** The titles of books, journals, magazines, newspapers, and movies should be underlined or italicized.

**PRACTICE 4**

*Using Quotation Marks*

Get a copy of any newspaper and write a paragraph about any article. Copy five quotations from the article. Mention the name of the newspaper and the article in your sentence and include the name of the speaker or writer.

**PRACTICE 5**

*Using Punctuation Marks*

Add punctuation to the following paragraph.

### Aging

People are more likely to live long enough to get old in wealthy countries than in poor countries. In rich countries people have nutritious food modern medical care good sanitation and clean drinking water but poor countries lack these things. As a result the mortality rate especially infant mortality is very
5    high. Citizens of Ethiopia and Yemen which are two of the world's poorest countries have an average life expectancy of 35–39 years. Citizens of Japan Norway Iceland and Sweden in contrast have an average life span of more than 75 years. Japan has the highest Yemen has the lowest. One exception is Saudi Arabia one of the world's wealthiest nations. Having an average life
10   expectancy of 45–49 years Saudi Arabians live about as long as Bangladeshis and Cambodians. Surprisingly the United States is not among the highest-rated nations having an average life expectancy of only 70–74 years.

Compared to other mammals humans have a relatively long life span. The average life span of elephants is 70 years of dogs 18 years of cats 14 years
15   and of horses 20 years. The life spans of other species are as follows eagles

parrots and owls 60 years parakeets 12 years guppies 5 years and box tortoises 100 years. Some plants such as trees live much longer than animals. Redwood trees for example live more than 3,000 years and bristlecone pine trees can live over 4,000 years.

20    The life expectancy of people who live in industrialized societies is increasing rapidly in fact it has doubled in the past one hundred years. When comparing males and females one finds that women generally live longer than men. The oldest person in the world until recently was a French woman Jeanne Calment. At her death in 1997 Madame Calment was both blind and
25    deaf but had not lost her sharp wit for which she had become quite famous. Asked what kind of future she expected she replied a very short one. Bragging about her smooth skin she said I've only had one wrinkle in my life and I'm sitting on it.

# APPENDIX

# Chart of Transition Signals

| MEANING/ FUNCTION | SENTENCE CONNECTORS[1] | CLAUSE CONNECTORS | | OTHERS (ADJECTIVES, VERBS, AND PREPOSITIONS) |
|---|---|---|---|---|
| | | COORDINATORS[2] | SUBORDINATORS | |
| To introduce a similar **additional** idea | also<br>besides<br>furthermore<br>in addition<br>moreover<br>too | and<br>nor<br>("and not") | | another<br>an additional |
| To **compare** things | also<br>likewise<br>similarly<br>too | and<br>both . . .and<br>not only . . .<br>  but also<br>neither . . .<br>  nor | as<br>just as | as . . .as<br>like/alike<br>just like<br>similar to<br>be alike<br>be similar |
| To introduce an **opposite** idea, and to **contrast** things | however<br>in contrast<br>instead<br>in/by comparison<br>nevertheless<br>nonetheless<br>on the other hand<br>on the contrary<br>still | but<br>yet | although<br>even though<br>though<br>whereas<br>while | despite<br>in spite of<br>compared to/with<br>be different (from)<br>be dissimilar<br>be unlike<br>differ (from) |

*(Chart continues on the next page.)*

---

[1] includes conjunctive adverbs
[2] includes correlative conjunctions

| MEANING/ FUNCTION | SENTENCE CONNECTORS[1] | CLAUSE CONNECTORS | | OTHERS (ADJECTIVES, VERBS, AND PREPOSITIONS) |
| --- | --- | --- | --- | --- |
| | | COORDINATORS | SUBORDINATORS | |
| To introduce an **example** | for example<br>for instance | | | such as<br>an example of |
| To **emphasize** | in fact | | | |
| To **explain** and **restate** | indeed<br>that is | | | |
| To introduce an **alternative** | otherwise | or | if<br>unless | |
| To signal **chronological order** | first, second, *etc.*<br>first of all<br>then, next<br>now, then, soon<br>last finally<br>meanwhile<br>gradually<br>after that<br>since then | | after<br>as<br>as soon as<br>before<br>since<br>until<br>when<br>while | the first, the second<br>the next, the last, the final<br>before lunch<br>after the war<br>since 19__<br>in the year 20__<br><br>(*any* time expression) |
| To indicate **order of importance** | above all<br>first and foremost<br>more/most importantly/<br>    significantly<br>primarily | | | a more important<br>the most important<br>the second most significant<br>the primary |
| To introduce a **cause** or **reason** | | for | because<br>since<br>as | result from<br>be the result of<br>due to<br>because of<br>the effect of<br>the consequence of<br>as a result of<br>as a consequence of |

| MEANING/ FUNCTION | SENTENCE CONNECTORS[1] | CLAUSE CONNECTORS | | OTHERS (ADJECTIVES, VERBS, AND PREPOSITIONS) |
| --- | --- | --- | --- | --- |
| | | COORDINATORS | SUBORDINATORS | |
| To introduce an **effect** or **result** | accordingly<br>as a result<br>as a consequence<br>consequently<br>hence, thus<br>therefore | so | | result in<br>cause<br>have an effect on<br>affect<br>the cause of<br>the reason for |
| To **conclude** | all in all<br>in brief<br>in conclusion<br>in short<br>in summary<br>indeed | | | It is clear that . . .<br>We can see that . . .<br>The evidence suggests<br>  that . . .<br>These examples show<br>  that . . . |

# Writing under Pressure

Writing under Pressure assignments give you practice in thinking and writing quickly, as you will have to do during essay examinations. Your goal is to complete each paragraph within twenty minutes, which is about the average time you might have to answer a typical essay question. For each Writing under Pressure assignment, follow this procedure:

**1.** Brainstorm for ideas by listing, clustering, or freewriting.

**2.** Make a simple outline.

**3.** Write a rough draft.

**4.** Check over your paragraph twice, once for content and organization and once for grammar and mechanics.

**5.** Make any necessary corrections before you hand it in.

*Suggested Time Limits*

| | |
|---|---|
| Brainstorming | 5 minutes |
| Outlining | 3 minutes |
| Writing | 10 minutes |
| Checking | 2 minutes |
| Total time | 20 minutes |

*Topics*

**1.** Your favorite place

**2.** A goal in your life

**3.** One problem you have

**4.** A perfect student/teacher/friend

**5.** An unusual pet

**6.** Your favorite leisure-time activity

**7.** The most exciting day in your life

**8.** The worst day in your life

**9.** An important person in your life

**10.** A present or past job you have had

**11.** The perfect job

**12.** The perfect husband/wife/parent

**13.** Your best friend

**14.** A bad habit

**15.** Important events in your life

**16.** Compare two family members or two friends

**17.** Make a generalization about one of the following groups of people:

| | | |
|---|---|---|
| Americans | Artists | Engineers |
| English teachers | Rock musicians | Politicians |
| Mothers | Astronauts | Teenagers |

Then write a paragraph supporting your opinion with specific supporting details. Examples of generalizations about Americans are as follows:

Americans are generally punctual.

Americans, in general, eat a lot of fast food.

# Correction Symbols

| Meaning | Incorrect | Correct |
|---|---|---|
| **P.** punctuation | *P.*<br>I live, and go to school here. *P.*<br>Where do you work. *P.* | I live and go to school here.<br>Where do you work? |
| ◯ word missing | ◯<br>I working in a restaurant.<br>∧ | I am working in a restaurant. |
| **Cap.** capitalization | *Cap.* *Cap.*<br>It is located at main and baker<br>*Cap.* *Cap.*<br>streets in the City. | It is located at Main and Baker<br>Streets in the city. |
| **V.t.** verb tense | *v.t.*<br>I never work as a cashier until<br>*v.t.*<br>I get a job there. | I had never worked as a cashier<br>until I got a job there. |
| **agr.** subject–verb agreement | *agr.*<br>The manager work hard.<br>*agr.*<br>There is five employees. | The manager works hard.<br>There are five employees. |
| ⌒ make one word or sentence | Every one works hard.<br>We work together. So we have<br>become friends. | Everyone works hard.<br>We work together, so we have<br>become friends. |
| **sp.** spelling | *sp.*<br>The maneger is a woman. | The manager is a woman. |
| **pl.** plural | *pl.*<br>She treats her employees like slave. | She treats her employees like slaves. |
| ✕ unnecessary word | My boss s̶h̶e̶ watches everyone all<br>the time. | My boss watches everyone all<br>the time. |
| **W.f.** wrong word form | *w.f.*<br>Her voice is irritated. | Her voice is irritating. |
| **W.W.** wrong word | *W.W.*<br>The food is delicious. Besides,<br>the restaurant is always crowded. | The food is delicious. Therefore,<br>the restaurant is always crowded. |

| | Meaning | Incorrect | Correct |
|---|---|---|---|
| ref. | pronoun reference error | The restaurant's specialty is fish. *ref.* They are always fresh. The food is delicious. Therefore, *ref.* <u>it</u> is always crowded. | The restaurant's specialty is fish. It is always fresh. The food is delicious. Therefore, the restaurant is always crowded. |
| ∽ | wrong word order | Friday always is our busiest night. | Friday is always our busiest night. |
| RO | run-on | *RO* Lily was fired she is upset. OR | Lily was fired, so she is upset. Lily was fired; therefore, she is upset. |
| CS | comma splice (incorrectly joined independent clauses) | *CS* Lily was fired, she is upset. | Because Lily was fired, she is upset. Lily is upset because she was fired. |
| FRAG | fragment (incomplete sentence) | She was fired. <u>Because she was always late.</u> | She was fired because she was always late. |
| Ⓣ | add a transition | She was also careless. ⓣ She frequently spilled coffee on the table. | She was also careless. For example, she frequently spilled coffee on the table. |
| S. | subject | *S.* ∧Is open from 6:00 P.M. until the last customer leaves. | The restaurant is open from 6:00 P.M. until the last customer leaves. |
| V. | verb | *V.* The employees∧on time and work hard. | The employees are on time and work hard. |
| prep. | preposition | *prep.* We start serving dinner∧6:00 P.M. | We start serving dinner at 6:00 P.M. |
| conj. | conjunction | *conj.* The garlic shrimp, fried clams,∧ broiled lobster are the most popular dishes. | The garlic shrimp, fried clams, and broiled lobster are the most popular dishes. |
| art. | article | *art.* Diners expect∧glass of water when *art.* they first sit down at∧table. | Diners expect a glass of water when they first sit down at the table. |
| ¶ | Symbol for a paragraph | | |

# Index

# Photo and Text Credits